THE HISTORY OF PHILOSOPHY:
A MARXIST PERSPECTIVE

Alan Woods was born in Swansea, South Wales, in 1944 into a working-class family with strong communist traditions. At the age of 16, he joined the Young Socialists and became a Marxist. He studied Russian at Sussex University and later in Sofia (Bulgaria) and the Moscow State University (MGU). He has a wide experience of the international labour movement and played an active role in building the Marxist tendency in Spain, where he participated in the struggle against the Franco dictatorship. He was later active in Pakistan, Mexico and other countries, including Venezuela, where he developed a close relationship with the late Hugo Chavez, and founded the international campaign, 'Hands off Venezuela'.

Alan Woods is the author of many works covering a wide spectrum of issues, including politics, economics, history, philosophy, art, music and science. He is also the political editor of the popular website 'In Defence of Marxism' (marxist.com) and a leading member of the International Marxist Tendency.

Highlights of the books he has authored are: *Lenin and Trotsky: What they Really Stood For* and *Reason in Revolt: Marxist Philosophy and Modern Science*, both in conjunction with the late Ted Grant; *Marxism and the USA*; *Reformism or Revolution*; *The Venezuelan Revolution: A Marxist Perspective*, *The Ideas of Karl Marx*, *Bolshevism: The Road to Revolution*, and *Spain's Revolution Against Franco: The Great Betrayal*. He also edited and completed Trotsky's last unfinished work, the biography of Stalin, which had remained incomplete for seventy years.

His books have been translated into many languages, including Spanish, Italian, German, Greek, Turkish, Urdu, Danish, Portuguese, Russian and Bahasa Indonesian.

THE HISTORY OF PHILOSOPHY

A MARXIST PERSPECTIVE

Alan Woods

Wellred Books
London

The History of Philosophy: A Marxist Perspective
Alan Woods

Wellred Books, September 2021

UK distribution: Wellred Books, wellredbooks.net
152-160 Kemp House, City Road
London, EC1V 2NX
books@wellredbooks.net

USA distribution: Marxist Books, marxistbooks.com
WR Books
250 44th Street #208
Brooklyn
New York, NY 11232
sales@marxistbooks.com

DK distribution: Forlaget Marx, forlagetmarx.dk
Degnestavnen 19, st. tv.
2400 København NV
forlag@forlagetmarx.dk

Cover design by Jesse Murray-Dean, based on '*Untitled*,
1919-1920' by El Lissitzky (public domain)

Layout by Wellred Books

ISBN: 978-1-913026-24-0

Printed and bound in Great Britain by Bell and Bain Ltd, Glasgow

CONTENTS

INTRODUCTION

THE STARTING POINT

I first started work on *The History of Philosophy* some twenty-seven years ago, when writing *Reason in Revolt*, a book that dealt with the relationship between Marxist philosophy and modern science. The book was a big success, but it turned out to be much longer than I had originally anticipated. Due to considerations of length, I was reluctantly obliged to omit the first part, which dealt with the history of philosophy, leading up to Marx's great revolution, the theory of dialectical materialism.

The intention had been to publish *The History of Philosophy* as a separate work sometime in the future. But for different reasons, that decision was delayed to make way for more pressing tasks. For more than two decades, the manuscript was put to one side, left to the gnawing criticism of the mice, as Marx once said, referring to the unpublished text of the *German Ideology*. It was eventually published on our website, and was favourably received, but the original intention of publishing it as a book remained unfulfilled until now.

I owe it to the pressure of a number of comrades with a special interest in philosophy that I have been spurred into action to publish this work. It represents a contribution to the ongoing campaign of the International Marxist Tendency to combat bourgeois ideology and to defend and propagate the ideas of Marxism. This was a timely and necessary decision. At a time when the capitalist system finds itself in a terminal crisis, the bankruptcy of the existing order inevitably finds its expression in an evident decline of every aspect of intellectual life.

This is particularly glaring in the field of philosophy, where bourgeois thought expresses its decay in a most scandalous manner. The struggle for socialism is not confined to politics and economics. It must be carried on at all levels, starting with the level of ideas. If the present work helps to arm the workers and youth in this necessary struggle, my aim will have been achieved.

Those who have read the original manuscript will see that, in all essential points, it has been maintained. But I have revised the text thoroughly with the assistance of comrades, and have added new sections, notably in the chapter on the Middle Ages, and also added a final chapter, which explains why philosophy – at least in the old sense of the word – comes to an end with Marxism.

You may also have noticed that the additional chapter on Indian philosophy that was included as an appendix has been omitted from the present edition, while the chapter on Islamic philosophy has been reduced, dealing mainly with the role it played in the Middle ages. This was neither accidental nor due to any lack of interest on my part. Quite the opposite, in fact. As you will appreciate, the presentation of two -and-a-half millennia of philosophy is a very daunting task, and for reasons of space I was compelled to omit many important aspects of the subject, which had to be stripped of all but the most basic essentials.

The evolution of Oriental philosophy (which would have to encompass Chinese philosophy – a vast topic in itself) proceeded on quite different lines to that of philosophy in the West, which reached its peak in Hegel and culminated in the philosophical revolution brought about by Marx and Engels. To do justice to that subject would have required not merely a huge (and quite unwarranted) expansion of the present book, but would have demanded one or more additional volumes. Therefore, rather than publish an unsatisfactory résumé of quite a complicated subject, which would please nobody, least of all myself, I decided to set this subject to one side, with the intention of perhaps returning to it when the pressure of time and work allows.

WHAT IS PHILOSOPHY?

Marxism began as a philosophy, and the philosophical method of Marxism is of fundamental importance in understanding the ideas of Marx and Engels. But what is philosophy?

Philosophy is a way of thinking, different from the kind of thinking we are used to in ordinary life. It does not confine itself to the immediate questions of daily life but attempts to grapple with the big questions of life and death, the universe, the nature of ideas and matter, and what is good and what is bad. These are issues that ultimately are of great importance to every one of us. Yet they do not normally occupy a central place in the thoughts of most people.

For the whole of history, at least up to the present time, the minds of most men and women have been mainly absorbed by the daily struggle for existence. They are fully occupied with such mundane questions as: will I have a job next week? Will I have enough money to last until the end of the month? Will I have a roof over my head, a school for my children, and so on and so forth.

Yet human thought is capable of far greater things. The history of thought includes the history of art, beginning with the wonderful cave paintings of Lascaux and Altamira; the history of science, which has enabled us to conquer nature and reach out our hands to the stars; and also the history of philosophy, with its many astonishing insights.

Philosophy emerges as soon as men and women begin to try to explain the world without the intervention of supernatural agencies: gods and goddesses and all the rest of the superstitious paraphernalia of religion that have been carried over from the most primitive times. It marks the beginning of a scientific understanding of nature and of ourselves.

A REVOLUTIONARY WORLD OUTLOOK

Marxism is first and foremost a world outlook, or philosophy if you prefer. It has a vast scope. It is a theory of history and of economics, and also a guide to revolutionary action. But where did Marx get his ideas from? They did not drop from the clouds. Marx himself explained that there were three main sources to his ideas: there was English classical bourgeois economics (Adam Smith and David Ricardo), then there were the bold pioneers of utopian socialism: the Frenchmen Saint-Simon and Fourier, and my fellow Welshman Robert Owen.

But the first and most important element in the formative stages of the ideas of Marx and Engels was without doubt German classical philosophy, particularly Hegel. And this, in turn, was the product of a lengthy period of the development of many different schools of philosophical thought. Now, it would be very easy to dismiss, for example, the ideas of the utopian socialists (as Dühring did). But surely it is more appropriate to pay tribute to their remarkable contribution to the history of socialism and to recognise the part their ideas played in the formative stage of Marxism?

I recently re-read parts of Robert Owen and I can tell you that some of his ideas are still quite revolutionary today. Does that mean that, in paying tribute to Owen, we advocate going back to the ideas of utopian socialism? Of course not! But it is impossible to deny that these ideas played an important role in the development of scientific socialism. This is a simple fact.

I have occasionally come across a rather childish prejudice that imagines that everything that came before Marx and Engels can be discarded as conservative and reactionary. It is quite true that not only Hegel but also Adam Smith and Ricardo were 'upper class thinkers'. Some foolish people imagine that this fact alone would be sufficient to disqualify them as great revolutionary thinkers. It is also true that some of them (though by no means all) held political views that tended towards conservatism, or even reaction. Hegel himself was conservative in his political views, although in his younger years he sympathised with the French Revolution. But that does not alter the fact that his dialectical method contained a very revolutionary element – a fact that was recognised by the reactionary Prussian authorities, who regarded Hegel with suspicion, and even suspected him of atheism and subversive views.

Marx explained long ago that the ruling ideas of every epoch are the ideas of the ruling class. These men represented the most advanced thought of their day and Marx based himself on these ideas. The law of value that was discovered by Adam Smith and developed by Ricardo led directly to Marx's theory of surplus value, and the idealist dialectic of Hegel led to dialectical materialism. The idea that Marxists can ignore the ideas of the past is as stupid as the prejudice held by some extreme anarchists that, in order to build a new classless society, it is necessary to destroy everything that has gone before and build it anew. This is the distilled essence of utopianism and, if we were to accept it, we would rule out the possibility of carrying out a socialist revolution in practice.

A socialist revolution would not destroy the existing achievements of capitalism but, on the contrary, would build on them, filling them with an entirely different social and class content. The achievements of science and technology would no longer serve the interests of a tiny parasitic ruling class, but would be planned harmoniously in the interests of the whole of society. We will build the new society, using the bricks left over by the old, for the simple reason that no other ready-made bricks exist for the purpose.

In the same way that we would make use of the existing productive forces – the land, the factories, science and technology – inherited from the old society, so we should base ourselves on the most advanced ideas developed in the past. Marxism negated Hegel's idealism, while simultaneously preserving all that was progressive and revolutionary in his dialectical method. The founders of scientific socialism rescued the dialectic, which in the hands of Hegel was presented in a distorted, idealist guise, and placed it for the first time on a sound materialist foundation. In doing so, they created a powerful weapon for changing society along revolutionary lines.

WHY STUDY THE HISTORY OF PHILOSOPHY?

All the writings of Marx and Engels are based on a definite philosophical method and cannot be understood without it, the method of dialectical materialism. The same is true of the works of Lenin and Trotsky, the most outstanding representatives of Marxist thought in the twentieth century. Dialectics was already known to the ancient Greeks and was later developed by Hegel. The basic ideas of dialectical materialism are not so difficult to grasp. Like all great ideas, they are essentially simple, and they are beautiful in their simplicity.

But all too many who regard themselves as Marxists are content to repeat a few basic ideas without giving any thought to the deeper meaning of what they are saying. Such 'Marxists' resemble a young child who has learned to recite the multiplication tables by rote, or rather, a parrot that has learned by imitating human speech to repeat certain sentences, without having the vaguest understanding of their meaning. In order to arrive at a full understanding of dialectical materialism, a great deal of careful study will be necessary. At the moment, I am working on a further comprehensive work on Marxist philosophy, which I hope will help to clarify the more complicated questions involved.

But there is a difficulty involved in the study of philosophy in general, and Marxist philosophy in particular, and one that lies at the heart of the present work. When Marx and Engels wrote about dialectical materialism, they could presuppose a basic knowledge of the history of philosophy on the part of at least the educated reading public of the day. Nowadays, it is impossible to make such an assumption.

HEGEL'S 'HISTORY OF PHILOSOPHY'

I first began reading Hegel's monumental, three-volume *History of Philosophy* when I was seventeen years old and still in school. I got through the whole of the first volume and half of the second before going to university. I found it absolutely riveting. Here, before my very eyes was two-and-a-half-thousand years of the most profound human thought, set forth in a compellingly clear and comprehensive dialectical manner.

I still possess several school notebooks full of the notes I made at the time on the *History of Philosophy*, the *Philosophy of History* and the *Phenomenology of Spirit*. I even had a notebook in which I had copied out extensive sections of Hegel's *Shorter Logic* from *The Encyclopaedia of Philosophical Science*. I had searched in vain for a copy of that remarkable work, but when I finally obtained one from a reference library, it turned out to be in the original German! But I was not to be put off by such a detail. At the time, my knowledge of the German language was pretty good, so I set about reading it and taking notes. Unfortunately, that particular notebook got lost in the course of my travels.

That enthusiasm for Hegel has remained with me ever since. What struck me about the *History of Philosophy* was the highly original way in which Hegel approached the subject. It is presented not as a series of accidental developments, but as an organic whole – a process that evolved through a series of contradictions, in which one set of ideas apparently negates a previous one, leading to an endless spiral of development of human thought.

Of course, one may find fault with Hegel's idealist approach to the history of philosophy. But the most important thing to see is the dialectical method that characterises all of his works. Where others only saw a mass of unconnected ideas, accidents and individual geniuses, Hegel was the first to see an organic process with a law and an inner logic of its own.

In the development of philosophy through a series of contradictions, Hegel saw not merely a negative process, whereby one set of ideas annihilated another. He understood that this process of negation also implied the preservation of all that was valid and true in previous stages. This idea of negation that at the same time preserves is what he called sublation, and it is expressed in the most sublime language in his introduction to the *Phenomenology of Spirit*:

The bud disappears when the blossom bursts forth, and one could say that the bud is refuted by the blossom; similarly, when the fruit appears, the blossom is declared to be a false Being-there [form] of the plant, and the fruit replaces the blossom as the truth of the plant. These forms are not only different, they also supplant one another as mutually incompatible. Yet at the same time their fluid nature makes them moments of the organic unity, in which they not only do not conflict, but each is as necessary as the other; and this shared necessity alone constitutes the life of the whole.[1]

Engels, commenting on Hegel's *Philosophy of History*, said this method represented a colossal step forward:

He was the first to try to demonstrate that there is development, an intrinsic coherence in history, and however strange some things in his philosophy of history may seem to us now, the grandeur of the basic conception is still admirable today, compared both with his predecessors or those who following him ventured to advance general observations on history.[2]

For all its faults, the grandeur of Hegel's *History of Philosophy* – its majestic sweep and profound insights – is still a source of wonder and admiration to me to this very day. As for the postmodern critics of Hegel, I will repeat what Lenin once wrote about Rosa Luxemburg, quoting the words of an old Russian proverb: "Eagles may at times fly lower than hens, but hens can never rise to the height of eagles."[3]

---

1   G. W. F. Hegel, *The Phenomenology of Spirit*, pp. 5-6.

2   F. Engels, 'Karl Marx, *A Contribution to the Critique of Political Economy*', *Marx and Engels Collected Works* (Henceforth referred to as MECW), Vol. 16, p. 474.

3   Quoted in V.I. Lenin, 'Notes of a Publicist', *Collected Works* (Henceforth referred to as LCW), Vol. 33, p. 210.

THE MARXIST VIEW OF THE HISTORY OF PHILOSOPHY

In the present work, I have attempted to make use of Hegel's innovation, but from a consistently materialist point of view. This is not a history of philosophy in the empirical notion of the word. Neither is it a compendium of all that everyone ever said on philosophy. Whoever seeks to find in this work, for example, a detailed study of Plato's *Republic*, will be sadly disappointed. Such a person I must direct to the nearest serious public reference library, where I trust they may find a sufficient number of erudite works that will satisfy their curiosity. This is a history of philosophy in its essence. That is, I have tried to follow the overarching line in the development of thought, which has its own immanent laws.

On the other hand, I fear that my book will not satisfy those mechanical 'Marxists' who imagine that it is possible to reduce everything under the sun to the development of the productive forces and/or the class struggle. Of course, in the final analysis, these are the fundamental motor forces of human history and determine the fate of countries, states and empires. But to try to find the explanation of, for example, works of art and music, or the fantastic twists and turns of philosophy and religion by imposing a direct link with this substratum would be a foolish waste of time.

However, insofar as philosophers (like everybody else) can be affected by the general state of society – the rise and fall of the productive forces and the resulting social and political tensions – a relationship can be discernible at certain stages, albeit an indirect one, as my work will point out.

As Engels wrote in a letter to the German economist Conrad Schmidt:

> As to the realms of ideology which soar still higher in the air, religion, philosophy, etc., these have a prehistoric stock, found already in existence and taken over in the historic period, of what we should to-day call bunk. These various false conceptions of nature, of man's own being, of spirits, magic forces, etc., have for the most part only a negative

economic basis; but the low economic development of the prehistoric period is supplemented and also partially conditioned and even caused by the false conceptions of nature.

And even though economic necessity was the main driving force of the progressive knowledge of nature and becomes ever more so, it would surely be pedantic to try and find economic causes for all this primitive nonsense. The history of science is the history of the gradual clearing away of this nonsense or of its replacement by fresh but already less absurd nonsense.

The people who deal with this belong in their turn to special spheres in the division of labour and appear to themselves to be working in an independent field. And in so far as they form an independent group within the social division of labour, in so far do their productions, including their errors, react back as an influence upon the whole development of society, even on its economic development.

But all the same they themselves remain under the dominating influence of economic development. In philosophy, for instance, this can be most readily proved in the bourgeois period. Hobbes was the first modern materialist (in the eighteenth-century sense) but he was an absolutist in a period when absolute monarchy was at its height throughout the whole of Europe and when the fight of absolute monarchy versus the people was beginning in England. Locke, both in religion and politics, was the child of the class compromise of 1688. The English deists and their more consistent successors, the French materialists, were the true philosophers of the bourgeoisie, the French even of the bourgeois revolution. The German petty bourgeois runs through German philosophy from Kant to Hegel, sometimes positively and sometimes negatively. But the philosophy of every epoch, since it is a definite sphere in the division of labour, has as its presupposition certain definite intellectual material handed down to it by its predecessors, from which it takes its start.

And that is why economically backward countries can still play first fiddle in philosophy: France in the eighteenth century compared with England, on whose philosophy the French based themselves, and later Germany in comparison with both. But the philosophy both of France and Germany and the general blossoming of literature at that time were also the result of a rising economic development.

I consider the ultimate supremacy of economic development established in these spheres too, but it comes to pass within conditions imposed by the particular sphere itself: in philosophy, for instance, through the operation of economic influences (which again generally only act under political, etc., disguises) upon the existing philosophic material handed down by predecessors.

Here economy creates nothing absolutely new (*a novo*), but it determines the way in which the existing material of thought is altered and further developed, and that too for the most part indirectly, for it is the political, legal and moral reflexes which exercise the greatest direct influence upon philosophy…

What these gentlemen all lack is dialectic. They never see anything but here cause and there effect. That this is a hollow abstraction, that such metaphysical polar opposites only exist in the real world during crises, while the whole vast process proceeds in the form of interaction (though of very unequal forces, the economic movement being by far the strongest, most elemental and most decisive) and that here everything is relative and nothing is absolute – this they never begin to see. Hegel has never existed for them.[4]

What I have attempted to do here is to draw out the essential and general course of the process of the advancement of knowledge, the full development of which in each epoch of history lays the ground for human thought to move on to the next stage.

The task of Marxists is not to assert and merely dissect every school of thought that ever existed. Rather, it is to draw out from the myriad of conflicting trends and ideas, the essential, rational principles, which have propelled humanity to the stage we are at now. This process has contributed mightily to the enormous advances in

4   F. Engels, 'Letter to Conrad Schmidt, 27 October 1890', *Marx and Engels Selected Correspondence, 1846-1895* (Henceforth referred to as MESC), pp. 482-484.

science and technology, which in turn lay the basis for humanity's progression to a qualitatively higher stage of development, under socialism.

THE POSTMODERN ATTITUDE TO THE PAST: WHERE IGNORANCE IS BLISS, 'TIS FOLLY TO BE WISE

Dialectics has a very long history, beginning with the Greeks, the pre-Socratic philosophers and particularly Heraclitus. It reaches its highest expression in the works of Hegel. But the dominant trend in modern bourgeois philosophy treats all past philosophy with contempt. Not only Marxism but all the great ideas of the past are frivolously dismissed, labelled as 'metanarratives' and consigned without a second thought to the dustbin of history.

In the past, when the bourgeoisie was still capable of playing a progressive role, it had a revolutionary ideology. It produced great and original thinkers: Locke and Hobbes, Rousseau and Diderot, and the other revolutionary thinkers of the French Enlightenment: Kant and Hegel, Adam Smith and David Ricardo, Newton and Darwin. But the intellectual production of the bourgeoisie in the period of decline displays all the evidence of advanced senile decay.

There are periods in history that are characterised by moods of pessimism, doubt and despair. In such periods, having lost faith in the existing society and its ideology, people have only two alternatives. One is to challenge the existing order and take the revolutionary road. The other is to turn inwards in a futile attempt to ignore the contradictions in society, seeking personal salvation, either in religion or in extreme philosophical subjectivism.

The old society is dying on its feet, but it refuses stubbornly to accept its fate. Powerful material interests continue to exert a determined effort to prop it up, and they command formidable resources and exert an irresistible influence on every aspect of social and intellectual life. Today, the ideology of the bourgeoisie is in the process of disintegration, not only in the fields of economics and politics but also in that of philosophy. It produces nothing of value. No longer commanding positive support, respect or authority, it emanates negative moods, as a corpse emits a bad odour. These moods inevitably find their expression in the prevailing philosophy. It is impossible to read the barren products of the university philosophy departments without a feeling of tedium and irritation in equal measure. Needless to say, this general retrogression finds its reflection in attitudes towards the history of philosophy.

The bright-eyed young students who enter the philosophy departments with high hopes of enlightenment are either swiftly disenchanted or else dragged into the poisonous cesspool of postmodern gibberish from whence no escape is possible. In either case, they will emerge without ever learning anything of value from the great thinkers of the past. Not content with filling the minds of young people with postmodernist rubbish, the philosophy departments have the audacity to introduce the same garbage into the study of the past. Evidently, the postmodern academic gang do not like to be reminded of the fact that there was once a time when philosophers actually had something profound and important to say about the real world.

THE DISTORTION OF PHILOSOPHICAL HISTORY

It was recently pointed out to me that a new (and highly praised) translation of Hegel contains a gross mistranslation from the German, which places the postmodernist terminology in the mouth of that great dialectical thinker. The prestigious new Cambridge University English translation of Hegel's *Science of Logic*, which is becoming canonised in universities across the world, consistently translates the German words *Denken* and *Denkend* (which in English plainly mean "thought" and "thinking") as "discourse" and "discursive".

This is a blatant falsification of Hegel's ideas and a transgression of all the ethical norms of translation. It is a criminal act of trying to sneak postmodernist subjectivism into Hegel. In defending this choice, the translator George di Giovanni casually asserts without any proof that: "The subject matter of the *Logic* is not the 'thing-in-itself' or its phenomenal manifestations, whether one conceives its 'in-itself' as a substance or as freedom, *but is discourse itself.*[5]

This is nothing short of a scandal. Yet it has passed unnoticed by the 'critics', who are all delighted by the new 'narrative'. It is an act of vandalism, more or less the equivalent of painting a moustache on the face of the Mona Lisa. This little detail should already put us on our guard.

A FALSE OBJECTIVITY

I have not the slightest doubt that the cleverdicks of the universities will lose no time in accusing me of presenting a one-sided version of the history of philosophy. To this accusation, I plead guilty. As a committed Marxist, I have every intention of defending a particular philosophical standpoint – that of dialectical materialism.

The university philosophy departments are not ivory towers of knowledge and culture, but merely trenches in the war between the classes. These trenches are carefully disguised with an artfully constructed camouflage of pseudo-scientific false objectivity. But behind this tangled web of lies one always finds material interests, class prejudice, and a cynical defence of the status quo.

The whole history of philosophy has been a constant struggle between two hostile and mutually exclusive viewpoints: philosophical materialism and philosophical idealism. That is to say, the scientific approach and the attempt to drag human consciousness backwards to the world of religious mysticism. Since the field of philosophy has always been divided into a whole series of 'one-sided versions', it is utterly impossible to avoid taking the side of one or other of these world views. The only difference between the present author and his critics is that I have been honest enough to declare my interest from the very outset, whereas my critics always hide behind a hypocritical and entirely spurious 'objectivity', which merely serves to disguise their partisan views and class standpoint.

---

5 G. W. F. Hegel, *The Science of Logic*, p. xxxv, my emphasis.

To this day, philosophy remains a battle with no holds barred between materialism and idealism, where the enemies of materialism are numerous and have many advantages. But does the fact that one takes up a definite philosophical and political standpoint rule out objectivity? That is an assumption which is contradicted by the facts.   That great Marxist Leon Trotsky answered these objections as follows:

> In the eyes of a philistine a revolutionary point of view is virtually equivalent to an absence of scientific objectivity. We think just the opposite: only a revolutionist – provided, of course, that he is equipped with the scientific method – is capable of laying bare the objective dynamics of the revolution. Apprehending thought in general is not contemplative, but active. The element of will is indispensable for penetrating the secrets of nature and society. Just as a surgeon, on whose scalpel a human life depends, distinguishes with extreme care between the various tissues of an organism, so a revolutionist, if he has a serious attitude toward his task, is obliged with strict conscientiousness to analyse the structure of society, its functions and reflexes.[6]

A WORD ON MY CRITICS

Ever since Marxism emerged as a significant force challenging the existing order, the establishment has been in a perpetual state of war against every aspect of Marxist ideology, starting with dialectical materialism. The very mention of Marxism is guaranteed to provoke a knee-jerk reaction in such circles. 'Out of date', 'unscientific', 'disproved long ago', 'metaphysics', and all the rest of the threadbare and tiresome litany of reaction.

I have no doubt that the present work will be greeted by a similar chorus of disapproval. This does not bother me in the slightest. I have listened to the same tedious torrent of abuse for the last six decades, and the arguments of the critics of Marx do not gain any greater strength from being so frequently and monotonously repeated. I understand that my opponents will be offended by this. They will

---

6   L. Trotsky, *The Chinese Revolution*, pp. xi–xii.

try to disprove my arguments by burrowing through old texts to try to prove that, after all, black is white and white is black. This is quite a natural reaction, since they themselves defend a particular philosophical standpoint, which is totally incompatible with my own. By that I mean the standpoint of philosophical idealism – either the objective or the subjective kind.

I naturally have no objection to this. They have every right to defend whatever mystical and irrational ideas appeal to them. But let them not try to conceal their partiality behind a façade of false objectivity, or attempt to distort the ideas of great thinkers of the past to fit in with their own narrow and reactionary outlook.

PHILOSOPHY AS A REVOLUTIONARY WEAPON

In spite of its aura of lofty superiority and contempt for the class struggle, official philosophy is only one more weapon in the hands of the ruling class, and it is used deliberately in order to confuse and disorient the youth, and divert them from the path of revolution. In the words of old Joseph Dietzgen, philosophy is not a science, but the safeguard against socialism.

In former times, philosophers were rebels, dangerous heretics bent on subverting the existing moral and social order. Socrates was forced to drink hemlock; Spinoza was accused of atheism, excommunicated and reviled; Giordano Bruno was burnt at the stake by the Inquisition; the French *philosophes* of the eighteenth century prepared the way for the storming of the Bastille. In our own times, however, most people regard philosophy and philosophers with either indifference or contempt, which is richly deserved. But it is a matter of the deepest regret that in turning aside from the present-day philosophical desert, people neglect the great thinkers of the past who, in contrast to the modern pygmies, were giants of human thought.

The old idealist philosophy stubbornly maintained its imaginary independence from social life. To this day, the philosophers of academia claim detachment from the grubby world of real human beings, social life and politics. But this is an illusion. In reality, they merely represent a reflection of that same world, albeit in a mystified form. In the last analysis, whether they are conscious of it or not, the ideas they defend are a thinly disguised defence of the existing society and, at bottom, the most sordid and cynical personal interest.

For my part, I have no intention of dancing a complicated minuet with academics who are guided only by a blind hatred of Marxism and a fervent desire to maintain the status quo. Only by clearing the decks of this ideological garbage can we clear the ground for the successful pursuit of the class struggle. Marxism has a duty to provide a comprehensive alternative to the old and discredited ideas. But we have no right to turn our backs on the great thinkers of the past: the Greeks, Spinoza, the French materialists of the Enlightenment and, above all, Hegel. These were heroic pioneers, who prepared the way for the brilliant achievements of Marxist philosophy, and can rightly be considered as an important part of our revolutionary heritage.

We have a duty to rescue all that was valuable in the history of philosophy, while discarding all that was false, outmoded and useless. Just as the October Revolution, the Paris Commune and the storming of the Bastille pointed the way to the future socialist revolution that will transform the entire world, so the great philosophical battles of the past laid the basis for dialectical materialism – the philosophy of the future. And just as we pay careful attention to the lessons afforded by the class struggles of the past, so we have a duty to study the great battle of ideas that constitutes the essential meaning of the history of philosophy.

* * *

PROFESSOR BENJAMIN FARRINGTON: A PERSONAL MEMOIR

In the early chapters of this work, you will notice that I quote from a book called *Greek Science*, a justly celebrated study written by Professor Benjamin Farrington. This was a pioneering work that has never been surpassed in its treatment of this subject. Nowadays it is generally seen as a classic, yet it provoked considerable controversy because it is written from the standpoint of Marxist historical materialism. I had the good fortune to meet with Professor Farrington in 1963, the year when I left Swansea to enter Sussex University, which had only recently opened. The reason for this meeting was as follows.

Professor Farrington was born in Ireland, but travelled to many countries to teach classics (Greek and Latin) which were his main specialities, although he also wrote important works on philosophy, such as his study of the English materialist, Francis Bacon. He taught in South Africa, where he soon became known for his radical views. Later, he moved to England, where he taught at Bristol University, until he finally settled in my hometown Swansea, where he was Professor of Classics from 1936 to 1956, when he retired.

The thirties was a period of severe depression, mass unemployment and poverty in South Wales. That affected my own family, where my grandfather – a tin plate worker – often had a hard time just feeding his children. He was an active trade unionist and a committed member of the Communist Party.

Although many people know that Benjamin Farrington was a Marxist, very few know that he also was a member of the Communist Party. Because of his position, this fact was not made public, as was the rule in the CP in those days. He got to know both my grandfather and my mother, who as a young girl used to sell *The Daily Worker* in Swansea. He soon became a firm friend of the family.

When I was preparing to go to Sussex, without saying a word to me, my mother sent him a letter in which she proudly announced that I was going to university (an unheard-of event in our family) and enclosed a couple of letters that I had sent to the *South Wales Evening Post*, in support of the Cuban Revolution. In view of the fact that Professor Farrington had retired and as far as I know had lost all contact with my family, I was astonished to learn that he had not only replied, but had invited me to join him for tea on my way to Brighton. He was now retired and living with his wife in Leamington Spa, where I went to meet him. He greeted me very warmly and enquired after my mother (my grandfather had recently passed away). I remember him as a very charming, friendly man, with no hint of the kind of lofty superiority that is the hallmark of so many pretentious academics. He spoke with that soft, gentle southern Irish accent that is music to the ear of us non-Irish inhabitants of these small islands. He asked me about my studies at Sussex and was very generous in his praise of the letters I had sent to *The Evening Post*. He noticed that I was fascinated by the shelves that were full of books on all sides. Seeing that I was interested in philosophy, he asked me who my favourite philosopher was. I replied without any hesitation: Hegel. He immediately stood up and reached for an old grey volume, which he handed to me. It was Hegel's *Philosophy of Law*. I opened it and started to glance through the pages, when he stopped me. "It's yours", he said. "You can keep it."

I have indeed kept that volume ever since and it is sitting on my desk as I write these lines. It is the only one of my books that I have not marked with numerous underlinings and comments in the margins. It remains a precious reminder of a brief encounter with a great man – a real exception in this life: an academic who was not only a genuine intellectual but also a committed Marxist who was not afraid to stand alone against the Philistine tribe.

Benjamin Farrington has long since passed away, but his spirit inspired every page of this book. And to this day, for anyone who is seriously interested in the history of ancient Greece, *Greek Science* is obligatory reading.

London,
20 August 2021

1. THE EMERGENCE
OF PHILOSOPHY

Before we start, you may be tempted to ask, "Well, what of it?" Is it really necessary for us to bother about complicated questions of science and philosophy? To such a question, two replies are possible. If what is meant is: do we need to know about such things in order to go about our daily life, then the answer is evidently no. But if we wish to gain a rational understanding of the world in which we live, and the fundamental processes at work in nature, society and our own way of thinking, then matters appear in quite a different light.

In reality, everyone has a 'philosophy', for a philosophy is a way of looking at the world. We all believe we know how to distinguish right from wrong, good from bad. These are, however, very complicated issues which have occupied the attention of the greatest minds in history. When confronted with the terrible fact of the existence of events like the fratricidal wars in Iraq and Afghanistan, the re-emergence of mass unemployment, or the civil war in Syria, many people will confess that they do not comprehend such things, and will frequently resort to vague references to 'human nature'. But what is this mysterious human nature which is seen as the source of all our ills, and is alleged to be eternally unchangeable? This is a profoundly philosophical question, to which not many would venture a reply, unless they were of a religious cast of mind, in which case they would say that God, in His wisdom, made us like that. Why anyone should worship a Being that played such tricks on His creations is another matter.

Those who stubbornly maintain that they have no philosophy are mistaken. Nature abhors a vacuum, it is said. Those who lack a coherently worked-out philosophical standpoint will inevitably reflect the ideas and prejudices of the society and the milieu in which they live. That means, in the given context, that their heads will be full of the ideas they imbibe from the newspapers, television, pulpit and schoolroom, which faithfully reflect the interests and morality of existing capitalist society.

Most people usually muddle through life until some great upheaval compels them to reconsider the kind of ideas and values they grew up with. The crisis of society forces them to question many things they took for granted. At such times, ideas which seemed remote suddenly become strikingly relevant. Anyone who wishes to understand life, not as a meaningless series of accidents or an unthinking routine, must occupy themselves with philosophy, that is, with thought at a higher level than the immediate problems of everyday existence. Only by this means do we raise ourselves to a height where we begin to fulfil our potential as conscious human beings, willing and able to take control of our own destinies.

It is generally understood that anything worthwhile in life requires some effort. The study of philosophy, by its very nature, involves certain difficulties, because it deals with matters far removed from the world of ordinary experience. Even the terminology used presents difficulties because words are used in a way which does not necessarily correspond to the common usage. But the same is true for any specialised subject, from engineering to psychology.

The second obstacle is more serious. As has been explained, in the nineteenth century, when Marx and Engels first published their writings on dialectical materialism, they could assume that many of their readers had at least a working knowledge of classical philosophy, including the ideas of Hegel. Nowadays, it is not possible to make such an assumption. Philosophy no longer occupies the place it had before, since the role of speculation about the nature of the universe and life has long since been occupied by the sciences. The possession of powerful radio telescopes and spacecraft renders guesses about the nature and extent of our solar system unnecessary. Even the mysteries of the human soul are being gradually laid bare by the progress of neurobiology and psychology.

The situation is far less satisfactory in the realm of the social sciences, mainly because the desire for accurate knowledge often decreases to the degree that science impinges on the powerful material interests which govern the lives of people. The great advances made by Marx and Engels in the sphere of social and historical analysis and economics fall outside the scope of this present work. Suffice it to point out that, despite the sustained and frequently malicious attacks to which they were subjected from the beginning, the theories of Marxism in the social sphere have been the decisive factor in the development of modern social sciences. The vitality of these ideas is testified to by the fact that the attacks not only continue, but tend to increase in intensity as time goes by.

In past ages, the development of science, which has always been closely linked to that of the productive forces, had not reached a sufficiently high level to permit men and women to understand the world in which they lived. In the absence of scientific knowledge, or the material means of obtaining it, they were compelled to rely upon the one instrument they possessed that could help them to make sense of the world, and thus gain power over it – the human mind. The struggle to understand the world was closely identified with humankind's struggle to tear itself away from a mere animal level of existence, to gain mastery over the blind forces of nature, and to become free in the real, rather than legalistic, sense of the word. This struggle is a thread running through the whole of human history.

ROLÈ OF RELIGION

> Man is quite insane. He wouldn't know how to create a maggot, and he creates Gods by the dozen.[1]

> All mythology overcomes and dominates and shapes the force of nature in the imagination and by the imagination; it therefore vanishes with the advent of real mastery over them.[2]

Animals have no religion, and in the past it was said that this constituted the main difference between humans and 'brutes'. But that is just another way of saying that only humans possess consciousness in the full sense of the word. In recent years, there has been a reaction against the idea of humanity as a special and unique Creation. This is undoubtedly correct, in the sense that humans developed from animals and, in many important respects, remain animals. Not only do we share many of the bodily functions with other animals, but the genetic difference between humans and chimpanzees is less than 2 per cent. That is a crushing answer to the nonsense of the Creationists.

Recent research with bonobo apes has proven beyond doubt that the primates closest to humans are capable of a level of mental activity similar, in some respects, to that of a human child. That is striking proof of the kinship between humans and the highest primates, but here the analogy begins to break down. Despite all the efforts of scientists, captive bonobos have not been able to speak or fashion a stone tool remotely similar to the simplest implements created by early hominids. The 2 per cent genetic difference between humans and apes marks the qualitative leap from the animal to the human. This was accomplished, not by a Creator, but by the development of the brain through manual labour.

The skill to make even the simplest stone tools involves a very high level of mental ability and abstract thought. The ability to select the right sort of stone and reject others; the choice of the correct angle to strike a blow, and the use of precisely the right amount of force – these

---

1   M. de Montaigne, *An Apology for Raymond Sebond*, p. 103.

2   K. Marx, *Grundrisse*, p. 110.

are highly complicated intellectual actions. They imply a degree of planning and foresight not found in even the most advanced primates. However, the use and manufacture of stone tools was not the result of conscious planning, but was something forced upon man's remote ancestors by necessity. It was not consciousness that created humanity, but the necessary conditions of human existence which led to an enlarged brain, speech and culture, including religion.

The need to understand the world was closely linked to the need to survive. Those early hominids who discovered the use of stone scrapers in butchering dead animals with thick hides got a considerable advantage over those who were denied access to this rich supply of fats and proteins. Those who perfected their stone implements, and worked out where to find the best materials stood a better chance of survival than those who did not. With the development of technique came the development of the mind, and the need to explain the phenomena of nature which governed their lives. Over millions of years, through trial and error, our ancestors began to establish certain relations between things. They began to make abstractions, that is, to generalise from experience and practice.

For centuries, the central question of philosophy has been the relation of thinking to being. Most people live their lives quite happily without even considering this problem. They think and act, talk and work, with not the slightest difficulty. Moreover, it would not occur to them to regard as incompatible the two most basic human activities, which are, in practice, inseparably linked. Even the most elementary action, if we exclude simple biologically determined reactions, demands a degree of thought. To a degree, this is true not only of humans but also of animals, as can be seen when watching a cat lying in wait for a mouse. In man, however, the kind of thought and planning has a qualitatively higher character than any of the mental activities of even the most advanced of the apes.

This fact is inseparably linked to the capacity for abstract thought, which enables humans to go far beyond the immediate situation given to us by our senses. We can envisage situations, not just in the past (animals also have memory, as a dog which cowers at the sight of a stick) but also the future. We can anticipate complex situations, plan, and thereby determine the outcome, and, to some extent, determine our own destinies.

Although we do not normally think about it, this represents a colossal conquest which sets humankind apart from the rest of nature. "What is distinctive of human reasoning", says the celebrated prehistorian Professor Gordon Childe, "is that it can go immensely farther from the actual present situation than any other animal's reasoning ever seems to get it".[3] From this capacity springs all the manifold creations of civilisation, culture, art, music, literature, science, philosophy and religion. We also take for granted that all this does not drop from the skies, but is the product of millions of years of development.

The Greek philosopher Anaxagoras, in a brilliant deduction, said that man's mental development depended upon the freeing of the hands. In his important article, 'The Part Played by Labour in the Transition from Ape to Man', Engels showed the exact way in which this transition was achieved. He proved that the upright stance, which freed the hands for labour, and the form of the hands – with the opposition of the thumb to the fingers, which allowed for clutching – were the physiological preconditions for toolmaking, which, in turn, was the main stimulus to the development of the brain. Speech itself – which is inseparable from thought – arose out of the demands of social production, the need to realise complicated functions by means of co-operation. These theories of Engels have been strikingly confirmed by the most recent discoveries of palaeontology, which show that hominid apes appeared in Africa far earlier than previously thought, and that they had brains no bigger than those of a modern chimpanzee. That is to say, the development of the brain came after the production of tools, and as a result of it. Thus, it is not true that "In the beginning was the Word", but, as the German poet Goethe proclaimed: "In the beginning was the Deed."

The ability to engage in abstract thought is inseparable from language. Gordon Childe observes:

---

3 V. G. Childe, *What Happened in History*, p. 19.

Reasoning, and all that we call thinking, including the chimpanzee's, must involve mental operations with what psychologists call images. A visual image, a mental picture of, say, a banana, is always liable to be a picture of a particular banana in a particular setting. A word on the contrary is, as explained, more general and abstract, having eliminated just those accidental features that give individuality to any real banana. Mental images of words (pictures of the sound or of the muscular movements entailed in uttering it) form very convenient counters for thinking with. Thinking with their aid necessarily possesses just that quality of abstractness and generality that animal thinking seems to lack. Men can think, as well as talk, about the class of objects called 'bananas'; the chimpanzee never gets further than 'that banana in that tube'. In this way the social instrument termed language has contributed to what is grandiloquently described as "man's emancipation from bondage to the concrete".[4]

Early humans, after a long period of time, formed the general idea of, say, a plant or an animal. This arose out of the concrete observation of many particular plants and animals. But when we arrive at the general concept 'plant', we no longer see before us this or that flower or bush, but that which is common to all of them. We grasp the essence of a plant, its innermost being. Compared with this, the peculiar features of individual plants seem secondary and unstable. What is permanent and universal is contained in the general conception. We can never actually see a plant as such, as opposed to particular flowers and bushes. It is an abstraction of the mind. Yet it is a deeper and truer expression of what is essential to the plant's nature, when stripped of all secondary features.

However, the abstractions of early humans were far from having a scientific character. They were tentative explorations, like the impressions of a child, guesses and hypotheses, sometimes incorrect, but always bold and imaginative. To early humans, the sun was a great being that sometimes warmed them, and sometimes burnt them. The earth was a sleeping giant. Fire was a fierce animal that bit them when they touched it.

---

4 Ibid., pp. 19-20.

Early humans experienced the phenomenon of thunder and lightning. This must have frightened them, as it still frightens animals and people today. But, unlike animals, humans looked for a general explanation of the phenomenon. Given the lack of any scientific knowledge, the explanation was invariably a supernatural one – some god, hitting an anvil with his hammer. To our eyes, such explanations seem merely amusing, like the naive explanations of children. Nevertheless, at this period they were extremely important hypotheses – an attempt to find a rational cause for the phenomenon, in which men distinguished between the immediate experience, and saw something entirely separate from it.

The most characteristic form of early religion is animism – the notion that everything, animate or inanimate has a spirit. We see the same kind of reaction in a child when it smacks a table against which it has banged its head. In the same way, early humans, and certain tribes today, will ask the spirit of a tree to forgive them before cutting it down. Animism belongs to a period when humankind has not yet fully separated itself from the animal world and nature in general. The closeness of humans to the world of animals is attested to by the freshness and beauty of cave art, where horses, deer and bison are depicted with a naturalness which can no longer be captured by the modern artist. It is the childhood of the human race, which has gone beyond recall. We can only imagine the psychology of these distant ancestors of ours. But by combining the discoveries of archaeology with anthropology, it is possible to reconstruct, at least in outline, the world from which we have emerged.

In his classic anthropological study of the origins of magic and religion, Sir James Frazer writes:

A savage hardly conceives the distinction commonly drawn by more advanced peoples between the natural and the supernatural. To him the world is to a great extent worked by supernatural agents, that is, by personal beings acting on impulses and motives like his own, liable like him to be moved by appeals to their pity, their hope, and their fears. In a world so conceived he sees no limit to this power of influencing the course of nature to his own advantage. Prayers, promises, or threats may secure him fine weather and an abundant crop from the gods; and if a god should happen, as he sometimes believes, to become incarnate in his own person, then he need appeal to no higher being; he, the savage, possesses in himself all the powers necessary to further his own well-being and that of his fellow-men.[5]

The notion that the soul exists separate and apart from the body comes down from the most remote period of savagery. The basis of it is quite clear. When we are asleep, the soul appears to leave the body and roam about in dreams. By extension, the similarity between death and sleep ("death's second self", as Shakespeare expressed it) suggested the idea that the soul could continue to exist after death. Early humans thus concluded that there is something inside them that is separate from their bodies. This is the soul, which commands the body, and can do all kinds of incredible things, even when the body is asleep. They also noticed how words of wisdom issued from the mouths of old people, and concluded that, whereas the body perishes, the soul lives on. To people used to the idea of migration, death was seen as the migration of the soul, which needed food and implements for the journey.

At first these spirits had no fixed abode. They merely wandered about, usually making trouble, which obliged the living to go to extraordinary lengths to appease them. Here we have the origin of religious ceremonies. Eventually, the idea arose that the assistance of these spirits could be enlisted by means of prayer. At this stage, religion (magic), art and science were not differentiated. Lacking the means to gain real power over their environment, early humans attempted to obtain their ends by means of magical intercourse with nature, and thus subject it to their will.

The attitude of early humans to their spirit-gods and fetishes was quite practical. Prayers were intended to get results. A man would make an image with his own hands, and prostrate himself before it. But if the desired result was not forthcoming, he would curse it and beat it, in order to extract by violence what he failed to do by entreaty. In this strange world of dreams and ghosts, this world of religion, the

---

5   S. J. G. Frazer, *The Golden Bough*, p. 13.

primitive mind saw every happening as the work of unseen spirits. Every bush and stream was a living creature, friendly or hostile. Every chance event, every dream, pain or sensation, was caused by a spirit. Religious explanations filled the gap left by lack of knowledge of the laws of nature. Even death was not seen as a natural occurrence, but a result of some offence caused to the gods.

For the great majority of the existence of the human race, the minds of men and women have been full of this kind of thing. And not only in what people like to regard as primitive societies. The same kind of superstitious beliefs continue to exist, in slightly different guises, today. Beneath the thin veneer of civilisation, lurk primitive irrational tendencies and ideas which have their roots in a remote past which has been half-forgotten, but is not yet overcome. Nor will they be finally rooted out of human consciousness until men and women establish firm control over their conditions of existence.

DIVISION OF LABOUR

Frazer points out that the division between manual and mental labour in early human society is invariably linked to the formation of a caste of priests, shamans or magicians:

> Social progress, as we know, consists mainly in a successive differentiation of functions, or, in simpler language, a division of labour. The work which in primitive society is done by all alike and by all equally ill, or nearly so, is gradually distributed among different classes of workers and executed more and more perfectly; and so far as the products, material or immaterial, of his specialised labour are shared by all, the whole community benefits by the increasing specialisation. Now magicians or medicine-men appear to constitute the oldest artificial or professional class in the evolution of society. For sorcerers are found in every savage tribe known to us; and among the lowest savages... they are the only professional class that exists.[6]

Of course, the language which Frazer uses is not the language we would use today, but the fundamental idea remains correct. The dualism which separates soul from body, mind from matter, thinking

6 Ibid., pp. 138-9.

from doing, received a powerful impulse from the development of the division of labour at a given stage of social evolution. The separation between mental and manual labour is a phenomenon which coincides with the division of society into classes. It marked a great advance in human development. For the first time, a minority of society was freed from the necessity to work to obtain the essentials of existence. The possession of that most precious commodity, leisure, meant that men could devote their lives to the study of the stars. As the German materialist philosopher Ludwig Feuerbach explains, real theoretical science begins with cosmology:

> The animal is sensible only of the beam which immediately affects life; while man perceives the ray, to him physically indifferent, of the remotest star. Man alone has purely intellectual, disinterested joys and passions; the eye of man alone keeps theoretic festivals. The eye which looks into the starry heavens, which gazes at that light, alike useless and harmless, having nothing in common with the earth and its necessities – this eye sees in that light its own nature, its own origin. The eye is heavenly in its nature. Hence man elevates himself above the earth only with the eye; hence theory begins with the contemplation of the heavens. The first philosophers were astronomers.[7]

Although at this early stage this was still mixed up with religion and the requirements and interests of a priest caste, it also signified the birth of human civilisation. This was already understood by Aristotle, who wrote:

> These theoretical arts, moreover, were evolved in places where men had plenty of free time: mathematics, for example, originated in Egypt, where a priestly caste enjoyed the necessary leisure.[8]

Knowledge is a source of power. In any society in which art, science and government is the monopoly of a few, that minority will use and abuse its power in its own interests. The annual flooding of the Nile

---

7 L. Feuerbach, *The Essence of Christianity*, p. 5.
8 Aristotle, *Metaphysics*, p. 53.

was a matter of life and death to the people of Egypt, whose crops depended on it. The ability of the priests in Egypt to predict, on the basis of astronomical observations, when the Nile would flood its banks must have greatly increased their prestige and power over society. The art of writing, a most powerful invention, was the jealously guarded secret of the priest-caste. As Prigogine and Stengers comment:

> Sumer discovered writing; the Sumerian priests speculated that the future might be written in some hidden way in the events taking place around us in the present. They even systematised this belief, mixing magical and rational elements.[9]

The further development of the division of labour gave rise to an unbridgeable gulf between the intellectual elite and the majority of humankind, condemned to labour with their hands. The intellectual, whether Babylonian priest or modern theoretical physicist, knows only one kind of labour, mental labour. Over the course of millennia, the superiority of the latter over 'crude' manual labour becomes deeply ingrained and acquires the force of a prejudice. Language, words and thoughts become endowed with almost mystical powers. Culture becomes the monopoly of a privileged elite, which jealously guards its secrets, and uses and abuses its position in its own interests.

In ancient times, the intellectual aristocracy made no attempt to conceal its contempt for physical labour. The following extract from an Egyptian text known as *The Satire on the Trades*, written about 2000 BC, is supposed to consist of a father's exhortation to his son, whom he is sending to the Writing School to train as a scribe:

> I have seen how the belaboured man is belaboured – thou shouldst set thy heart in pursuit of writing. And I have observed how one may be rescued from his duties [sic!] – behold, there is nothing which surpasses writing…

> I have seen the metalworker at his work at the mouth of his furnace. His fingers were somewhat like crocodiles; he stank more than fish-roe…

---

9   I. Prigogine and I. Stengers, *Order Out of Chaos: Man's New Dialogue with Nature*, p. 4.

The small building contractor carries mud ... He is dirtier than vines or pigs from treading under his mud. His clothes are stiff with clay...

The arrow-maker, he is very miserable as he goes out into the desert [to get flint points]. Greater is that which he gives to his donkey than its work thereafter [is worth]...

The laundry man launders on the [river] bank, a neighbour of the crocodile...

Behold, there is no profession free of a boss – except for the scribe: he is the boss...

Behold, there is no scribe who lacks food from the property of the House of the King – life, prosperity, health! ... His father and his mother praise god, he being set upon the way of the living. Behold these things – I [have set them] before thee and thy children's children.[10]

The same attitude was prevalent among the Greeks, as can be seen in this passage from Xenophon of Athens:

What are called the mechanical arts, carry a social stigma and are rightly dishonoured in our cities, for these arts damage the bodies of those who work in them or who act as overseers, by compelling them to a sedentary life and to an indoor life, and, in some cases, to spend the whole day by the fire. This physical degeneration results also in deterioration of the soul. Furthermore, the workers at these trades simply have not got the time to perform the offices of friendship or citizenship. Consequently they are looked upon as bad friends and bad patriots, and in some cities, especially the warlike ones, it is not legal for a citizen to ply a mechanical trade.[11]

The radical divorce between mental and manual labour deepens the illusion that ideas, thoughts and words have an independent existence. This misconception lies at the heart of all religion and philosophical idealism.

It was not God who created man after his own image, but, on the contrary, men and women who created gods in their own image and

---

10 Quoted in M. Donaldson, *Children's Minds*, p. 84.
11 Quoted in B. Farrington, *Greek Science*, pp. 28-9.

likeness. Ludwig Feuerbach said that if birds had a religion, their God would have wings.

> Religion is a dream, in which our own conceptions and emotions appear to us as separate existences, beings out of ourselves. The religious mind does not distinguish between subjective and objective – it has no doubts; it has the faculty, not of discerning other things than itself, but of seeing its own conceptions out of itself as distinct beings.[12]

This was already understood by men like Xenophanes of Colophon, who wrote:

> Homer and Hesiod have ascribed to the gods every deed that is shameful and dishonourable among men: stealing and adultery and deceiving each other ... The Ethiopians make their gods black and snub-nosed, and the Thracians theirs grey-eyed and red-haired ... If animals could paint and make things, like men, horses and oxen too would fashion the gods in their own image.[13]

The Creation myths which exist in almost all religions invariably take their images from real life, for example, the image of the potter who gives form to formless clay. In the opinion of Gordon Childe, the story of the Creation in the first book of Genesis reflects the fact that, in Mesopotamia the land was indeed separated from the waters "in the Beginning", but not by divine intervention:

> The land on which the great cities of Babylonia were to rise had literally to be created; the prehistoric forerunner of the biblical Erech was built on a sort of platform of reeds, laid criss-cross upon the alluvial mud. The Hebrew book of Genesis has familiarised us with much older traditions of the pristine condition of Sumer – a 'chaos' in which the boundaries between water and dry land were still fluid. An essential incident in 'The Creation' is the separation of these elements. Yet it was no god, but the proto-Sumerian themselves who created the land; they dug channels to water the fields and drain the marsh; they built dykes and mounded platforms to protect men

---

12 L. Feuerbach, *The Essence of Christianity*, pp. 204-5.
13 Quoted in A. R. Burn, *The Pelican History of Greece*, p. 132.

and cattle from the waters and raise them above the flood; they made the first clearings in the reed brakes and explored the channels between them. The tenacity with which the memory of this struggle persisted in tradition is some measure of the exertion imposed upon the ancient Sumerians. Their reward was an assured supply of nourishing dates, a bounteous harvest from the fields they had drained, and permanent pastures for flocks and herds.[14]

Man's earliest attempts to explain the world and his place in it were mixed up with mythology. The Babylonians believed that the god Marduk created 'Order out of Chaos', separating the land from the water, heaven from earth. The biblical Creation myth was taken from the Babylonians by the Jews, and later passed into the culture of Christianity. The true history of scientific thought commences when men and women learn to dispense with mythology, and attempt to obtain a rational understanding of nature, without the intervention of the gods. From that moment, the real struggle for the emancipation of humanity from material and spiritual bondage begins.

A REVOLUTION IN THOUGHT

The advent of philosophy represents a genuine revolution in human thought. Like so much of modern civilisation, we owe it to the ancient Greeks. Although important advances were also made by the Indians and Chinese, and later the Arabs, it was the Greeks who developed philosophy and science to its highest point prior to the Renaissance. The history of Greek thought in the four hundred year period, from the middle of the seventh century BC, constitutes one of the most imposing pages in the annals of human history.

Here we have a long line of heroes who pioneered the development of thought. The Greeks discovered that the world was round long before Columbus. They explained that humans had evolved from fishes long before Darwin. They made extraordinary discoveries in mathematics, especially geometry, which were not greatly improved upon for one-and-a-half millennia. They invented mechanics and even invented the steam engine.

---

14 V. G. Childe, *Man Makes Himself*, pp. 107-8.

What was startlingly new about this way of looking at the world was that it was not religious. In complete contrast to the Egyptians and Babylonians, from whom they had learnt a lot, the Greek thinkers did not resort to gods and goddesses to explain natural phenomena. For the first time, men and women sought to explain the workings of nature purely in terms of nature. This was one of the greatest turning points in the entire history of human thought. True science starts here.

THE BIRTH OF PHILOSOPHY

Western philosophy was born under the clear blue skies of the early Aegean period. The eighth and seventh centuries BC were a period of rapid economic expansion in the eastern Mediterranean. These were stirring times. The Greeks of the Ionian islands, which lie off the coast of present-day Turkey, conducted a thriving trade with Egypt, Babylon and Lydia. The Lydian invention of money was introduced into Europe via Aegina at about 625 BC, greatly stimulating trade, bringing in its wake great riches for some and indebtedness and slavery for others.

The earliest Greek philosophy represents the true starting point of philosophy. It is an attempt to struggle free from the age-old bounds of superstition and myth, to dispense with gods and goddesses, so that, for the first time, human beings could stand face to face with nature and with real men and women.

The economic revolution gave rise to new social contradictions. The breakdown of the old patriarchal society provoked a clash between rich and poor. The old aristocracy was faced with the discontent of the masses and the opposition of the 'tyrants' – frequently dissident nobles themselves – who were always willing to put themselves at the head of popular risings. A period of instability opened up, in which men and women began to question the old beliefs.

The situation in Athens at this time is described in the following passage:

> In the bad years they [the peasants] had to borrow from rich neighbours; but with the coming of money, this meant that, instead of borrowing a

sack of corn in the good old neighbourly way, one had to borrow the price of enough corn to tide one over, before the harvest, when it was cheap; or alternatively, to pay heavy interest, of the kind that raised such indignation at Megara. By 600 [BC], while rich men exported to good markets in Aegina or Corinth, poor men were going hungry. Many, too, were losing their land, pledged as security for debts, and even their liberty; for the debtor's last recourse against the insolvent debtor was to seize him and his family as slaves.

The law was harsh; it was rich man's law.[15]

These laws were put into a code by Drakon, from which the phrase 'Draconian laws' has become proverbial.

The turbulent sixth century BC was a period of decline of the Greek Ionian republics of Asia Minor, characterised by social crisis and ferocious class struggle between rich and poor, masters and slaves. Rostovtsev writes: "At Miletus [in Asia Minor] the people were at first victorious and murdered the wives and children of the aristocrats; then the aristocrats prevailed and burned their opponents alive, lighting up the open spaces of the city with live torches".[16]

These conditions were typical of most other Greek cities of Asia Minor at the time. The heroes of this age had nothing in common with the later idea of the philosopher, isolated from the rest of humanity in his ivory tower. These 'wise men' were not only thinkers, but doers, not only theoreticians, but practical men of the world. Of the first of them, Thales of Miletus (c. 640-546 BC), we know next to nothing, but it is expressly stated that it was only late in life that he took to philosophy. He was also involved in commerce, engineering, geometry and astronomy (he is said to have predicted an eclipse, which must have occurred in 585 BC).

What is indisputable is that all the early Greek philosophers were materialists. Turning their backs on mythology, they sought to find a general principle for the workings of nature from an observation of

---

15 A. R. Burn, *The Pelican History of Greece*, p. 119.
16 Quoted in B. Russell, *History of Western Philosophy*, p. 44.

nature itself. The later Greeks refer to them as *hylozoists*, which can be translated as "those who think that matter is alive". This conception of matter as self-moving is strikingly modern, and far superior to the mechanical physics of the eighteenth century. Given the absence of modern scientific instruments, their theories frequently had the character of inspired guesswork. But, taking into account the lack of resources, the amazing thing is how close they came to a real understanding of the workings of nature. Thus the philosopher Anaximander (c. 610-545 BC) worked out that man and all other animals had developed from a fish, which abandoned water for the land.

It is misleading to suppose that these philosophers were religious just because they used the word 'god' (*theos*) in relation to primary substance. J. Burnet states that this meant no more than the old Homeric epithets like 'ageless', 'deathless', etc. Even in Homer, the word is used in several different senses. From Hesiod's *Theogony* it is clear that many of the 'gods' were never worshipped, but were merely convenient personifications of natural phenomena or even human passions. Primitive religions looked on the heavens as divine and set apart from the earth. The Ionian philosophers radically broke with this standpoint. While basing themselves on the many discoveries of Babylonian and Egyptian cosmology, they rejected the mythical element, which confused astronomy with astrology.

The general tendency of Greek philosophy before Socrates was to search for the underlying principles of nature:

> Nature it was – that which is most immediately present to us, that which lies nearest the eye, that which is palpablest – that first attracted the spirit of inquiry. Under its changeful forms, its multiplex phenomena, there must lie, it was thought, a first and permanent fundamental principle. What is this principle? What, it was asked, is the primitive ground of things? Or, more precisely, what natural element is the basal element?[17]

They gave different explanations for this. For example, Thales claimed that the basis of all things is water. This was a great advance for human

---

17 A. Schwegler, *Handbook of the History of Philosophy*, p. 6.

thought. True, the Babylonians had long before put forward the idea that all things came from water in their Creation myth, which was the model for the Hebrew story of the Creation in the first book of Genesis. "All lands were sea", says the legend, until Marduk, the Babylonian creator, separated the land from the sea. The difference here is that there is no Marduk, no divine creator standing outside nature. Instead, for the first time, nature is explained in purely materialist terms, that is, in terms of nature itself.

Nor is the idea of nature as reducible to water as far-fetched as it might appear. Apart from the fact that the great majority of the earth's surface is made up of water, something the Ionian Greeks above all were aware of, water is essential for all forms of life. The bulk of our body consists of water, and we would quickly die if deprived of it. Moreover, water changes its form, passing from a liquid to a solid, to a vapour. On this Burnet comments:

> Nor is it hard to see how the meteorological considerations may have led Thales to adopt the views he did. Of all the things we know, water seems to take the most various shapes. It is familiar to us in a solid, a liquid, and a vaporous form, and so, Thales may well have thought he saw the world-process from water and back to water again going on before his eyes. The phenomenon of evaporation naturally suggests that the fire of the heavenly bodies is kept up by the moisture they draw from the sea. Even at the present day, people speak of the 'sun drawing up water'. Water comes down again in rain; and lastly, so the early cosmologists thought, it turns to earth. This may have seemed natural enough to men who were familiar with the rivers of Egypt which had formed the Delta, and the torrents of Asia Minor which bring down large alluvial deposits.[18]

ANAXIMANDER

Thales was followed by other philosophers who advanced different theories as to the basic structure of matter. Anaximander is said to have come from Samos, where the famous Pythagoras also lived. He is said to have written about nature, the fixed stars, the earth's sphere

---

18 J. Burnet, *Early Greek Philosophy*, pp. 48-9.

and other matters. He produced something like a map, showing the boundary of land and sea, and was responsible for a number of mathematical inventions, including a sundial and an astronomical chart.

Like Thales, Anaximander considered what the nature of reality was. Like him, he approached this question from a strictly materialist point of view, without recourse to the gods or any supernatural elements. But, unlike his contemporary, Thales, he did not seek to find the answer in a particular form of matter, such as water. According to Diogenes:

> He adduced the Infinite (the undetermined) as principle and element; he neither determined it as air or water or any such thing.
>
> …
>
> It is the principle of all becoming and passing away; at long intervals infinite worlds or gods rise out of it, and again they pass away into the same.[19]

This put the study of the universe on a scientific footing for the first time, and enabled the early Greek philosophers to make outstanding discoveries, far in advance of their time. They first discovered that the world is round and does not rest on anything, that the earth was not the centre of the universe, but revolves with the other planets around the centre. According to another contemporary, Hippolitos, Anaximander said that the earth swings free, held in place by nothing, because it is equidistant from everything, and is round in shape and hollow, like a pillar, so that we are on one side of the earth, and others on the other. They also discovered the true theory of lunar and solar eclipses.

With all their gaps and deficiencies, these ideas represent a startlingly bold and original conception of nature and the universe, certainly far nearer to the truth than the blinkered mysticism of the Middle Ages, when human thought was again shackled by religious dogma. Moreover, these important advances were not merely the result

---

19 Quoted in G. W. F. Hegel, *Lectures on the History of Philosophy*, Vol. 1, p. 186.

of guesswork, but the result of careful thought, investigation and experiment. 2000 years before Darwin, Anaximander anticipated the theory of evolution, with his amazing discoveries in marine biology. The historian A. R. Burn believes that this was no accident, but the result of scientific investigation: "It looks as though he had made observations on embryos and also on fossils, as one of his successors certainly did; but we are not positively told."[20]

Anaximander effected a great revolution in human thought. Instead of limiting himself to this or that concrete form of matter, he arrived at the concept of matter in general, matter as a philosophical concept. This universal substance is eternal and infinite, constantly changing and evolving. All the myriad forms of being we perceive through our senses are different expressions of the same basic substance. This idea was so novel that for many it proved incomprehensible. Plutarch complained that Anaximander did not specify which one of the elements his Infinite was – water, earth, air or fire. But precisely in this lay the epoch-making character of the theory.

ANAXIMENES

The last of the great trio of Ionian materialists was Anaximenes (c. 585-528 BC). He is said to have been born when Thales 'flourished', and to have 'flourished' when Thales died. He was younger than Anaximander. Unlike Anaximander, and following Thales, he took a single element – air – as the absolute substance, from which everything comes forth and to which everything is ultimately reduced. In fact, Anaximenes' use of the word 'air' (*aer*) differs substantially from the modern usage. It includes vapour, mist and even darkness. Many translators prefer the word 'mist'.

At first sight, this idea represents a step back in comparison to the position of matter in general arrived at by Anaximander. In fact, his world view was a step forward.

Anaximenes attempted to show how 'air', the universal substance, becomes transformed through a process of what he called rarification

20 A. R. Burn, *The Pelican History of Greece*, p. 130.

and condensation. When it is rarefied, it becomes fire, when condensed, wind. By further condensation, we get clouds, water, earth and stones. But, although in details his view of the universe compares unfavourably with that of Anaximander (he thought the world was shaped like a table, for instance), nevertheless, his philosophy represented an advance, inasmuch as he tried to move beyond a general statement of the nature of matter. He attempted to give it a more precise determination, not only qualitatively, but quantitatively, through the process of rarification and condensation. In the words of Professor Farrington:

> Observe, in following this succession of thinkers, how their logic, their stock of ideas, their power of abstraction, increase as they grapple with their problem. It was a great advance in human thinking when Thales reduced the manifold appearances of things to one First Principle. Another great step was taken when Anaximander chose, as his First Principle, not a visible form of things like water, but a concept like the Indeterminate. But Anaximenes was still not content. When Anaximander sought to explain how the different things emerged from the Indeterminate, he gave a reply that was a mere metaphor. He said it was a process of 'separating out'. Anaximenes felt that something more was needed, and came forward with the complementary ideas of Rarification and Condensation, which offered an explanation of how quantitative changes could produce qualitative ones.[21]

Given the existing level of technique, it was impossible for Anaximenes to arrive at a more precise characterisation of the phenomena under consideration. It is easy to point to the deficiencies and even absurdities of his views. But this would miss the point. The early Greek philosophers cannot be blamed for failing to provide their world picture with a detailed content, which was only possible on the basis of over 2000 years of subsequent economic, technological and scientific advance. These great pioneers of human thought rendered humanity the unique service of breaking away from the age-

---

21 B. Farrington, *Greek Science*, p. 39.

old habits of religious superstition, and thereby laid the foundation without which all scientific and cultural advance would have been unthinkable.

Moreover, the general view of the universe and nature elaborated by these great revolutionary thinkers was in many respects close to the truth. Their problem was that, given the level of development of production and technology, they did not have the means of testing their hypotheses, and putting them on a solid footing. They anticipated many things which could only be fully worked out by modern science, resting on a far higher development of science and technique. Thus, for Anaximenes, 'air' is only shorthand for matter in its simplest, most basic form. As Erwin Schrödinger, one of the founders of modern physics shrewdly remarked: "Had he said dissociated hydrogen gas", (which he could hardly be expected to say), "he would not be so far from our present view".[22]

The earlier Ionian philosophers of nature had probably gone as far as they could to explain the workings of nature by means of speculative reason. These were truly great generalisations, which pointed in the right direction. But, in order to carry the process further, it was necessary to examine things in greater detail, to proceed to analyse nature piece by piece. This was later begun by Aristotle and the Alexandrine Greek thinkers. But an important part of this task was to consider nature from a quantitative point of view. Here the Pythagorean philosophers undoubtedly played a major role.

Already, Anaximenes had pointed in this direction in attempting to pose the question of the relation between changes of quantity and quality in nature (rarification and condensation). But this method had by now reached its limits and exhausted itself. As J. D. Bernal puts it:

> The triumph of the Ionian school was that it had set up a picture of how the universe had come into being and how it worked without the intervention of gods or design. Its basic weakness was its vagueness and qualitative character. By itself it could lead nowhere; nothing concrete

22 Quoted in A. R. Burn, *The Pelican History of Greece*, p. 131.

could be done with it. What was needed was the introduction of *number* and *quantity* into philosophy.[23]

FROM MATERIALISM TO IDEALISM

The period of the ascent of ancient Greek philosophy was characterised by a profound crisis of society, marked by a general questioning of the old beliefs, including the established religion. The crisis of religious belief gave rise to atheist tendencies and the birth of a genuinely scientific outlook, based on materialism. However, as always in society, the process took place in a contradictory way. Alongside the rationalist and scientific tendencies, we also see the opposite – a growing trend towards mysticism and irrationality. A very similar phenomenon occurred at the time of the crisis of Roman society, with the rapid spread of oriental religions, of which Christianity was originally only one among many.

To the mass of peasants and slaves, living in a time of social crisis, the gods of Olympus seemed remote. This was a religion for the upper classes. There was no prospect of a future reward for present suffering in the afterlife. The Greek underworld was a cheerless place inhabited by lost souls. The newer cults, with their mimetic dancing and choral singing (the real origin of Greek tragedy), their mysteries (from the verb *myo*, meaning to keep your mouth shut), and the promise of life after death, was far more attractive to the masses. Particularly popular was the cult of Dionysius, the god of wine (known to the Romans as Bacchus), which involved drunken orgies. This was much more appealing than the old gods of Olympia.

As in the period of decline of the Roman Empire, and in the present period of capitalist decline, there was a spread of all kinds of mystery cults, mixed with new exotic rites imported from Thrace and Asia Minor and possibly Egypt. Of particular importance was the cult of Orpheus, a refinement of the cult of Dionysius, with many points in common with the Pythagorean movement. Like the Pythagoreans, the followers of the cult of Orpheus believed in the transmigration of souls. They had rites of purification, including abstaining from

23 J. D. Bernal, *Science in History*, p. 122.

meat, except for sacramental purposes. Their view of man was based on dualism – the idea of the cleavage of body and soul. For them, man was partly of heaven, partly of earth.

So close are these ideas to the Pythagorean doctrines that some authors, such as Bury, maintain that the Pythagoreans were really a branch of the Orphean movement. This is an exaggeration. Despite its mystical elements, the Pythagorean school made an important contribution to the development of human thought, especially mathematics. It cannot be dismissed as a religious sect. Nevertheless, it is impossible to resist the conclusion that the idealist conceptions of Pythagoreanism are not just an echo of a religious world outlook, but stem directly from it. Bertrand Russell traces the development of idealism back to the mysticism of the Orphean religion:

> This mystical element entered into Greek philosophy with Pythagoras, who was a reformer of Orphism as Orpheus was a reformer of the religion of Dionysius. From Pythagoras Orphic elements entered into the philosophy of Plato, and from Plato into most later philosophy that was in any degree religious.[24]

The division between mental and manual labour reaches an extreme expression with the growth of slavery. This phenomenon was directly related to the spread of Orphism. Slavery is an extreme form of alienation. Under capitalism, the 'free' worker is alienated from his labour-power, which presents itself to him as a separate and hostile force – capital. Under slavery, however, the slave loses his very existence as a human being. He is nothing. Not a person, but a 'tool with a voice'. The product of his labour, his body, his mind, his soul are the property of another, who disposes of them without regard to his wishes. The unfulfilled desires of the slave, his extreme alienation from the world and himself, gives rise to a feeling of rejection towards the world and all its works. The material world is evil. Life is a vale of tears. Happiness is not to be found there, only in death, which gives release from toil. The soul, freed from its prison in the body, can become free.

---

24 B. Russell, *History of Western Philosophy*, p. 39.

In all periods of social decline, men and women have two options: either to confront reality, and fight to change it, or to accept that there is no way out, and resign themselves to their fate. These two contrasting outlooks are inevitably reflected in two antagonistic philosophies – materialism and idealism. If we desire to change the world, it is necessary to understand it. We must look reality in the face. The cheerful optimism of the early Greek materialists was typical of this outlook. They wanted to know. Later, all that changed. The break-up of the old order, the rise of slavery and a general sense of insecurity led to a certain introversion and pessimism. In the absence of a clear alternative, the tendency to look away from reality, to seek individual salvation in mysticism, gradually gained ground. The lower orders looked to mystery cults, like those of Demeter, giver of corn, Dionysius, giver of wine, and later the cult of Orpheus. But the upper classes were not immune to the problems of the period. These were troubled times. Prosperous cities could be turned to ashes overnight, and their citizens killed or sold into slavery.

The city of Sybaris, Croton's powerful commercial rival, was renowned for its wealth and luxury. So wealthy were the upper class that all kinds of tall stories were told about the 'Sybarite' lifestyle. A typical example was the young Sybarite who, upon rising, complained of a crumpled rose-leaf in his bed. It is said that they piped their wine to the quay. Allowing for an element of exaggeration, it is clear that this was a most prosperous city, where the rich lived a life of great luxury. However, the growth of inequality gave rise to a ferocious class struggle.

This was a period in which the division of labour was enormously intensified, accompanied by the rapid growth of slavery, and an ever-increasing gulf between rich and poor. The industrial and residential quarters were completely segregated. But high walls and guards did not save the rich citizens of Sybaris. As in other city states, a revolution erupted in which the 'tyrant', Telys, seized power with the support of the masses. This gave Croton the excuse to declare war on its rival, at a moment when it was weakened by internal divisions. After a seventy-day campaign, the city fell into their hands. A. R. Burn comments:

They utterly destroyed it, turning the local river across its site, while survivors scattered, largely to the west coast. The particular savagery of this war is more easily understood when it is seen as a class war.[25]

It is in this specific context that we must see the rise of the Pythagorean school of philosophy. As in the period of decline of the Roman Empire, a section of the ruling class was filled with a feeling of anxiety, fear and perplexity. The old gods offered no solace or hope of delivery, either to rich or poor. Even the good things in life lost some of their appeal to men and women who felt they were sitting on the edge of an abyss. Under such conditions of general insecurity, when even the strongest and most prosperous states could be overthrown in a short time, the doctrines of Pythagoras struck a chord with a section of the ruling class, despite their ascetic character, or even because of it. The esoteric and intellectual nature of this movement gave it no appeal to the masses, where the Orphic cult had gained a huge following.

PYTHAGORAS AND HIS SCHOOL

It is safer to speak of the school rather than of its founder, since it is difficult to disentangle the philosophy of Pythagoras from the myths and obscurantism of his followers. No written fragments of his have survived, and it is doubtful if they ever existed. Even the existence of Pythagoras has been questioned. However, the influence of his school on Greek thought was profound.

Pythagoras is said to have been a native of the island of Samos, a thriving commercial power, like Miletus. Its local dictator ('tyrant'), Polycrates, had overthrown the landed aristocracy and was ruling with the support of the merchant class. Of him, the historian Herodotos reports that he robbed all men indiscriminately, for he said that his friends were more grateful if he gave them their property back than they would have been if he had never taken it! In his youth, Pythagoras apparently worked as a *philo-sophos* (lover of wisdom) under the patronage of Polycrates. He travelled to Phoenicia and Egypt, where he is said to have been initiated into an Egyptian priest caste. In 530

---

25 A. R. Burn, *The Pelican History of Greece*, p. 140.

BC, he fled to Croton in southern Italy to escape from civil strife and the threat posed by the Persians to Ionia.

The luxuriant overgrowth of myth and fable makes it almost impossible to say anything certain about the man. His school certainly was a remarkable mixture of mathematical and scientific investigation and a religious-monastic sect. The community was run on monastic lines, with strict rules which included, for instance: not to eat beans; not to pick up what was fallen; not to stir the fire with iron; not to step over a crowbar, etc. The whole idea was to escape from the world, to seek salvation in a life of peaceful contemplation based on mathematics, which was invested with supposedly mystical qualities. Probably reflecting oriental influences, the Pythagoreans also preached the transmigration of souls.

In contrast to the cheerful worldliness of the Ionian materialists, here we have all the elements of the future idealist world outlook later developed by Plato, and taken over by Christianity, which bedevilled the growth of the spirit of scientific inquiry for many centuries. The moving spirit behind this ideology is aptly expressed by J. Burnet in the following lines:

> We are strangers in this world, and the body is the tomb of the soul, and yet we must not seek to escape by self-murder; for we are the chattels of God who is our herdsman, and without His command we have no right to make our escape. In this life, there are three kinds of men, just as there are three sorts of people who come to the Olympic Games. The lowest class is made up of those who come to buy and sell, the next above them are those who come to compete. Best of all, however, are those who come simply to look on. The greatest purification of all is, therefore, disinterested science, and it is the man who devotes himself to that, the true philosopher, who has most effectually released himself from the 'wheel of birth'.[26]

This philosophy, with its strong elitist and monastic overtones, proved popular with the wealthy classes of Croton, although how many really gave up eating beans, or anything else, may be open to doubt! The

---

26 Quoted in B. Russell, *History of Western Philosophy*, p. 52.

common thread in all this is the radical separation of the soul from the body. This idea, with its roots in a prehistoric conception of man's place in nature, has been passed down in different forms throughout history. It even resurfaces in one of the Hippocratic treatises:

> While the body is awake, the soul is not under its own control, but is split into various portions each being devoted to some special bodily function such as hearing, vision, touch, locomotion and all the various actions of the body. But when the body is at rest, the soul is stirred and roused and becomes its own master, and itself performs all the functions of the body. When the body is sleeping it receives no sensations, but the soul being awake at that time perceives everything; it sees what is visible, it hears what is audible, it walks, it touches, it feels pain and thinks. In short, during sleep the soul performs all the functions of both body and soul. A correct appreciation of these things implies considerable wisdom.[27]

In contrast to the Ionian materialist philosophers, who deliberately turned their backs on religion and mythology, the Pythagoreans took over the idea of the Orphic mystery cult, that the soul could free itself from the body by means of an 'ecstasy' (the word *ekstasis* means 'stepping out'). Only when the soul left the prison of the body was it deemed to express its true nature. Death was life and life was death. Thus, from its inception, philosophical idealism, in common with its conjoined twin, religion, represented an inversion of the real relation between thought and being, man and nature, people and things. Such idealism has persisted down to the present time, in one form or another, with the most pernicious results.

THE PYTHAGOREAN DOCTRINE

In spite of its mystical character, the Pythagorean doctrine marked a step forward in the development of philosophy. There is nothing strange about this. In the evolution of human thought, there are many instances in which the pursuit of irrational and unscientific goals nevertheless have furthered the cause of science. For centuries, the alchemists exerted themselves fruitlessly in an attempt to discover

---

27 Dreams (Regimen IV), *Hippocratic writings*, p. 252.

the 'philosopher's stone'. This ended in failure. But in the process, they made extremely important discoveries in the field of experiment which provided the basis upon which modern science, especially chemistry, later developed.

The basic tendency of Ionian philosophy was an attempt to generalise from the experience of the real world. Pythagoras and his followers attempted to arrive at an understanding of the nature of things by a different route. Schwegler puts it thus:

> We have the same abstraction, but on a higher stage, when the sensuous concretion of matter *in general* is looked away from; when attention is turned no longer to the qualitative aspect of matter, as water, air, etc., but to its quantitative measure and relations; when reflection is directed, not to the material, but to the form and order of things as they exist in space.[28]

The progress of human thought in general is closely linked to the capacity to make abstractions from reality, to be able to draw general conclusions from a host of particulars. Since reality is many-sided, it is possible to interpret it in many different ways, reflecting this or that element of the truth. This we see many times in the history of philosophy, where great thinkers laid hold of one aspect of reality, and held it up as an absolute and final truth, only to be swept away by the next generation of thinkers, who in turn repeat the process. Yet the rise and fall of great philosophical schools and scientific theories represents the development and enrichment of human thought by a process of endless successive approximations.

The Pythagoreans approached the world from the standpoint of number and quantity relations. For Pythagoras, all things are numbers. This idea was linked to the search for the underlying harmony of the universe. They believed that number was the element out of which all things developed. Despite the mystical element, they made important discoveries which greatly stimulated the development of mathematics, especially geometry. They invented the terms odd and even numbers, odd numbers being male and even ones female. Since no women were

---

28 A. Schwegler, *History of Philosophy*, p. 11.

allowed in the community, they naturally declared odd numbers to be divine and even ones earthly! Likewise, our terms squares and cubes of numbers come from the Pythagoreans, who also discovered harmonic progression in the musical scale, linking the length of a string and the pitch of its vibrating note.

These important discoveries were not put to any practical use by the Pythagoreans, who were interested in geometry purely from an abstract mystical point of view. Yet they had a determining influence on subsequent thought. The mystique of mathematics as an esoteric subject, inaccessible to ordinary mortals, has persisted down to the present day. It was transmitted through the idealist philosophy of Plato, who placed over the entrance of his school the inscription: "Let no man destitute of geometry enter my doors."

Professor Farrington writes:

> The cosmology of the Pythagoreans is very curious and very important. They did not, like the Ionians, try to describe the universe in terms of the behaviour of certain material elements and physical processes. They described it exclusively in terms of number. Aristotle said long afterwards that they took number to be the matter as well as the form of the universe. Numbers constituted the actual stuff of which their world was made. They called a point One, a line Two, a surface Three, a solid Four, according to the minimum number of points necessary to define each of these dimensions.[29]

They attached magical significance to particular numbers – three, four, seven. Of particular significance was the number ten, which is the sum of one, two, three and four. These superstitions still persist in the Holy Trinity, the four horsemen of the Apocalypse, the seven deadly sins, and the like. "It is also apparent", adds Bernal, "in modern mathematical physics whenever its adepts try to make God the supreme mathematician."[30]

The history of science is characterised by the most fierce partisanship, at times bordering on fanaticism, in defence of particular schools of

---

29 B. Farrington, *Greek Science*, p. 47.
30 J. D. Bernal, *Science in History*, p. 124.

thought, which put themselves forward as the protagonists of an absolute truth, and who do in fact embody the maximum point reached by human knowledge at a given point in time. Only the further development of science itself reveals the limitations and inner contradictions of a given theory, which is then negated by its opposite, which is itself negated, and so on *ad infinitum*. This process is precisely the dialectic of the history of science, which for centuries proceeded in tandem with the history of philosophy, and initially was virtually indistinguishable from it.

'ALL THINGS ARE NUMBERS'

The development of the quantitative side of investigating nature was obviously of crucial importance. Without it, science would have remained on the level of mere generalities, incapable of further development. However, when such a breakthrough takes place, there is inevitably a tendency to make exaggerated claims on its behalf. This is particularly true in this case, where science is still entangled with religion.

The Pythagoreans saw number – quantitative relations – as the essence of all things: all things are numbers. Indeed, it is possible to explain many natural phenomena in mathematical terms. Nevertheless, even the most advanced mathematical models are only approximations of the real world. The inadequacy of the purely quantitative approach, however, was evident long ago. Hegel, who was a convinced idealist and a formidable mathematician, might have been expected to be enthusiastic about the Pythagorean school. However, this was far from the case. Hegel poured scorn on the idea that the world could be reduced to quantitative relations.

From Pythagoras onwards, the most extravagant claims have been made on behalf of mathematics, which has been portrayed as the queen of the sciences, the magic key opening all doors of the universe. Breaking free from all contact with crude material reality, mathematics appeared to soar into the heavens, where it acquired a god-like existence, obeying no rule but its own. Thus, the great mathematician Henri Poincaré, in the early years of the twentieth century, could claim that the laws of science did not relate to the real world at all, but represented arbitrary conventions destined to promote a more convenient and 'useful' description of the corresponding phenomena. Many physicists now openly state that the validity of their mathematical models does not depend upon empirical verification, but on the aesthetic qualities of their equations.

Thus, the theories of mathematics have been, on the one side, the source of tremendous scientific advance and, on the other, the origin of numerous errors and misconceptions which have had, and are still having, profoundly negative consequences. The central error is to attempt to reduce the complex, dynamic and contradictory workings of nature to static, orderly quantitative formulae. Starting with the Pythagoreans, nature is presented in a formalistic manner, as a single-dimensional point, which becomes a line, which becomes a plane, a cube, a sphere, and so on. At first sight, the world of pure mathematics is one of absolute thought, unsullied by contact with material things. But this is far from the truth, as Engels points out. We use the decimal system, not because of logical deduction or 'free will', but because we have ten fingers. The word 'digital' comes from the Latin word for fingers. And to this day, a schoolboy will secretly count his material fingers beneath a material desk, before arriving at the answer to an abstract mathematical problem. In so doing, the child is unconsciously retracing the way in which early humans learned to count.

The material origins of the abstractions of mathematics were no secret to Aristotle:

> The mathematician investigates abstractions. He eliminates all sensible qualities like weight, density, temperature, etc., leaving only the quantitative and continuous (in one, two or three dimensions) and its essential attributes.[31]

Elsewhere, he says:

> Mathematical objects cannot exist apart from sensible (i.e. material) things.[32]

---

31 Aristotle, *Metaphysics*, p. 120.
32 Ibid., p. 251.

We have no experience of anything which consists of lines or planes or points, as we should have if these things were material substances, lines, etc., may be prior in definition to body, but they are not on that account prior in substance.[33]

The development of mathematics is the result of very material human needs. Early man at first had only ten number sounds, precisely because he counted, like a small child, on his fingers. The exception was the Mayas of Central America, who had a numerical system based on twenty instead of ten, probably because they counted their toes as well as their fingers. Early man, living in a simple hunter-gatherer society, without money or private property, had no need of large numbers. To convey a number larger than ten, he merely combined some of the ten sounds connected with his fingers. Thus, one more than ten is expressed by 'one-ten' (*undecim*, in Latin, or *ein-lifon* – 'one over' – in early Teutonic, which becomes eleven in modern English). All the other numbers are only combinations of the original ten sounds, with the exception of five additions – hundred, thousand, million, billion and trillion.

The real origin of numbers was already understood by the great English materialist philosopher of the seventeenth century, Thomas Hobbes:

> And it seems, there was a time when those names of number were not in use; and men were fayn to apply their fingers of one or both hands, to those things they desired to keep account of; and that thence it proceeded, that now our numerall words are but ten, in any Nation, and in some but five, and then they begin again.[34]

Alfred Hooper explains:

> Just because primitive man invented the same number of number-sounds as he had fingers, our number-scale today is a *decimal* one, that is, a scale based on *ten*, and consisting of endless repetitions of the first ten basic

---

33 Ibid., p. 253.
34 T. Hobbes, *Leviathan*, p. 14.

number-sounds ... Had men been given twelve fingers instead of ten, we should doubtless have a *duo-decimal* number-scale today, one based on twelve, consisting of endless repetitions of twelve basic number-sounds.[35]

In fact, a duodecimal system has certain advantages in comparison to the decimal one. Whereas ten can only be exactly divided by two and five, twelve can be divided exactly by two, three, four and six. The proof of this can be found in the ancient Sumerian sexagesimal system, which produced a solar year of twelve months and 360 days, and from which we have taken our twenty-four-hour days and sixty minute hours. A recent study of a 3,700 year-old tablet from Senkereh, modern Iraq, has proven that the ancient Babylonians had developed a superior form of trigonometry to our own, over 1,000 years before the Greeks, on the basis of this system.

But while the ancient Sumerians did not have twelve fingers, the origin of this seeming exception to the decimal rule is still thought to have been in the counting of fingers and toes, up to twenty, forty and then sixty before beginning the sequence again. Numbers one to nine in the Sumerian cuneiform script are pictorial representations of fingers, not unlike the Roman system, in which numbers one to four are representations of fingers, and the symbols for five likely represented the gap between thumb and index fingers. The word 'calculus' (from which we derive 'calculate') means 'pebble' in Latin, connected with the method of counting stone beads on an abacus. These and countless other examples serve to illustrate how mathematics did not arise from the free operation of the human mind, but is the product of a lengthy process of social evolution, trial and error, observation and experiment, which gradually becomes separated out as a body of knowledge of an apparently abstract character.

Similarly, our present systems of weights and measures have been derived from material objects. The origin of the English unit of measurement, the foot, is self-evident, as is the Spanish word for an inch, *pulgada*, which means a thumb. The origin of the most basic mathematical symbols + and – has nothing to do with mathematics.

35 A. Hooper, *Makers of Mathematics*, pp. 4-5.

They were the signs used in the Middle Ages by the merchants to calculate excess or deficiency of quantities of goods in warehouses.

The need to build dwellings to protect themselves from the elements forced early man to find the best and most practical way of cutting wood so that their ends fitted closely together. This meant the discovery of the right angle and the carpenters' square. The need to build a house on level ground led to the invention of the kind of levelling instrument depicted in Egyptian and Roman tombs, consisting of three pieces of wood joined together in an isosceles triangle, with a cord fastened at the apex. Such simple practical tools were used in the construction of the pyramids. The Egyptian priests accumulated a huge body of mathematical knowledge derived ultimately from such practical activity.

The very word 'geometry' betrays its practical origins. It means simply 'earth-measurement'. The virtue of the Greeks was to give a finished theoretical expression to these discoveries. However, in presenting their theorems as the pure product of logical deduction, they were misleading themselves and future generations. Ultimately, mathematics derives from material reality and, indeed, could have no application if this were not the case. Even the famous theorem of Pythagoras, known to every school pupil, that a square drawn on the longest side of a right triangle is equal to the sum of the squares drawn on the other two sides, had been already worked out in practice by the Egyptians.

The Pythagoreans, breaking with the Ionian materialist tradition which attempted to generalise on the basis of experience of the real world, asserted that the higher truths of mathematics could not be derived from the world of sensuous experience, but only from the workings of pure reason, by deduction. Beginning with certain first principles, which have to be taken as true, the philosopher argues them through a series of logical stages until he arrives at a conclusion, using only facts that are agreed first principles, or are derived from such. This was known as *a priori* reasoning, from the Latin phrase denoting 'from what comes first'.

Using deduction and *a priori* reasoning, the Pythagoreans attempted to establish a model of the universe based on perfect forms and

governed by divine harmony. The problem is that the forms of the
real world are anything but perfect. For instance, they thought that
the heavenly bodies were perfect spheres moving in perfect circles.
This was a revolutionary advance for its time, but neither of these
assertions is really true. The attempt to impose a perfect harmony on
the universe, to free it from contradiction, soon broke down even in
mathematical terms. Internal contradictions began to surface which
led to a crisis of the Pythagorean school.

About the middle of the fifth century, Hippius of Metapontum
discovered that the quantitative relations between the side and the
diagonal of simple figures like the square and the regular pentagon
are incommensurable, that is, they cannot be expressed as a ratio of
whole numbers, no matter how great. The square root of two cannot
be expressed by any number. It is, in fact, what mathematicians call
an 'irrational' number. This discovery threw the whole theory into
confusion. Hitherto, the Pythagoreans had taught that the world was
constructed out of points with magnitude. While it might not be
possible to say how many points there were on a given line, still they
were assumed to be finite in number. Now if the diagonal and the side
of a square are incommensurable, it follows that lines are infinitely
divisible, and that the little points from which the universe was built
do not exist.

From that time on, the Pythagorean school entered into decline.
It split into two rival factions, one of which buried itself in ever
more abstruse mathematical speculation, while the other attempted
to overcome the contradiction by means of ingenious mathematical
innovations which laid the basis for the development of the
quantitative sciences.

2. THE FIRST DIALECTICIANS

Over 100 years after Darwin, the idea that everything changes is generally accepted amongst educated people. It was not always so. The theory of evolution by natural selection had to fight a long and bitter struggle against those who defended the biblical view that God created all species in seven days, and that the species were fixed and immutable.

For many centuries, the Church dominated science and taught that the earth was fixed at the centre of the universe. Those who disagreed were burnt at the stake.

Even today, however, the idea of change is understood in a one-sided and superficial way. Evolution is interpreted to mean slow, gradual change which precludes sudden leaps. Contradictions are not supposed to exist in nature, and where they arise in human thought are attributed to subjective error. In point of fact, contradictions abound in nature at all levels, and are the basis of all movement and change. This fact was understood by thinkers from the earliest times. It is reflected in some elements of Buddhist philosophy. It underlies the ancient Chinese idea of the principles of yin and yang. In the fourth century BC, Hui Shih wrote the following lines: "The sky is as low as the earth; mountains are level with marshes. The sun is just setting at noon; each creature is just dying at birth."[1]

Compare this to the following fragments of the founder of Greek dialectical philosophy, Heraclitus (c. 544-484 BC):

> Fire lives the death of air, and air lives the death of fire; Water lives the death of earth, earth that of water.
>
> It is the same thing in us that is living and dead, asleep and awake, young and old; each changes place and becomes the other.
>
> We step and we do not step into the same stream; we are and are not.[2]

With Heraclitus, the contradictory assertions of the Ionian philosophers for the first time are given a dialectical expression. "Here we see land", commented Hegel, "there is no proposition of Heraclitus which I have not adopted in my *Logic*."[3]

For all his importance, Heraclitus' philosophy has only come down to us in about 130 fragments, written in a difficult aphoristic style. Even in his lifetime, Heraclitus was known as 'the Dark' for the obscurity of his sayings. It is almost as if he deliberately chose to make his philosophy inaccessible. Socrates wryly commented: "What he understood was excellent, what not he believed to be equally so; but that the book required a tough swimmer."[4]

In *Anti-Dühring*, Engels gives the following appraisal of Heraclitus' dialectical world outlook:

> When we consider and reflect upon nature at large or the history of mankind or our own intellectual activity, at first we see the picture of an endless entanglement of relations and reactions, permutations and combinations, in which nothing remains what, where and as it was, but everything moves, changes, comes into being and passes away. [We see, therefore, at first the picture as a whole, with its individual parts

---

1   Quoted in G. Thomson, *The First Philosophers*, p. 69.
2   Quoted in J. Burnet, *Early Greek Philosophy*, pp. 135-9.
3   G. W. F. Hegel, *Lectures on the History of Philosophy*, Vol. 1, p. 279.
4   Quoted in A. Schwegler, *Handbook of the History of Philosophy*, p. 20.

still more or less kept in the background; we observe the movements, transitions, connections, rather than the things that move, combine and are connected.] This primitive, naive but intrinsically correct conception of the world is that of ancient Greek philosophy, and was first clearly formulated by Heraclitus: everything is and is not, for everything is *fluid*, is constantly changing, constantly coming into being and passing away.[5]

Heraclitus lived in Ephesus in the violent period of the fifth century BC, a period of war and civil strife. Little is known of his life, except that he came from an aristocratic family. But the nature of the period in which he lived is well reflected in one of his fragments:

War is the father of all things and the king of all; and some he has made gods and some men, some bond and some free.[6]

But Heraclitus here does not just refer to war in human society, but to the role of inner contradiction at all levels of nature as well. Indeed, it is better translated as 'strife'. He states that:

We must know that war is common to all and strife is justice, and that all things come into being and pass away through strife.[7]

All things contain a contradiction, which impels their development. Indeed, without contradiction, there would be no movement and no life.

Heraclitus was the first to give a clear exposition of the idea of the unity of opposites.

The Pythagoreans had worked out a table of ten antitheses:

1. The finite and the infinite
2. The odd and the even
3. The one and the many
4. The right and the left
5. The male and the female
6. The quiescent and the moving

5 F. Engels, *Anti-Dühring*, p. 30.
6 Quoted in J. Burnet, *Early Greek Philosophy*, p. 136.
7 Quoted ibid., p. 137.

7. The straight and the crooked
8. Light and darkness
9. Good and evil
10. The square and the parallelogram

These are important concepts, but they were not developed by the Pythagoreans, who satisfied themselves with a mere enumeration. In fact, the Pythagoreans had the position of the fusion of opposites through a 'mean', eliminating contradiction by seeking the middle ground. Polemicising against this view, Heraclitus uses a most striking and beautiful image:

> Men do not know how what is at variance agrees with itself. It is an attunement of opposite tensions, like that of the bow and the lyre.[8]

Contradiction lies at the root of everything. The desire to eliminate contradiction would actually presuppose the elimination of all movement and life, consequently:

> Homer was wrong in saying: "Would that strife might perish from among gods and men!" He did not see that he was praying for the destruction of the universe; for, if his prayer were heard, all things would pass away…[9]

These are profound thoughts, but are clearly at variance to everyday experience and 'common sense'. How can something be itself and something else at the same time? How can a thing be both alive and dead? On this kind of argument, Heraclitus poured scorn:

> It is wise to hearken, not to me, but to my Word, and to confess that all things are one…

> Though this Word is true evermore, yet men are unable to understand it when they hear it for the first time as before they have heard it at all. For, though all things come to pass in accordance to this Word, men seem as if they have no experience of them, when they make trial of words and deeds such as I set forth, dividing each thing according to its kind and showing

8 Quoted ibid., p. 136.
9 Quoted ibid.

how it truly is. But other men know not what they are doing when they awake, even as they forget what they do in sleep...

Fools when they do hear are like the deaf; of them does the saying bear witness that they are absent when present...

Eyes and ears are bad witnesses to men if they have souls that understand not their language.[10]

What does this mean? The Greek for Word is '*Logos*', from which logic is derived. Despite its mystical appearance, Heraclitus' opening remark is an appeal to rational objectivity. Do not listen to me, he is saying, but to the objective laws of nature which I describe. That is the essential meaning. And "all things are one"? Throughout the history of philosophy, there have been two ways of interpreting reality – either as one single substance, embodied in different forms (monism, from the Greek word meaning single); or as two entirely different substances, spirit and matter (known as dualism). The early Greek philosophers were materialist monists. Later, the Pythagoreans adopted a dualist position, based upon a supposedly unbridgeable gulf between mind (spirit) and matter. This is the hallmark of all idealism. As we have seen, it has its roots in the primitive superstitions of savages who believed that the soul left the body in dreams.

The above passage is a polemic against the philosophical dualism of the Pythagoreans, against which Heraclitus defends the position of earlier Ionic monism – that there is an underlying material unity of nature. The universe has not been created, but has always existed, in a process of continuous flux and change, whereby things change into their opposites, cause becomes effect, and effect cause. Thus, contradiction lies at the root of everything. In order to get at the truth, it is necessary to go beyond the appearances, and lay bare the inner conflicting tendencies of a given phenomenon, in order to understand its inner motive forces.

The ordinary intelligence, by contrast, is content to take things at face value, the reality of sense perception, the 'given', the 'facts', are accepted without more ado. However, such perception is at best limited,

---

10 Quoted ibid., pp. 132-133.

and can be the source of endless errors. To give just one example: for 'sound common sense', the world is flat and the sun goes around the earth. The true nature of things is not always evident. As Heraclitus puts it: "Nature loves to hide." In order to arrive at the truth, it is necessary to know how to interpret the information of the senses. "If you do not expect the unexpected, you will not find it", he wrote, and again: "Those who seek for gold dig up much earth and find a little."[11]

"Everything flows," was the basis of his philosophy. "You cannot step twice into the same river; for fresh waters are ever flowing in upon you."[12] This was a dynamic view of the universe, the exact opposite of the static idealist conception of the Pythagoreans. And when Heraclitus looked for a material substance to underpin the universe, following in the footsteps of Thales and Anaximenes, he chose that most elusive and fleeting element, fire.

The idea that everything is in a constant state of flux, that there is nothing fixed and permanent except motion and change, is an uncomfortable one for the ordinary cast of mind to accept. Human thinking is, in general, innately conservative. The desire to cling to what is solid, concrete and reliable is rooted in a profound instinct, akin to that of self-preservation. The hope for an afterlife, the belief in an immortal soul, flows from a rejection of the fact that all things come into existence and also pass away – '*panta rhei*', everything flows. Man has stubbornly sought to attain freedom by denying the laws of nature, inventing certain imaginary privileges for himself. True freedom, however, as Hegel explained, consists in correctly understanding these laws, and acting accordingly. It was the great role of Heraclitus to provide the first more or less fully worked-out picture of the dialectical world outlook.

Heraclitus' philosophy was greeted by incredulity and hostility even in his own lifetime. It challenged the assumptions, not only of all religion and tradition, but of the 'common sense' mentality which sees no further than the end of its nose. For the next 2,500 years,

---

11 Quoted ibid., p. 133, all quotes.
12 Quoted ibid., p. 139.

2. THE FIRST DIALECTICIANS

attempts have been made to disprove it. As the British philosopher
Bertrand Russell comments:

> Science, like philosophy, has sought to escape from the doctrine of
> perpetual flux by finding some permanent substratum amid changing
> phenomena. Chemistry seemed to satisfy this desire. It was found that fire,
> which appears to destroy, only transmutes: elements are recombined, but
> each atom that existed before combustion still exists when the process is
> completed. Accordingly it was supposed that atoms are indestructible, and
> that all change in the physical world consists merely in re-arrangement of
> persistent elements. This view prevailed until the discovery of radioactivity,
> when it was found that atoms could disintegrate.
>
> Nothing daunted, the physicists invented new and smaller units, called
> electrons and protons, out of which atoms were composed; and these
> units were supposed, for a few years, to have the indestructibility formerly
> attributed to atoms. Unfortunately it seemed that protons and electrons
> could meet and explode, forming, not new matter, but a wave of energy
> spreading through the universe with the velocity of light. Energy had to
> replace matter as what is permanent. But energy, unlike matter, is not
> a refinement of the common-sense notion of a 'thing'; it is merely a
> characteristic of physical processes. It might be fancifully identified with
> the Heraclitean Fire, but it is the burning, not what burns. 'What burns'
> has disappeared from modern physics.
>
> Passing from the small to the large, astronomy no longer allows us to
> regard the heavenly bodies as everlasting. The planets came out of the
> sun, and the sun came out of a nebula. It has lasted some time, and will
> last some time longer; but sooner or later – probably in about a million
> million years – it will explode, destroying all the planets. So at least the
> astronomers say; perhaps as the fatal day draws nearer they will find some
> mistake in their calculations.[13]

THE ELEATICS

In the past it was thought that Heraclitus' philosophy was a reaction
against the views of Parmenides (c. 540-470 BC). The prevailing

13 B. Russell, *History of Western Philosophy*, pp. 64-5.

opinion now is that, on the contrary, the Eleatic school represented a reaction against Heraclitus. The Eleatics attempted to disprove the idea that 'everything flows' by asserting the direct opposite: that nothing changes, that movement is an illusion. This is a good example of the dialectical character of the evolution of human thought in general, and the history of philosophy in particular. It does not unfold in a straight line, but develops through contradiction, where one theory is put forward, is challenged by its opposite, until this, in turn, is overturned by a new theory, which frequently appears to signify a return to the starting point. However, this apparent return to old ideas does not mean that intellectual development is merely a closed circle. On the contrary, the dialectical process never repeats itself in exactly the same way, since the very process of scientific controversy, discussion, constant re-examination of positions, backed up by observation and experiment, leads to a deepening of our understanding and a closer approximation to the truth.

Elia (or Velia) was a Greek colony in southern Italy founded about 540 BC by emigrants fleeing from the Persian invasion of Ionia. According to tradition, the Eleatic school was founded by Xenophones. However, his connection with the school is unclear, and his contribution was overshadowed by its most prominent representatives, Parmenides and Zeno (born 460 BC). Whereas the Pythagoreans abstracted from matter all determinate qualities except number, the Eleatics went one step further, taking the process to an extreme, arriving at a totally abstract conception of being, stripped of all concrete manifestations except bare existence. Only being is; non-being (becoming) is not at all: pure, unlimited, unchanging, featureless being – this is the essence of the Eleatic thought.

This view of the universe is designed to eliminate all contradictions, all mutability and motion. It is a very consistent philosophy, within its own frame of reference. There is only one snag. It is directly contradicted by the whole of human experience. Not that this worried Parmenides. If human understanding cannot grasp this idea, so much the worse for understanding! Zeno elaborated a famous series of paradoxes designed to prove the impossibility of movement. According to legend, Diogenes the Cynic disproved Zeno's argument by simply walking up and down the room! However, as generations of logicians have found to their cost, Zeno's arguments are not so easy to dispose of in theoretical terms.

Hegel points out that the real intention of Zeno was not to deny the reality of motion, but to bring out the contradiction present in movement, and the way it is reflected in thought. In this sense, the Eleatics were, paradoxically, also dialectical philosophers. Defending Zeno against Aristotle's criticism that he denied the existence of motion, he explains:

> The point is not that there is movement and that this phenomenon exists; the fact that there is movement is as sensuously certain as that there are elephants; it is not in this sense that Zeno meant to deny movement. The point in question concerns its truth. Movement, however, is held to be untrue, because the conception of it involves a contradiction; by that he meant to say that no true Being can be predicated of it.[14]

In order to disprove Zeno's argument, it is not enough to demonstrate that movement exists, as Diogenes did, just by walking around. It is necessary to proceed from his own premises, to exhaust his own analysis of motion, and carry it to its limits, to the point where it turns into its opposite. That is the real method of dialectical argument, not merely asserting the opposite, still less resorting to ridicule. And, in fact, there is a rational basis for Zeno's paradoxes, which cannot be resolved by the method of formal logic, but only dialectically.

'ACHILLES THE SWIFT'

Zeno 'disproved' motion in different ways. Thus, he argued that a body in motion, before reaching a given point, must first have travelled half the distance. But, before this, it must have travelled half of that half, and so on *ad infinitum*. Thus, when two bodies are moving in the same direction, and the one behind at a fixed distance from the one in front is moving faster, we assume that it will overtake the other. Not so, says Zeno: "The slower one can never be overtaken by the

---

14 G. W. F. Hegel, *Lectures on the History of Philosophy*, Vol. 1, p. 266.

quicker."[15] This is the famous paradox of Achilles the Swift. Imagine a race between Achilles and a tortoise. Suppose that Achilles can run ten times faster than the tortoise which has a 1,000 metre head start. By the time Achilles has covered 1,000 metres, the tortoise will be 100 metres ahead; when Achilles has covered that 100 metres, the tortoise will be one metre ahead; when he covers that distance, the tortoise will be one-tenth of a metre ahead, and so on to infinity.

From the standpoint of everyday common sense, this seems absurd. Of course Achilles will overtake the tortoise! Aristotle remarked that: "This proof asserts the same endless divisibility, but it is untrue, for the quick will overtake the slow body if the limits to be traversed be granted to it."[16]

Hegel quotes these words, and comments:

This answer is correct and contains all that can be said; that is, there are in this representation two periods of time and two distances, which are separated from one another, i.e. they are limited in relation to one another...

But then he adds:

...when, on the contrary, we admit that time and space are related to one another as continuous, they are, while being two, not two, but identical.[17]

The paradoxes of Zeno do not prove that movement is an illusion, or that Achilles, in practice, will not overtake the tortoise, but they do reveal brilliantly the limitations of the kind of thinking now known as formal logic. The attempt to eliminate all contradiction from reality, as the Eleatics did, inevitably leads to this kind of insoluble paradox, or antinomy, as Kant later called it. In order to prove that a line could not consist of an infinite number of points, Zeno claimed that, if it were really so, then Achilles would never overtake the tortoise. There really is a logical problem here. As Alfred Hooper explains:

---

15 Quoted ibid., p. 272.
16 Quoted ibid., pp. 272-3.
17 Ibid., p. 273.

This paradox still perplexes even those who know that it is possible to find the sum of an infinite series of numbers forming a geometrical progression whose common ratio is less than 1, and whose terms consequently become smaller and smaller and thus 'converge' on some limiting value.[18]

In fact, Zeno had uncovered a contradiction in mathematical thought which would have to wait 2,000 years for a solution. The contradiction relates to the use of the infinite. From Pythagoras right up to the discovery of the differential and integral calculus in the seventeenth century, mathematicians went to great lengths to avoid the use of the concept of infinity. Only the great genius Archimedes approached the subject, but still avoided it by using a roundabout method.

The Pythagoreans stumbled on the fact that the square root of two cannot be expressed as a number. They invented ingenious ways of finding successive approximations for it. But, no matter how far the process is taken, you never get an exact answer. The result is always midway between two numbers. The further down the list you go, the closer you get to the value of the square root of two. But the process of successive approximation may be continued forever, without getting a precise result that can be expressed in a whole number.

The Pythagoreans thus had to abandon the idea of a line made up of a finite number of very small points, and accept that a line is made up of an infinite number of points with no dimension. Parmenides approached the issue from a different angle, arguing that a line was indivisible. In order to prove the point, Zeno tried to show the absurd consequences that would follow from the concept of infinite divisibility. For centuries after, mathematicians steered clear of the idea of infinity.

Ultimately, all these paradoxes are derived from the problem of the continuum. All the attempts to resolve them by means of mathematical theorems, such as the theory of convergent series and the theory of sets have only given rise to new contradictions. In the end, Zeno's arguments have not been refuted, because they are based

18 A. Hooper, *Makers of Mathematics*, p. 237.

on a real contradiction which, from the standpoint of formal logic, cannot be answered.

Hooper continues:

> Even the abstruse arguments put forward by Dedekind (1831-1916), Cantor (1845-1918) and Russell (1872-1970) in their mighty efforts to straighten out the paradoxical problems of infinity into which we are led by our concept of 'numbers,' have resulted in the creation of still further paradoxes.[19]

The breakthrough came in the seventeenth and eighteenth centuries, when men like Kepler, Cavalieri, Pascal, Wallis, Newton and Leibniz decided to ignore the numerous difficulties raised by formal logic, and deal with infinitesimal quantities. The results were epoch-making. Without the use of infinity, the whole of modern mathematics, and with it physics, would be unable to function.

The essential problem, highlighted by Zeno's paradoxes, is the inability of formal logic to grasp movement. Zeno's Paradox of the Arrow takes as an example of movement the parabola traced by an arrow in flight. At any given point in this trajectory, the arrow is considered to be still. But since, by definition, a line consists of a series of points, at each of which the arrow is still, movement is an illusion. The answer to this paradox was given by Hegel.

The notion of movement necessarily involves a contradiction. Consider the movement of a body, Zeno's arrow for example, from one point to another. When it starts to move, it is no longer at point A. At the same time, it is not yet at point B. Where is it, then? To say that it is 'in the middle' conveys nothing, for then it would still be at a point, and therefore at rest. "But," says Hegel, "movement means to be in this place and not to be in it, and thus to be in both alike; this is the continuity of space and time which first makes motion possible."[20] As Aristotle shrewdly observed, "It arises from the fact that it is taken for granted that time consists of the Now; for if this is not conceded,

19 Ibid., p. 238.
20 G. W. F. Hegel, *Lectures on the History of Philosophy*, Vol. 1, pp. 273-74.

the conclusions will not follow." But what is this 'now'? If we say the arrow is 'here', 'now', it has already gone.

Engels writes:

> Motion itself is a contradiction: even simple mechanical change of place can only come about through a body being both in one place and in another place at one and the same moment of time, being in one and the same place and also not in it. And the continual assertion and simultaneous solution of this contradiction is precisely what motion is.[21]

THE FIRST ATOMISTS

Anaxagoras of Clazomenae was born around 500 BC, in Asia Minor, in the period of wars with the Medes, and the rise of Athens under Pericles. Anaxagoras moved to Athens, where he was a contemporary of Aeschylus, Sophocles, Aristophanes, Diogenes and Protagoras. He was a far more original and profound thinker, who had a tremendous impact on philosophy in Athens. Aristotle said that he was like "a sober man among drunkards".[22] Anaxagoras, following the best Ionian tradition, believed in experiment and observation. "There can be no question," says Benjamin Farrington, "but that he regarded sense-evidence as indispensable for the investigation of nature, but, like Empedocles, he was concerned to show that there were physical processes too subtle for our senses to perceive directly."[23]

His scientific discoveries were of the first order. He believed that the sun was a mass of molten elements, as also were the stars, although these were too far away for their heat to be felt. The moon was nearer, and made of the same material as the earth. The light of the moon was a reflection of the sun, and eclipses were caused by the moon blocking off the sun's light. Like Socrates later, he was accused of atheism, probably accurately, since he scarcely mentions religion in his cosmology. These revolutionary ideas shocked the conservative Athenians, eventually leading to Anaxagoras' banishment.

---

21 F. Engels, *Anti-Dühring*, pp. 144-145.

22 G. W. F. Hegel, *Lectures on the History of Philosophy*, Vol. 1, p. 319.

23 B. Farrington, *Greek Science*, p. 62.

In opposition to Parmenides, Anaxagoras held that everything is infinitely divisible, and that even the smallest amount of matter contains some of each element. He also considered that matter was made up of particles of many kinds. Thus, he asked how it occurs that bread, when eaten, turns into bones, flesh, blood, skin, and the rest. The only explanation was that the particles of wheat must contain, in some hidden form, all the elements necessary for the makeup of the body, which are rearranged in the digestive process.

He believed there to be an infinite number of elements or 'seeds'. But there was one of them which played a special role. This was the *nous*, usually translated as 'mind'. Lighter than the other elements, it is, unlike the rest, unmixed, and permeates all matter, as an organising and animating principle. For this reason, Anaxagoras is usually regarded as an idealist. But this is far from certain. The arch-idealist Hegel considered that, while the *nous* was an important step in the direction of idealism, "with Anaxagoras it was not fully worked out."[24] Anaxagoras' *nous* can also have a materialistic interpretation, as the inner moving spirit of matter, or, more correctly expressed, energy. Hegel himself understood that it did not mean an external intelligence, but the objective processes which take place within nature, providing it with form and definition.

The idea that matter consists of an infinity of tiny particles, invisible to the senses, represents a most important generalisation, and a transition to the atomic theory, that remarkable anticipation of modern science, first expounded by Leucippus (c. 500-440 BC) and Democritus (c. 460-370 BC). The breakthrough was even more astonishing when we bear in mind that these thinkers had no access to electron microscopes, or any other technological aids. There was therefore no means of corroborating the theory, let alone developing it at that time. More importantly, it incurred the wrath of the religious, and the scorn of the idealists, and was allowed to sink without trace in the long, dark night of the Middle Ages. This was until, like so many ideas of antiquity, it was rediscovered by the thinkers of the

---

24 G. W. F. Hegel, *Lectures on the History of Philosophy*, Vol. 1, p. 330.

Renaissance, like Gassendi, where it played an important role in stimulating the new scientific outlook.

About Leucippus, so little is known that some even doubted his existence, which, however, was proved by the discovery of papyri at Herculaneum. Most of his sayings have come down to us through the writings of other philosophers. In a startlingly modern hypothesis, Leucippus stated that the whole universe was made up of just two things, atoms and the void, an absolute vacuum. He was also the first to establish what later became known as the law of causality and the law of sufficient reason. The one authentic fragment which has survived says: "Naught happens for nothing, but everything from a ground and of necessity."[25] The early atomists were determinists. They placed causality firmly at the centre of all natural processes, but they did so in an unbending way, reminiscent of the later mechanical determinism of Laplace. This rigidity of the earliest atomists was later corrected by Epicurus, who put forward the idea that atoms falling through the void swerve slightly, thus introducing the element of accident into the framework of necessity.

The atomists derived all things from an infinite number of fundamental particles, the *atoma* (which means 'that which cannot be divided'). These atoms were alike in quality, but unlike in quantity, differing only in size, shape and weight, although the smallness of their size made it impossible to see them. In essence, this was correct. The entire physical world, from coal to diamonds, from the human body to the scent of roses, is composed of atoms of different sizes and weights, arranged in molecules. Present day science can give a precise quantitative expression to this assertion. The Greek atomists were in no position to do this, because the limitation upon the development of technology inherent in the slave method of production prevented the proper utilisation of the brilliant inventions of the time, including the steam engine, which mostly remained on the level of toys and curiosities. All the more remarkable, then, was the way in which they anticipated one of the most important principles of twentieth-century science.

---

25 J. Burnet, *Early Greek Philosophy*, p. 340.

The celebrated American physicist Richard P. Feynman underlines the place of atomic theory in present day science:

> If, in some cataclysm, all of scientific knowledge were to be destroyed, and only one sentence passed onto the next generations of creatures, what statement would contain the most information in the fewest words? I believe it is the *atomic hypothesis* (or the atomic *fact*, or whatever you wish to call it) that *all things are made of atoms – little particles that move around in perpetual motion, attracting each other when they are a little distance apart, but repelling upon being squeezed into one another.* In that one sentence, you will see, there is an *enormous* amount of information about the world, if just a little imagination and thinking are applied.[26]

And again:

> *Everything is made of atoms.* That is the key hypothesis. The most important hypothesis in all of biology, for example, is that *everything that animals do, atoms do.* In other words, *there is nothing that living things do that cannot be understood from the point of view that they are made of atoms acting according to the laws of physics.* This was not known from the beginning: it took some experimenting and theorising to suggest this hypothesis, but now it is accepted, and it is the most useful theory for producing new ideas in the field of biology.
>
> If a piece of steel or a piece of salt, consisting of atoms one next to the other, can have such interesting properties; if water – which is nothing but these little blobs, mile upon mile of the same thing over the earth – can form waves and foam, and make rushing noises and strange patterns as it runs over cement; if all of this, all the life of a stream of water, can be nothing but a pile of atoms, *how much more is possible?* If instead of arranging the atoms in some definite pattern, again and again repeated, on and on, or even forming little lumps of complexity like the odour of violets, we make an arrangement which is always different from place to place, with different kinds of atoms arranged in many ways, continually changing, not repeating, how much more marvellously is it possible that this thing might behave? Is it possible that that 'thing' walking back and

26 R. P. Feynman, *The Feynman Lectures on Physics*, p. 1–2.

forth in front of you, talking to you, is a great glob of these atoms in a very complex arrangement, such that the sheer complexity of it staggers the imagination as to what it can do? When we say we are a pile of atoms, we do not mean we are *merely* a pile of atoms, because a pile of atoms which is not repeated from one to the other might well have the possibilities which you see before you in the mirror.[27]

The world outlook of the Greek atomists was naturally materialist. This earned them the hatred of the idealists and the religiously-inclined. A particularly spiteful campaign of calumny was directed against Epicurus, whose philosophical views were so distorted for centuries as to turn them into their exact opposite in the popular imagination. They were self-confessed atheists. There is no room for God in this view of the universe. Democritus found the cause of mutation and change in the nature of the atoms themselves: falling through the vacuum (the 'void'), they impinge on one another, arranging themselves in different ways, like combining with like.

Through an endless series of different combinations, we get the constant changes which are everywhere to be seen in nature, and which give rise to the transitoriness of worldly things. There was an infinite number of worlds 'born and dying', not created by God, but arising and being destroyed out of necessity, in accordance with natural laws. Knowledge of these things is derived mainly from sensory perception, but this gives us only a 'dim' understanding of nature. It must be supplemented and transcended by 'bright' reason, which leads to the cognition of the essence of things, the atoms and the void. The fundamental elements of a scientific materialist world outlook are all present in these few lines.

The philosophy of Democritus was further developed and deepened by Epicurus. Like his mentor, he explicitly denied the interference of the gods in the affairs of the world, basing himself on the eternity of matter, in a state of continual motion. However, he rejected the mechanistic determinism of Leucippus and Democritus, introducing the idea of a spontaneous (internally conditioned) 'deviation' of the

27 Ibid., pp. 1–8, 1–9.

atoms from their course, in order to explain the possibility of collisions between atoms moving at equal speed through empty space. This was an important step forward, posing the dialectical relation between necessity and chance – one of the key theoretical questions over which modern physics is still wracking its brains, although the solution was found long ago by Hegel.

Epicurus' theory of knowledge is based entirely on acceptance of the information given to us by the senses. "All senses are heralds of the true",[28] nor is there anything that can refute the senses. Here his presentation, while starting from a correct assumption – I interpret the world through my senses – represents a step back in relation to Democritus. It is too one-sided. Sense perception is undoubtedly the basis of all knowledge, but it is necessary to know how to interpret correctly the information of the senses. That is what Heraclitus meant when he said that: "Eyes and ears are bad witnesses to men if they have souls that understand not their language."[29] The narrow empirical approach invariably leads to errors. Thus, according to Cicero, Democritus thought that the sun was immensely large, whereas Epicurus believed it to be only about two feet in diameter. In other respects, however, Epicurus made some startling discoveries. Gassendi, who may be considered the father of modern atomism, praised Epicurus because, exclusively by reasoning, he showed the fact later demonstrated by experiment, that all bodies, irrespective of their mass and weight, have the same velocity when falling from above to below.

LUCRETIUS ON RELIGION

Epicurus and his followers declared war upon religion which feeds off men's fear and ignorance. The first book of Lucretius' great philosophical poem *On The Nature of the Universe* contains what amounts to a materialist and atheist manifesto:

---

28 Quoted in K. Marx, 'Difference Between the Democritean and Epicurean Philosophy of Nature', MECW, Vol. 1, p. 48.

29 Quoted in J. Burnet, *Early Greek Philosophy*, p. 133.

When human life lay grovelling in all men's sight, crushed to the earth under the dead weight of superstition whose grim features loured menacingly upon mortals from the four quarters of the sky, a man of Greece was first to raise mortal eyes in defiance, first to stand erect and brave the challenge. Fables of the gods did not crush him, nor the lightning flash and the growling menace of the sky. Rather, they quickened his manhood, so that he, first of all men, longed to smash the constraining locks of nature's doors. The vital vigour of his mind prevailed. He ventured far out beyond the flaming ramparts of the world and voyaged in mind throughout infinity. Returning victorious, he proclaimed to us what can be and what cannot: how a limit is fixed to the power of everything and an immovable frontier post. Therefore superstition in its turn lies crushed beneath his feet, and we by his triumph are lifted level with the skies.[30]

Even here, the religious prejudices of the translator are apparent. He cannot bring himself to translate the word *religio* as religion, preferring to render it as 'superstition'. This, in 1951! The materialist philosophy of Epicurus made a big impact on the young Karl Marx, who chose it as the subject of his doctoral dissertation while at university. Marx considered that the Roman philosopher-poet Lucretius was "the only one in general of all the ancients who has understood Epicurean physics", who has written "a more profound exposition".[31]

In the most striking poetic language, Lucretius defends the indestructibility of matter, the correct idea that matter can neither be created nor destroyed:

This dread and darkness of the mind cannot be dispelled by the sunbeams, the shining shafts of day, but only by an understanding of the outward form and inner workings of nature. In tackling this theme, our starting-point will be this principle: *Nothing can ever be created by divine power out of nothing.* The reason why all mortals are so gripped by fear is that they see all sorts of things happening on the earth and in the sky with no

---

30 Lucretius, *On The Nature of the Universe*, p. 29.

31 K. Marx, 'Difference Between the Democritean and Epicurean Philosophy of Nature', MECW, Vol. 1, p. 48.

discernible cause, and these they attribute to the will of a god. Accordingly, when we have seen that nothing can be created out of nothing, we shall then have a clearer picture of the path ahead, the problem of how things are created and occasioned without the aid of the gods.[32]

The law of the conservation of energy, proved by Mayer, Joule, Helmholz and others in the mid-nineteenth century shows that the total amount of energy neither disappears nor is created, when changing from one kind to another. This provides an unshakeable basis for the materialist position that matter can neither be created nor destroyed. This idea is also brilliantly conveyed by Lucretius:

> The second great principle is this: *nature resolves everything into its component atoms and never reduces anything to nothing.* If anything were perishable in all its parts, anything might perish all of a sudden and vanish from sight. There would be no need of any force to separate its parts and loosen their links. In actual fact, since everything is composed of indestructible seeds, nature obviously does not allow anything to perish till it has encountered a force that shatters it with a blow or creeps into chinks and unknits it.[33]

The Epicurean world view maintains that the universe is infinite, and matter has no limit, either externally or internally:

> If there are no such least parts, even the smallest bodies will consist of an infinite number of parts, since they can always be halved and their halves halved again without limit. On this showing, what difference will there be between the whole universe and the very least of things? None at all. For, however endlessly infinite the universe may be, yet the smallest things will equally consist of an infinite number of parts.[34]

And:

> Learn, therefore, that *the universe is not bounded in any direction.* If it were, it would necessarily have a limit somewhere. But clearly a thing cannot

---

32 Lucretius, *On The Nature of the Universe,* p. 31.

33 Ibid., p. 33.

34 Ibid., p. 45.

have a limit unless there is something outside to limit it, so that the eye can follow it up to a certain point but not beyond. Since you must admit that there is nothing outside the universe, it can have no limit and is accordingly without end or measure.[35]

If the scientists of our own era had had an equally sound philosophical outlook, we would have been spared the most glaring errors of method, such as the search for the 'bricks of matter', the 'big bang' with its finite universe, the 'birth of time', the equally absurd 'continuous creation of matter', and the like. In relation to time, Democritus stated that time had no origin, that it does not exist in itself, apart from the movement of things or things at rest. How infinitely more scientific than certain present-day physicists who talk about the alleged 'beginning of time' twenty billion years ago! In their apparatus, they are more advanced, but in their mode of thinking, they are worlds behind the early materialists.

The consistent materialist outlook of Epicurus earned him the most venomous attacks of the Church from the earliest times. The apostle Paul specifically mentions them in the Acts of the Apostles.[36] In Dante's time, the accusation of Epicureanism meant someone who denied the Holy Ghost and the immortality of the soul. In general, Epicurus is thought to have advocated an amoral and hedonistic philosophy, in which all manner of gluttony and licentiousness was permitted. All this is just a crude slander against Epicurus and his philosophy.

In terms of morality and ethics, the Epicurean philosophy represents one of the noblest products of the human spirit. It resembles the famous dictum of Spinoza: *Neither weep nor laugh, but understand.* Epicurus sought to free humanity from fear by promoting a clear understanding of nature and man's place in it. He asked himself what is the basis of all fear, and answered, the fear of death. His main aim was to eliminate this fear, by explaining that death is nothing for me in the present, for I am alive, and will be nothing to me in the future,

---

35 Ibid., p. 55.
36 See Acts of the Apostles 17:18.

since, after death, I can know nothing about it. Therefore, he urged men to set aside fear of death and live life to the full. This beautiful and humane philosophy has always been anathema to those who wish to direct the eyes of men and women away from the problems of the real world to an alleged world after death, which is supposed to reward or punish us according to our just deserts.

The accusation of grossness and hedonism against Epicurus stems from the vengeful attitude of the Christian apologists against a cheerful and life-enhancing philosophy – the exact opposite of their own. They sought to bury their enemy under a heap of slander. In fact, Epicurus, like Spinoza, identified the good with pleasure, or the absence of pain. He considered human relations from the point of view of utility, which finds its highest expression in friendship. In a period of great social turbulence and uncertainty, he preached withdrawal from the world, and a life of peaceful meditation. He recommended men to reduce their needs to a minimum, away from the world of strife, competition and war. This was, of course, a utopian idea, but it is nothing to do with the ugly and spiteful caricature put in circulation by the opponents of materialism. Epicurus remained true to his ideals on his deathbed, from where he wrote:

> A happy day is this on which I write to you ... The pains which I feel ... could not be greater. But all of this is opposed by the happiness which the soul experiences, remembering our conversations of a bygone time.[37]

THE RISE OF IDEALISM

The term 'dialectics' comes from the Greek '*dialektike*', derived from '*dialegomai*', to converse, or discuss. Originally, it signified the art of discussion, which may be seen in its highest form in the Socratic dialogues of Plato. This was no accident, but flowed from the very nature of Athenian democracy, with its ample scope for oratory and debate in public assemblies. This gave rise to a new breed of public figures, professional teachers and speakers of all kinds, from

---

37 Quoted in *The New Encyclopaedia Britannica: Macropaedia*, p. 574.

courageous freethinkers and profound philosophers to unscrupulous demagogues.

To modern ears, the words 'sophist' and 'sophistry' have a thoroughly disreputable ring about them, suggesting intellectual dishonesty, trickery and lies, masked by clever turns of phrase. That, indeed, was how sophism ended up. But it was not always so. In a way, they can be compared to the philosophers of the French Enlightenment in the eighteenth century. They were rationalists and freethinkers, who stood opposed to all existing dogmas and orthodoxy. Their maxim was 'Doubt Everything'. All existing things and ideas had to be subjected to the most far-reaching criticism. This undoubtedly contained a revolutionary and dialectical kernel.

Schwegler writes:

> On this new-won field now the Sophists disported, enjoying with boyish exuberance the exercise of the power of subjectivity, and destroying, by means of a subjective dialectic, all that had been ever objectively established.[38]

The activities of the sophists reflected life in Athens during the period of the Peloponnesian War between Athens and Sparta. They were both scholars and practical men, the first ones to charge a fee for teaching. Plato remarks in the *Republic* that the doctrines of the Sophists express only the same principles which guided the practice of the multitude in their civil and social relations. The hate with which they were persecuted by the statesmen proves the jealousy with which the latter saw them. The sophists were attacked for saying that morality and truth were subjective concepts, which could be determined by anyone, according to his personal preferences and interests. But they were only saying what was already the established norm in practice. We see the same thing today. Professional politicians do not like to be reminded of the moral code which really operates in the corridors of power!

Schwegler continues:

---

38 A. Schwegler, *History of Philosophy*, p. 30.

Public life was become an arena of passion and self-seeking; the party-strifes, which agitated Athens during the Peloponnesian war, had blunted and stifled the moral sentiment; every one accustomed himself to set his own private interest above that of the state and of the common good, and to seek in his own self-will and his own advantage the standard of his action and the principle of his guidance. The axiom of Protagoras, man is the measure of all things, was in practice only all too truly followed, while the influence of rhetoric in public assemblies and decisions, the corruption of the masses and their leaders, the weak points which cupidity, vanity, and party-spirit betrayed to the crafty, offered only all too much occasion for its exercise.

What was established, and had come down so, had lost its authority, political regulation appeared as arbitrary restriction, moral principle as a result of calculated political training, faith in the gods as human invention for the intimidation of free activity, piety as a statute of human origin which every man had a right to alter by the art of persuasion. This reduction of the necessity and universality of nature and reason to the contingency of mere human appointment, is mainly the point where the Sophists are in contact with the general consciousness of the cultivated classes of the time; and it is impossible to decide what share theory had here, and what practice; whether the Sophists only found practical life in a theoretical formula, or whether the social corruption was rather a consequence of the destructive influence which the Sophists exercised over the entire circle of the opinions of their contemporaries.[39]

The turbulence of the times, with constant changes, wars, destruction and unrest, found a reflection in the restless spirit of dialectical contradiction. The unsettling movement of thought, upsetting existing ideas, mirrored the actual conditions of Greece at the time of the Peloponnesian wars. Likewise, the need to win over the assembly or law-court by clever argument provided a material base for the rise of a generation of professional orators and dialecticians. But that is not to say that the initial content of sophism was determined by

---

39 Ibid., pp. 31-32.

considerations of personal advantage or pecuniary gain, any more than was, say, Calvinism. But, given the prevailing social conditions, the later development of sophism was determined in advance.

The first generation of sophists were genuine philosophers, often identified with democratic politics and with a materialist understanding of nature. They were rationalists and encyclopaedists, just as their French equivalents in the decades before 1789. And in the same way, they were clever and witty, with an ability to deal with all sides of a problem. Protagoras was celebrated as a teacher of morals, Gorgias as a rhetorician and politician, Prodicus as a grammarian and etymologist, and Hippias as a polymath. They were to be found in all the professions and spheres of knowledge. But gradually the movement, which really never constituted a real school, began to degenerate. The wandering 'wise man' going from town to town in search of good pay and a rich patron became a figure of contempt and ridicule.

The common feature of all the previous schools of thought examined here is their objectivity, the assumption that the validity of our ideas depends on the degree to which they correspond to objective reality, to the world outside us. The sophists broke entirely from this, advancing instead the position of philosophical subjectivity. This is well summed up in the celebrated phrase of Protagoras (481-411 BC), "Man is the measure of all things; of that which is, that is; of that which is not, that is not.[40]

There is some dispute about the exact meaning of this phrase, which may also be put in a way which implies that Protagoras was a materialist, a view which fits in with a remark of Sextus Empiricus, to the effect that Protagoras said that the main causes ('*logoses*') of all things are in matter. But there can be no doubt that the general trend of sophism was in the direction of extreme subjectivism. As a result of their withering attacks on existing beliefs and prejudices, they were regarded as subversives in conservative circles. Protagoras

---

40 Quoted in G. W. F. Hegel, *Lectures on the History of Philosophy*, Vol. 1, p. 373.

himself was expelled from Athens for atheism, and his book *On the Gods* was burnt.

Religious conviction and its philosophical counterpart, dogmatism, is not culture. Even Heraclitus, despite his great wisdom, was not free from a dogmatic and narrow cast of mind, as shown by the tone of his utterances. But no real progress is possible along this path. Sophism, therefore, at least in its first period, played a positive role in breaking down the old universal dogmas into their component parts and counterposing each of the parts to the others. There was a negative side, in that the isolated elements were open to be twisted and turned out of context, in a typically 'sophist' way. Yet, as Hegel says: "A man of culture ... knows how to say something of everything, to find points of view in all."[41] In fact, Hegel thought that the arguments of Protagoras in Plato's dialogue of that name were superior to those of Socrates.

This kind of *esprit* (wit) is entirely foreign to the Anglo-Saxon tradition and mentality, which generally regards it with ill-concealed suspicion, and distaste. Yet, as Hegel, penetratingly observes, sophism marks the beginning of culture in the modern sense of the word. For culture presupposes a rational consideration of things and a choice.

> In fact, what is most striking in a man or people of culture is the art of speaking well, or of turning subjects round and considering them in many aspects. The uncultivated man finds it unpleasant to associate with people who know how to grasp and express every point of view with ease. The French are good speakers in this sense, and the Germans call their talking prattle; but it is not mere talk that brings about this result, for culture is also wanted. We may have mastered a speech quite completely, but if we have not culture, it is not good speaking. Men thus learn French, not only to be able to speak French well, but to acquire French culture. What is to be obtained from the Sophists is thus the power of keeping the manifold points of view present to the mind, so that the wealth of categories by which an object may be considered, immediately occurs to it.[42]

---

41 Ibid., p. 356.
42 Ibid., p. 359.

Despite the disrepute in which sophism is supposed to be held nowadays, it is the true father of modern professional politics, law and diplomacy. We observe with tedious regularity how bourgeois politicians are prepared to defend with apparently total conviction, now one position, now precisely the opposite, adducing in either case the most impressive moral and practical arguments. The same procedure may be observed in the law courts any day of the week. And why bother the reader with a list of examples of the consummate lying, manoeuvring deceit practised by the diplomatic corps of every government in the world? These people have all the faults of the sophists and none of their virtues!

It is true that the sophists made a living out of their nimble wits and ability to argue for or against almost anything, as a lawyer argues for the defence or the prosecution, irrespective of the intrinsic rights and wrongs of the case (the verb '*sophizesthai*' meant 'making a career by being clever'). They were the prototype of the smart lawyer and the professional politician. But they were much more than that. Even in the more morally questionable activities of the sophists, there was a real philosophical principle involved. As Hegel wittily observes:

> In the worst action there exists a point of view which is essentially real; if this is brought to the front, men excuse and vindicate the action...

> A man does not require to make great progress in his education to have good reasons ready for the worst action; all that has happened in the world since the time of Adam has been justified by some good reason.[43]

The basic idea which underlies the dialectic of sophism is that truth is many-sided. This is an extremely important truth, and fundamental to the dialectical method in general. The difference lies in the use to which it is put. Scientific, objective dialectics strives to grasp every phenomenon in an all-round manner. Subjective dialectics, the dialectic of sophism, takes one or another aspect of the whole, and counterposes it to the rest. In this way, it is possible to deny the whole by insisting on the part, which, in itself, is perfectly sound. This is the

---

43 Ibid., p. 369.

method of the legal charlatan, the eclectic, and also, in a cruder way, of 'common sense', which makes arbitrary assumptions based upon particulars.

They tried to use the arguments of Zeno and Heraclitus to justify their views, but did so in a negative and one-sided way. For example, Heraclitus had said that it is impossible to step in the same stream twice. One of his disciples went further, saying that you could not even step into it once! This, however, is false. The idea of Heraclitus was that everything is and is not, because everything is in flux, constantly changing. The second view merely takes one half of the equation – that everything is not. This is not at all what Heraclitus meant. The objective world certainly exists, but it is in a permanent process of motion, development and change, in which nothing remains as it was before.

The sophists were sceptics. Protagoras wrote:

> As to the gods, I am not able to say whether they are or are not; for there is much which prevents this knowledge, both in the obscurity of the matter, and in the life of man which is so short.[44]

That sentence got him banished from Athens. The fundamental difference with the earlier philosophy is the subjective character of the sophist outlook. "Man is the measure of all things" – this statement may be taken in two ways, practical and theoretical. In the first sense, it can be taken as a defence of egotism, self-interest, and the like. In the second sense, it represents a theory of knowledge (epistemology) which is subjective. Man counterposes himself to the objective world, and, at least in his imagination, subjects it to himself. His own reason decides what is what. The essential thing is not what is, but how I see it. This is the basis of all forms of subjective idealism, from Protagoras to Bishop Berkeley, from Kant to Werner Heisenberg.

Basically, the subjective idealist claims that the world is unknowable. We can have no real grasp of the truth, but only opinions, based on subjective criteria. "The truth?" asked Pontius Pilate ironically,

---

44 Quoted ibid., p. 373.

"What is the truth?" That is the language of the cynical politician and bureaucrat, who hides his self-interest behind a thin veneer of 'cultured' sophistry. Philosophically speaking, however, it is an expression of subjective idealism, which denies the possibility of really knowing the world outside us. This outlook was most clearly expressed by one of the most famous sophists, Gorgias of Leontini (483-375 BC), who wrote a provocatively-titled book: *On Nature, or On That Which Is Not*. The title already says it all. Gorgias based himself on three propositions: a) nothing is real, b) if anything were real, it could not be known, and c) if it could be known, it could not be expressed.

Such opinions seem absurd. Yet they have repeatedly surfaced in the history of philosophy in different forms, including in our own times, when even respected scientists can permit themselves to assert that humans cannot comprehend the quantum world of subatomic particles, and that photons and electrons only materialise in a given spot when they are observed by someone; that is, the observer creates his result through the subjective act of observation. Here we once again depart from the world of objectivity, and return, through the tradesman's entrance of subjective idealism, to the realms of religious mysticism.

The present-day scientists who advocate such views have far less excuse than the sophists, who were the children of their time. The early attempts to find a rational explanation for the processes of nature had reached a point where they could not be taken any further by thought alone. The thinkers of that period arrived at a series of brilliant generalisations about the nature of the universe. But in order to test them and develop them further, it was necessary to examine them in detail, to break them down into their component parts, to analyse them one by one. This work was started by the sophists, and later put on a more rigorous basis by Aristotle. The heroic period of great generalisations gradually gave way to the slow and painstaking accumulation of facts, experiment and observation. Only in this way could the truth or falsehood of the different hypotheses be finally demonstrated. Before we reach this stage, however, we come to the high point of classical philosophical idealism.

SOCRATES AND PLATO

By subordinating the objective world to subjectivity, the sophists had stripped it of all inherent law and necessity. The sole source of order, rationality and causation was the perceiving subject. Everything was declared to be relative. For example, they held that morality and social conduct was determined by convenience (a similar view is held by the Pragmatists, a philosophy which enjoyed a lot of support in the United States, and which fits in nicely with the need to make morality compatible with the ethics of the 'free enterprise' jungle). Thrasymachus of Chalcedon in the late fifth century BC openly declared that "justice or right is simply what is in the interest of the stronger party".[45]

This was another period of war, revolution and counter-revolution. In 411 BC, after a 100 years of slave-owning democracy, there was a revolution in Athens, followed by a counter-coup two years later. There followed a disastrous war with Sparta, which imposed the rule of the 'Thirty Tyrants', under which numerous atrocities were perpetrated by the aristocratic party in power. But by 399 BC, the Thirty had been overthrown, and Socrates, who had the misfortune to have had several of them as his pupils and friends, was put on trial and sentenced to death.

Socrates (469-399 BC) was regarded by his contemporaries as a sophist, although he did not teach for money. Though he wrote nothing – his ideas have come down to us through the writings of Plato and Aristotle – he had a huge influence on the development of philosophy. His origins were humble; he was the son of a stonemason and a midwife. The driving force of his life was a burning desire to get at the truth, tearing aside all pretences and sophistry by a relentless process of question and answer. It is said that, in his attempt to get people to think about universal principles, he went about the

---

45 Quoted in Plato, *Republic*, p. 77.

The Socratic Method

workplaces of artisans and merchants, as well as the haunts of sophists and youths, subjecting all to the same procedure.

The method was always the same: setting out from a particular idea or opinion, usually derived from the concrete experiences and problems of life of the person involved, he would, step-by-step, by a rigorous process of argument, bring to light the inner contradictions contained on the original proposition, show its limitations, and take the discussion to a higher level, involving an entirely different proposition. This is the dialectic of discussion in its classical form. An initial argument (thesis) is advanced. This is answered by a contrary argument (antithesis). Finally, after examining the question thoroughly, dissecting it to reveal its inner contradictions, we arrive at a conclusion on a higher level (synthesis). This may or may not mean that the two sides reach agreement. But in the very process of developing the discussion itself, the understanding of both sides is deepened, and the discussion proceeds from a lower to a higher level.

The same dialectical process of the development of thought through contradiction can be seen in the history of science and philosophy. It was graphically expressed by Hegel in the Preface to his pioneering work *The Phenomenology of Spirit*:

> The bud disappears when the blossom bursts forth, and one could say that the bud is refuted by the blossom; similarly, when the fruit appears, the blossom is declared to be a false Being-there [form] of the plant, and the fruit replaces the blossom as the truth of the plant. These forms are not only different, they also supplant one another as mutually incompatible. Yet at the same time their fluid nature makes them moments of the organic unity, in which they not only do not conflict, but each is as necessary as the other; and this shared necessity alone constitutes the life of the whole.[46]

It is possible to say that in the Socratic dialogues we do not find a worked-out exposition of dialectics, but we do find many important examples of the dialectical method in action. The celebrated Socratic irony, for example, is not just a stylistic trick, but a reflection of the

---

46 G. W. F Hegel, *The Phenomenology of Spirit*, pp. 5-6.

The Marxist Method

dialectic itself. Socrates wished to make other people become aware of the contradictions underlying their own ideas, beliefs and prejudices. From each definite proposition, he deduced as a direct result, the exact opposite of what the proposition stated. Instead of merely attacking his opponents' ideas, he would put them in a position where they themselves would draw the opposite conclusion. This is precisely the basis of irony, not just here, but in general. This dialectic of discussion is an art which was perfected by Socrates. He himself likens it to the art of midwifery, which he jokingly claimed to have learnt from his mother. It is, to quote Hegel:

> [T]he assisting into the world of the thought which is already contained in the consciousness of the individual – the showing from the concrete, unreflected consciousness, the universality of the concrete, or from the universally posited, the opposite which already is within it.[47]

In just the same way, the task of Marxists is not to introduce into the working class a socialist consciousness 'from without', as some have imagined, but to proceed from the existing state of awareness of the class, and show concretely, step-by-step, how the problems which workers face can only be resolved by a radical transformation of society. It is not a question of preaching from without, but of making conscious the unconscious aspiration of working people to change society. The difference is that this process is not brought to fruition exclusively in the debating chamber, but by practical activity, struggle and the experience of the class itself. The problem, nevertheless, remains essentially the same: how to break down existing prejudices and get people to see the contradictions present, not only in their heads, but in the world in which they live – to get them to see things as they really are, not as they imagine them to be.

Socrates would begin with the most self-evident, everyday, even trivial facts given to us by our senses. Then he would compare these with other facts, proceeding from one detail to the next, and in this way, gradually eliminating all accidental and secondary aspects, until,

---

47 G. W. F. Hegel, *Lectures on the History of Philosophy*, Vol. 1, p. 402.

finally, we are brought face to face with the essence of the question. This is the method of induction, proceeding from the particular to the universal, a most important method for the development of science. Aristotle explicitly credits Socrates with the invention (or, at least, perfection) of the method of induction and logical definitions which are closely related to it.

The search for the general which lies hidden within the particular is one of the most important aspects of the development of human thought in general. Starting with elementary sense perception which registers individual facts and circumstances, the human mind begins slowly and painfully to abstract from these particulars, discarding the inessential, until it finally arrives at a series of more or less abstract generalisations. Though these 'universals' have no existence separate and apart from the particular things that embody them, they nonetheless represent the essential being of things, expressing a far deeper and more profound truth than the particular. The progress of human thought in general is closely related to the ability to generalise on the basis of experience, and to arrive at abstract ideas which correspond to the nature of reality.

In his autobiography, Trotsky touches on this question:

> Later, the feeling of the supremacy of the general over the particular became an integral part of my literary and political work. The dull empiricism, the unashamed, cringing worship of the fact which is so often only imaginary, and falsely interpreted at that, were odious to me. Beyond the facts, I looked for laws. Naturally, this led me more than once into hasty and incorrect generalisations, especially in my younger years when my knowledge, book-acquired, and my experience in life were still inadequate. But in every sphere, barring none, I felt that I could move and act only when I held in my hand the thread of the general.[48]

The aim of Socrates was to proceed, by means of logical argumentation, from the particular to the general, to arrive at the 'universal'. For him, this was no longer a question of getting to the most general laws

---

48 L. Trotsky, *My Life*, pp. 75-76.

governing nature, as was the case with earlier Greek philosophers, but rather of man examining himself, his own nature, his thought and actions. The philosophy of Socrates is not the philosophy of nature but the philosophy of society, above all of ethics and morality. His favourite subject is 'what is the Good?' In reality, this question can only be answered concretely, with reference to the historical development of society, since there is no such thing as a supra-historical morality. This can be seen clearly in the case of ancient Greece, where the very language betrays the historical relativity of morality. The Greek word for goodness '*arete*', like its Latin equivalent, '*virtus*' (from which we get the English 'virtue') originally meant something like combative manliness. As J. D. Bernal points out: "It took a long time to soften into the ideal of citizenship and still longer to Christian submissiveness."[49]

Nonetheless, what is important is not the subject matter of these dialogues, but the method. This really represents the birth of logic, which was originally the handling of words (Greek '*logoi*'). Thus, logic and dialectics were originally the same – a technique for getting at the truth. The method involved breaking up concepts into their constituent parts, revealing their inner contradictions, and putting them back together again. It was a dynamic process, with even a certain element of drama and surprise. The first reaction to the discovery of a fundamental contradiction in previously held ideas is one of surprise. For example, the idea that motion implies being and not being in the same place at the same time. The dialectic constantly challenges what appeared at first sight to be unquestionable. It shows the limitations of vulgar thinking, 'common sense' and superficial appeals to the 'facts', which, as Trotsky rightly remarked, are so often only imaginary, and falsely interpreted.

The task of going beyond the particular, of breaking down the information provided by our eyes and ears, and arriving at abstract generalisations lies at the root of the development and growth of human thought, not only in a historical sense, but in the evolution

---

49 J. D. Bernal, *Science in History*, p. 135.

of every individual in the arduous struggle to pass from childhood to conscious maturity. In the writings of Plato (428-348 BC) the search for the general, the 'universal', becomes the central issue of philosophy to the exclusion of all else, one might say almost an obsession. In these works, profound thoughts, a brilliant style and some masterly examples of the dialectic of discussion are mixed up with the most blatant and mystifying idealism ever produced by the human mind.

For Plato, the universals of thought, for example, the idea of a circle, had an independent existence, separate and apart from particular round objects. From a materialist standpoint, as we have seen, the idea of a circle was originally derived from the observation of round objects over a long period of time. Not so, says Plato. If one looks at any example of a round object, for instance the plate on this table, it will be seen to be imperfect. It is therefore only a poor copy of the perfect circle that existed before the world began. For a class of wealthy intellectuals, used to working only with thoughts and words, it was logical that these should appear to them to be endowed with a life and a power of their own:

> The emphasis on the discussion of words and their true meanings tended to give to words a reality independent of the things and actions to which they referred. Because there is a word for beauty, beauty itself must be real. Indeed it must be more real than any beautiful thing. This is because no beautiful thing is altogether beautiful, and so whether it is beautiful or not is a matter of opinion, whereas beauty contains nothing but itself and must exist independently of anything in this changing and imperfect material world. The same logic applies to concrete things: a stone in general must be more real than any particular stone.[50]

PLATO'S IDEALISM

In his work *Phaedo*, Plato develops this idea in a consistent way. If we ask what the cause of a thing is, we end up with its essence – the Greek word is '*eidos*', which can be variously translated as form or idea, although Aristotle interprets it as 'species', which is obviously

---

50 Ibid., p. 138.

preferable from a materialist standpoint. To go back to our dinner plate, what makes it round? Or – to use Platonic language – what is the cause of its roundness? One might answer: that it was caused by a potter rotating a lump of clay on a wheel and moulding it with his hand. But for Plato, the plate, like all other crude material objects, is merely an imperfect manifestation of the Idea, which, put in plain language, is God.

Plato's theory of knowledge, which Aristotle says is different from that of Socrates, was based on the idea that the object of knowledge must be permanent, eternal, and since nothing under the sun is permanent, we must seek stable knowledge outside this fleeting and deceitful world of material things. When Diogenes ridiculed the theory of Ideas, by saying he could see the cup, but not 'cupness', Plato retorted that that was because he had eyes to see, but no intellect. And it is true that merely to base oneself on sense-perception is not enough. It is necessary to go from the particular to the universal. The fundamental flaw here is to think that the generalisations of the intellect can stand on their own, divorced from, and counterposed to, the material world from which, ultimately, they are derived.

Marx and Engels, in *The Holy Family*, explained: in the philosophy of Idealism, the real relations between thought and being are stood on their head:

> [F]or the *absolute* idealist, in order to be an absolute idealist, must necessarily constantly go through the *sophistical process* of first transforming the world *outside himself* into an *appearance*, a mere fancy of *his* brain, and afterwards declaring this *fantasy* to be what it really is, i.e., a mere fantasy, so as finally to be able to proclaim his sole, exclusive existence, which is no longer disturbed even by the semblance of an external world.[51]

The sophistical trick whereby this is done was wittily explained in the same work:

> If from real apples, pears, strawberries and almonds I form the general idea '*Fruit*', if I go further and *imagine* that my abstract idea '*Fruit*',

---

51 K. Marx and F. Engels, *The Holy Family*, MECW, Vol. 4, p. 140.

derived from real fruit, is an entity existing outside me, is indeed the true essence of the pear, the apple, etc., then – in the *language* of *speculative* philosophy – I am declaring that '*Fruit*' is the '*Substance*' of the pear, the apple, the almond, etc. I am saying, therefore, that to be a pear is not essential to the pear, that to be an apple is not essential to the apple; that what is essential to these things is not their real existence, perceptible to the senses, but the essence that I have abstracted from them and then foisted on them, the essence of my idea – '*Fruit*'. I therefore declare apples, pears, almonds, etc., to be mere forms of existence, *modi*, of '*Fruit*'. My finite understanding supported by my senses does of course *distinguish* an apple from a pear and a pear from an almond, but my speculative reason declares these sensuous differences inessential and irrelevant. It sees in the apple *the same* as in the pear, and in the pear the same as in the almond, namely 'Fruit'. Particular real fruits are no more than *semblances* whose true essence is "*the* substance" – '*Fruit*'.[52]

Far from advancing the cause of human understanding, the idealist method does not take us a single step forward. Only a study of the real, that is to say, material world, can deepen our understanding of nature and our place in it. By directing men's eyes away from 'crude' material things towards the realm of so-called 'pure' abstraction, the idealists played havoc with the development of science for centuries.

By this method one attains no particular *wealth of definition*. The mineralogist whose science was limited to the statement that all minerals are really '*the* Mineral' would be a mineralogist only in *his imagination*. For every mineral the speculative mineralogist says '*the* Mineral', and his science is reduced to repeating this word as many times as there are real minerals.[53]

As opposed to the earlier Greek philosophers, who were generally materialists and set out from a study of nature, Plato consciously turned his back on the world of the senses. Not experiment and observation, but only pure deduction and mathematics was the road to truth. Above

---

52 Ibid., pp. 57-8.
53 Ibid., p. 58.

the entrance of his Academy in Athens he placed the inscription: "Let no man destitute of geometry enter my doors." Plato encouraged his students, for example, to study the stars, not as they are, but as they ought to be. Following in the footsteps of the Pythagoreans, he alleged that the planets showed their divine nature by their eternally unchanging orbits, the perfect regularity of their circular motion being an expression of the harmony of the universe. This cosmology, together with that of Aristotle, his great successor, held back the development of astronomy for 2,000 years. It represented a retreat from science to Pythagorean mysticism. Thus, in an Alexandrian handbook on astronomy written by Geminus, we read:

> There underlies the whole science of astronomy… the assumption that the sun and the moon and the five planets move at even speeds in perfect circles in an opposite direction to the cosmos. It was the Pythagoreans, the first to approach these questions, who laid down the hypothesis of a circular and uniform motion for the sun, moon, and planets. Their view was that, in regard of divine and eternal beings, a supposition of such disorder as that these bodies should move now more quickly and now more slowly, or should even stop, as in what are called the stations of the planets, is inadmissible. Even in the human sphere such irregularity is incompatible with the orderly procedure of a gentleman. And even if the crude necessities of life often impose upon men occasions of haste or loitering, it is not to be supposed that such occasions inhere in the incorruptible nature of the stars. For this reason they defined their problem as the explanation of the phenomena on the hypothesis of circular and uniform motion.[54]

Kepler discovered that the planets moved, not in circles, but in ellipses. Even this was not completely true, as Newton later showed. The ellipses are not perfect, either. But for the previous two millennia, the idealist picture of the universe held the force of an unchallengeable dogma. For much of that time it was backed by the formidable power of the Church.

---

54 B. Farrington, *Greek Science*, pp. 95-6.

It is significant that the ideas of Plato were known in the Middle Ages through only one work, *The Timaeus*, his worst book. This represents a complete counter-revolution in philosophy. From Thales on, Greek philosophy was characterised by an attempt to explain the world in natural terms, without recourse to the gods or any supernatural phenomena. *The Timaeus* is not a work of philosophy but a religious tract. Here we see a revival of "all the old crap", as Marx once put it. It is, in effect, the revival of the old creation myth. The world was created by a Supreme Craftsman. Matter consists of triangles because solids are bounded by planes, and planes can be resolved into triangles.

The world is spherical and moves in circles because the circle is the most perfect form. Men who live badly are reborn as women in the next reincarnation, and so on and so forth.

In a passage strikingly similar to some of the statements of the present-day defenders of the 'big bang', Plato writes about the 'beginning of time':

> Time, then, and the heaven came into being at the same instant in order that, having been created together, if ever there was to be a dissolution of them, they might be dissolved together. It was framed after the pattern of the eternal nature, that it might resemble this as far as was possible; for the pattern exists from eternity, and the created heaven has been, and is, and will be, in all time. Such was the mind and thought of God in the creation of time.[55]

No wonder the Christian Church welcomed this with open arms!

Despite its dialectical side, the Platonic philosophy is essentially a conservative one, reflecting the world outlook of an aristocratic elite, who felt, correctly, that their world was crumbling about them. The urge to turn one's back on reality, to deny the evidence of one's senses, to cling to some kind of stability in the midst of turbulence and upheaval, to deny change, all this clearly corresponded to a powerful psychological and moral need.

---

55 Plato, *Timaeus*, p. 457.

3. ARISTOTLE AND THE END OF CLASSICAL GREEK PHILOSOPHY

"[T]he greatest thinker of antiquity",[1] Marx called him. Aristotle lived from 384 to 322 BC and was born, not in Athens, but in Stagira, Thrace. Originally a pupil of Plato, he made a thorough study of his philosophy over a period of twenty years, but evidently became dissatisfied with it. After Plato's death, he left the Academy and later became the tutor of Alexander. He returned to Athens in 335 BC to found his own school, the Lyceum. His was an encyclopaedic mind, encompassing a huge number of subjects – logic, rhetoric, ethics, political sciences, biology, physics and metaphysics ('what comes after physics' – the study of first principles and presuppositions). He is the real founder of logic, natural history, the theory of morals, and even of economics.

The philosophy of Aristotle marks a sharp break with that of Plato. In many ways it is diametrically opposed to it. Instead of the idealist method, which turns its back upon reality in order to take refuge in a world of perfect ideas and forms, Aristotle proceeds from the concrete facts of sense perception, and from these arrives at ultimate grounds

---

1 K. Marx, *Capital,* Vol. 1, MECW, Vol. 35, p. 411.

and principles. Whereas Plato started with ideas and tried to explain reality from them, Aristotle sets out from reality, carefully examining a large number of facts and phenomena in order to derive from them a series of general inferences. That is to say, he used the method of induction.

Aristotle's interest in physics and biology is an illustration of his general approach, his love of experiment and observation as the main source of knowledge. In this, he was a pioneer of the modern scientific method. When Alexander the Great was engaged in his wars of conquest, he arranged to send back to Aristotle details and drawings of all new discoveries of plants and animals. What a difference to Plato, who regarded the crude material world of nature as unworthy of his attention! Aristotle spent many years collecting, arranging, and classifying information from all manner of spheres.

Aristotle, however, did not merely collect facts. Basing himself on information derived from the objective material world, he proceeded to generalise. In his most profound work, the *Metaphysics*, he speculates on the meaning of universal notions. In the process, he sums up and criticises previous philosophies, and therefore may also be regarded as the first historian of philosophy. It should be borne in mind that this has nothing to do with the use of the word 'metaphysics' in the writings of Marx and Engels, where it is used in an entirely different sense – as a way of describing the narrow mechanical outlook of the non-dialectical materialist philosophers of the eighteenth and nineteenth centuries. In fact, the 'metaphysics' of Aristotle occupies a similar place to dialectics in the philosophy of Plato.

In the *Metaphysics*, Aristotle for the first time provides a systematic account of some of the basic categories of dialectics. This fact is often overlooked, because he also laid down the laws of formal ('Aristotelian') logic, which, at first sight, appear to stand in contradiction to dialectics. In point of fact, for Aristotle, logic and dialectics were both valid ways of thinking. This is, in fact, the case. Dialectical thinking does not contradict formal logic, but complements it. More correctly, the laws of formal logic hold good within certain limits, beyond which they break down. In particular, formal logic, based on the law of identity, cannot adequately deal with motion, which involves a contradiction – something which formal logic explicitly rules out. For a whole series of operations in everyday life, the rules of formal logic hold good and play a useful role. But when the attempt is made to apply these laws and thought-forms to areas where they conflict with reality, they turn into their opposite. Far from helping us to understand the workings of nature, they become an endless source of error, holding back the development of science and knowledge.

The whole of formal logic is based on three propositions, which make up the basic Aristotelian syllogism:

1.   The law of identity ('A' = 'A')
2.   The law of contradiction ('A' is not 'not-A')
3.   The law of the excluded middle ('A' is not 'B')

For more than 2,000 years, this has been the cornerstone of all logic. Towards the end of the eighteenth century, Kant was able to say that logic, since Aristotle, had not made any step forward or any step back. Despite all the changes experienced by science in that period, the rules of logic remained petrified in the forms worked out by Aristotle, and later converted into a dogma by the mediaeval Church. Yet the basic Aristotelian syllogism upon which the whole edifice is constructed is based on a false premise. In the first place, despite the appearance of a logical progression, this is an illusion. All three assertions are, in fact, already contained in the first one: 'A' is equal to 'A'. Everything stands or falls with this, the 'law of identity'.

At first sight, the truth of this proposition would appear to be self-evident. Like the law of contradiction, which is merely a negative way of saying the same thing, it seems to brook no dissent. As Aristotle says:

> There are some who maintain (a) that the same thing can be and not be, and (b) that it is possible so to judge. Many physicists too, have used language to this effect. Now we have just assumed that a thing cannot both be and not be, and have also shown this to be the most indubitable of all principles. The demand that we should prove the law argues a defective

education in logic – a science which enables one to recognise what requires proof and what does not. It is absolutely impossible to have proof of everything: the process would continue indefinitely, and the result would be no proof of anything whatsoever. Granted, on the other hand, that there are some things which do not call for proof, what principle, I ask, is more self-evident than the law of contradiction?[2]

It is interesting to note that here Aristotle, who is normally most concerned to prove each of his postulates by a rigorous process of argument, makes no attempt to prove the law of contradiction, but merely asserts it dogmatically. It is just to be accepted as 'common sense'. But, upon closer examination, the matter is not at all as simple as it is presented. In real life, a thing is and is not equal to itself, because it is constantly changing. You are in no doubt that you are you. But in the time you have taken to read these lines, billions of changes have taken place in your body – cells have died and been replaced. The body consists of tissue, which is constantly breaking down and being replaced, eliminating waste matter and bacteria, excreting carbon dioxide through the lungs, losing water in sweat and urine, and so on. These constant changes are the basis of all life. They mean that, at any moment, the body is itself and also something different to itself, so you are not the same person you were. Nor is it possible to get round this by arguing that you are you at this precise moment in time, since even in the smallest portion of time, change takes place.

For normal purposes, we can accept that 'A' = 'A', that you are you, and nobody else. The reason is that the kind of change we are referring to is so small that it can be ignored for normal purposes. However, over a longer period, twenty years, for instance, a difference would be noticed. And in 100 years, the difference would be quite sufficient for one to conclude that you are not you at all! Moreover, this does not only apply to living things. Inorganic matter is also in a state of constant change, so that everything is and is not, because, to use Heraclitus' marvellous expression: *everything is in flux.*

---

2 Aristotle, *Metaphysics*, p. 125.

For ordinary everyday purposes, we can accept the law of identity. Indeed, it is absolutely indispensable if thought is not to dissolve into utter confusion. But for more accurate calculations, or higher velocities approaching the speed of light, or for a whole series of critical situations, it proves inadequate. At a certain point, an accumulation of small, quantitative changes gives rise to a fundamental change in quality. All of this remains a closed book to formal logic, the fundamental weakness of which is an inability to deal with things in their movement and life.

Similarly with the law of the excluded middle, which states that it is necessary either to assert or deny, that a thing must be either black or white, either alive or dead, either 'A' or 'B'. It cannot be both at the same time. For normal everyday purposes, we can take this to be true. Indeed, without such assumptions, clear and consistent thought would be impossible. In the period of decadence of sophism, it became customary to play with dialectics in an arbitrary way, which so twisted the method of reasoning as to be able to prove practically any opinion. Aristotle was determined to clear up the mess caused by the subjective dialectics of sophism, hence his insistence on elementary logical propositions.

Nevertheless, when we depart from the realm of everyday experience and consider more complex processes, it is by no means such a simple matter to distinguish 'A' from 'B'. The dogmatic insistence on eliminating contradiction leads precisely to the metaphysical mode of thought in the specific sense understood by Marx and Engels, as explained in *Anti-Dühring*. It points out the limitations of the laws of formal logic when faced with the contradictory reality of nature:

> To the metaphysician, things and their mental reflexes, ideas, are isolated, are to be considered one after the other and apart from each other, are objects of investigation fixed, rigid, given once for all. He thinks in absolutely irreconcilable antitheses. "His communication is 'yea, yea; nay, nay'; for whatsoever is more than these cometh of evil." For him a thing either exists or does not exist; a thing cannot at the same time be itself

and something else. Positive and negative absolutely exclude one another; cause and effect stand in a rigid antithesis one to the other.

At first sight this mode of thinking seems to us very luminous, because it is that of so-called sound common sense. Only sound common sense, respectable fellow that he is, in the homely realm of his own four walls, has very wonderful adventures directly he ventures out into the wide world of research. And the metaphysical mode of thought, justifiable and even necessary as it is in a number of domains whose extent varies according to the nature of the particular object of investigation, sooner or later reaches a limit, beyond which it becomes one-sided, restricted, abstract, lost in insoluble contradictions. In the contemplation of individual things, it forgets the connection between them; in the contemplation of their existence, it forgets the beginning and end of that existence; of their repose, it forgets their motion. It cannot see the wood for the trees. For everyday purposes we know and can say, e.g., whether an animal is alive or not. But, upon closer inquiry, we find that this is, in many cases, a very complex question, as the jurists know very well. They have cudgelled their brains in vain to discover a rational limit beyond which the killing of the child in its mother's womb is murder. It is just as impossible to determine absolutely the moment of death, for physiology proves that death is not an instantaneous, momentary phenomenon, but a very protracted process.

In like manner, every organic being is every moment the same and not the same; every moment it assimilates matter supplied from without, and gets rid of other matter; every moment some cells of its body die and others build themselves anew; in a longer or shorter time the matter of its body is completely renewed, and is replaced by other molecules of matter, so that every organic being is always itself, and yet something other than itself.

Further, we find upon closer investigation that the two poles of an antithesis, like positive and negative, e.g., are as inseparable as they are opposed, and that despite all their opposition, they mutually interpenetrate. And we find, in like manner, that cause and effect are conceptions which only hold good in their application to individual cases; but as soon as we consider the individual cases in their general connection with the universe as a whole, they run into each other, and they become confounded when we contemplate that universal action and reaction in which causes and effects are eternally changing places, so that what is effect here and now will be cause there and then, and vice-versa.

None of these processes and modes of thought enters into the framework of metaphysical reasoning. Dialectics, on the other hand, comprehends things and their representations, in their essential connection, concatenation, motion, origin, and ending. Such processes as those mentioned above are, therefore, so many corroborations of its own method of procedure.[3]

It is unfortunate, but not unique, that the brilliant, original thought of a genius became ossified and impoverished in the hands of his successors. The flexible, dialectical aspect of Aristotle's method, with its emphasis on observation and experiment was lost sight of for a long time. The mediaeval Schoolmen, interested only in providing an ideological basis for the doctrines of the Church, concentrated on his logic, interpreted in a lifeless and formalistic way, to the exclusion of practically all else. Thus, a body of ideas which ought to have provided a healthy stimulus to the development of science, was turned into its opposite – a set of chains for the intellect, which was only shattered by the revolutionary upsurge of the Renaissance.

There is something profoundly ironic about the hijacking of Aristotle by the Church. In fact, his writings are impregnated with a strongly materialist spirit. Lenin considered that "Aristotle comes very close to materialism".[4]

Thus, unlike Plato, in Aristotle, formal logic is closely connected to the theory of being and the theory of knowledge, because he saw the forms of thought as being, not independently existing phenomena, but forms of being, expressed in human consciousness.

Aristotle totally rejected Plato's theory of ideas as disembodied forms. The aim of science is, of course, to generalise on the basis of experience. But the general only exists in and through the material

---

3   F. Engels, *Anti-Dühring*, pp. 31-3.

4   V. I. Lenin, 'Conspectus of Hegel's *Lectures on the History of Philosophy*', LCW, Vol. 38, p. 287.

things given to us in sense perception. He rightly understood the limitations of the early materialists like Thales who attempted to express the material world in terms of a single concrete manifestation, such as water. He saw matter as an eternal substance, which is always changing, which cannot be created or destroyed, with neither beginning or end, but which is in a constant process of change and transformation. One of his main objections to Plato's idealism is that non-material ('non-sensible') things can have no movement: "But this is quite inadmissible; a heaven ... without movement is unthinkable; yet a non-sensible heaven can have no movement."[5]

Aristotle's penetrating mind detected an insoluble contradiction in Plato's idealism. If there really existed unchanging, eternal forms, how did they succeed in giving rise to the constantly moving, changing material world we see before us? Out of such an immobile idea, entirely devoid of any principle of motion, one can derive nothing at all, except a complete standstill. Nothing comes into being without a moving force, either from within itself or from without, as Newton found out when he assigned God the task of providing the initial impulse to get his mechanical universe moving. But here there is nothing of the sort. Plato's Ideas have no motion in them. But since all things move and change, these allegedly perfect ideas suffer from the greatest imperfection of all: they do not exist. More correctly, they do not exist anywhere except as phantoms in the brains of philosophers.

The absolute separation between thought and being, that peculiar schizophrenia which afflicts all brands of idealism, ultimately leads it to impotence. This is because there is no real way in which the 'Absolute Idea', which is supposed to stand above the world of crude material reality, can affect the latter, or impinge upon it in any way whatsoever. As Schwegler remarks:

> The supporters of the Ideal Theory, then, are not in a position logically to determine any idea; their ideas are indefinable. Plato has left in complete obscurity the relation in general of things to the ideas. He terms the ideas archetypes, and supposes things to participate in them; but such

---

5 Aristotle, *Metaphysics*, p. 94.

expressions are only hollow poetical metaphors. How are we to conceive this 'participation' in, this copying of, these patterns thus remote, absent in an alien region? It is in vain to seek in Plato any definite explanation here. It is wholly unintelligible how and why matter comes to participate in the ideas.[6]

In his struggle against the subjectivism of the sophists, Socrates laid stress on the need to look for universal ideas, and arrive at correct conceptions and definitions which really correspond to the subject matter under consideration. This was an advance as against the arbitrary method of the sophists. Indeed, without such universals, science in general would be impossible. However, Plato's attempt to transform these general notions into independent entities led straight into the swamp of religious mysticism. What we are really dealing with here, under the heading of 'universals', is the *genus* and *species* of things. The notion that a genus or species can exist separate and apart from the individuals that comprise it, or vice versa, is self-evident nonsense. Aristotle rejected the notion that forms and ideas can exist separate from material things:

> While the Ideal Theory involves us in numerous difficulties, its greatest absurdity is the doctrine that there are entities apart from those in the sensible universe, and that they are the same as sensible things except that the former are eternal while the latter are perishable. Those who uphold this view are saying in effect that there is an absolute Man, and Horse, and Hearth. They follow closely in the footsteps of those who teach that there are gods, but in human form; for as the latter merely set up eternal men, so the former do no more than make the Forms eternal sensibles.[7]

With enormous patience and intellectual rigour, Aristotle went through all the categories of thought, which he expressed in a far more developed and explicit way than had hitherto been the case. Many of the categories of dialectical thought later developed in Hegel's *Logic* are already dealt with in outline by Aristotle –

6 A. Schwegler, *History of Philosophy*, p. 104.

7 Aristotle, *Metaphysics*, pp. 93-4.

Being, Quantity and Quality, Part and Whole, Necessity and Accident, Potential and Actual, and so on. There are many important insights here. For example, in the discussion of the relation between potentiality ('*dynamis*') and actuality ('*energeia*'), Aristotle anticipates the idea of the unity of matter and energy. For Aristotle, matter consists of two aspects, substance, which contains within itself the potential for an infinite number of transformations, and a kind of active principle, '*energeia*', which is an innate and spontaneous moving force. In developing the idea of the movement of potential being into actual being, Aristotle gives a more concrete version of the 'becoming' of Heraclitus. Here we have the main point of difference between the philosophy of Aristotle and that of Plato. In place of the static, lifeless 'Idea', we have an inherent tendency of matter towards movement and development, which realises itself by constantly passing from potentiality to actuality.

In relation to time, Aristotle shows himself to be superior, not only to Plato, but to many modern scientists, who talk mystical nonsense about the 'beginning of time'. He points out that time, like motion, has always existed, and that, consequently, it is absurd to talk of the beginning or end of time:

> It is impossible, however, that motion should be generable or perishable; it must always have existed. Nor can time come into being or cease to be; for there cannot be a 'before' or 'after' where there is no time. Movement, then, is also continuous in the sense in which time is, for time is either the same thing as motion or an attribute of it.[8]

This is a profound thought, and one that anticipates the position of dialectical materialism, that time, space and motion are the mode of existence of matter, although Aristotle was unable to develop this idea in a satisfactory way.

Starting out from the position of objective idealism, Aristotle came quite close to materialism, although he never managed to make

---

8   Ibid., p. 342.

a complete break; as Lenin comments: "Aristotle *wavers* between idealism and materialism".[9] In the writings of Aristotle, we find the germs of a materialist conception of history and the development of thought and culture. He explains that, while the actions of animals are determined by immediate sense-impressions (the things they can see, hear, etc.) and memory, only the human race lives by shared, social experience, art and science. While the starting point of all knowledge is experience and sense-perception, that is not enough:

> Wisdom, again, is not to be identified with sense-perception which, though it is our primary source of knowledge of particulars, can never tell us *why* anything is so (e.g., why fire is hot), but only that it *is* so.[10]

The theory of knowledge of Aristotle also comes close to a materialist position. The starting point is the facts and phenomena given to us through our senses (in sense-perception), passing from the particular to the universal:

> [S]o that in this case we have to start from what is more intelligible to ourselves (i.e., the complex facts and objects of experience) and advance to the understanding of what is *of its nature* intelligible (i.e., the simple, universal principles of scientific knowledge).[11]

The inconsistency of Aristotle's position is revealed in the concessions he makes to religion, in assigning to God the role of the 'First Cause'. Anticipating Newton, he argued that there must be something which originates motion, and this something must itself be unmoved. This 'something', however, must be an eternal substance and actuality. The concept is ambiguous, rather like the 'substance' of Spinoza. It is open to the same objections levelled by Aristotle against Plato. For if the universe was once without motion – something which is impossible – there is no way it could be made

---

9 V. I. Lenin, 'Conspectus of Hegel's *Lectures on the History of Philosophy*', LCW, Vol. 38, p. 286.

10 Aristotle, *Metaphysics*, p. 52.

11 Ibid., p. 172.

to move, unless by an external impulse. But if the 'unmoved First Mover' is not material, it is impossible that it should impart motion to a material universe.

Moreover, this line of argument does not solve the problem posed, but merely shifts it back one stage. Let us accept that the 'First Cause' set the universe in motion. What caused the 'First Cause'? This question is not supposed to be asked. The answer is allegedly given in advance by the phrase 'unmoved First Mover', which, of course, answers nothing. The weakness of the whole argument is self-evident, and flows from Aristotle's preoccupation with the search for final causes (as opposed to what he called material, formal and efficient causes). Within certain limits, for everyday purposes, it is possible to do this with a fair degree of satisfaction. For example, the causes of the existence of a house can be traced to the building materials, the builders, the architect, and so on.

In fact, however, it is possible to go on tracing the causes of even the simplest phenomenon indefinitely. Even in the given example, we could go on to specify the demand for housing, the state of the world economy, the atomic composition of the bricks and cement, the parents and grandparents of all the people involved, and so on and so forth. For practical purposes, we choose not to do this, placing a definite limit on causality. But, in reality, the chain of causation is endless, cause becoming effect, and vice versa, *ad infinitum*. Thus, the very conception of a 'First Cause' is unscientific and mystical. Naturally, this weakest side of Aristotle was seized upon and elevated to the rank of dogma by the Church.

Another misconception in Aristotle, related to the above, was the teleological interpretation of nature. Teleology (from the Greek word *telos*, an end) holds that all natural phenomena, including man, are determined by an ultimate goal or purpose. This mistaken notion played a negative role in holding back science, since it cannot really explain anything. Moreover, it leads to religious conclusions, because one has to say where this 'purpose' came from. The conclusion is drawn that the goal of things is determined by God.

Aristotle himself did not approach things in this way, although it suited the Church later on to give it a religious interpretation. To him, everything contained within itself an active principle, or 'soul' ('entelechy'), and the whole of nature is guided by a single supreme goal. This idea probably comes from Aristotle's investigations of biology. In his works, he mentions some 500 different types of animals, of which he himself dissected about fifty different types. From close observation, he noted how the body structure of animals is perfectly adapted to their environment and mode of existence. From such observations, Darwin arrived at the theory of evolution. But Aristotle drew a different conclusion, namely that the nature of each animal is predetermined by Nature in accordance with a given order, a plan almost, which is inherent in the nature of things. Thus, Aristotle ascribes the body to a divine plan:

> Man alone of all the animals is erect, because his nature and his substance are divine. To think, to exercise intelligence, is the characteristic of that which is most divine. This is not easy if much of the body is situated in the upper part. For weight renders the exercise of thought and perception sluggish. Accordingly, if the weight and the bodily element increase, bodies must bow down to earth; then, for security, nature must substitute forelegs for hands and arms, and we get quadrupeds ... But man being erect has no need of forelegs; instead of them nature has given him hands and arms. Now Anaxagoras has said that it is the possession of hands that has made man the most intelligent of the animals. The probability is that it was because he was the most intelligent that he got hands. For hands are a tool, and nature, like an intelligent man, always distributes tools to those that can use them. The proper thing is to give a genuine flute-player a flute rather than to give a man who happens to have a flute the skill to play; for that is to add the lesser to the greater and more august instead of adding the greater and more precious to the lesser. If, then, it is best that it should be so, and if nature, out of what is possible always does the best, it

is not because he has hands that man is wise, but because he is the wisest of the animals he has hands.[12]

The idea of Anaxagoras, that the development of human intelligence was made possible by the freeing of the hands was a marvellous insight, but Aristotle completely stands it on its head. His teleological approach prevented him from arriving at a genuinely scientific appraisal of nature, in spite of the vast extent of his research. Taken over by Thomas Aquinas and the Church, it held back the study of nature for centuries, until Darwin's discoveries gave a rational explanation of the relative purpose of living creatures. Even so, teleological conceptions in biology resurfaced in different guises – neo-vitalism, neo-Lamarckism, etc. The same tendency is often expressed even today by people who, when attempting to describe natural phenomena, unconsciously endow 'Nature' with human characteristics, as if it 'made' animals and plants, and got them to behave in a certain way. In reality, the 'purposefulness' displayed by plants and animals is the process of optimum adaptation of living objects to their surroundings, and not at all the product of a preordained plan.

GREEK SCIENCE IN THE ALEXANDRIAN PERIOD

The barrenness of idealist philosophy is shown by the fact that it was incapable of further development. Plato's philosophy ended with the death of Plato. His Academy was taken over by a series of second-raters, who contributed nothing new to the development of thought. This was not the case with Aristotle's Lyceum. His emphasis on investigation stimulated his pupils to engage in fruitful practical research. The voluminous studies in different fields bequeathed by the Master laid the basis for the development of various sciences. The great museum of Alexandria was an offshoot of the Lyceum, which produced important treatises on botany, physics, anatomy, physiology, mathematics, astronomy, geography, mechanics, music and grammar.

---

12 Aristotle, *Parts of Animals*, quoted in Farrington, *Greek Science*, pp. 129-130.

Aristotle's first successor, Theophrastus, made a breakthrough in biology, being the first to draw a firm distinction between plants and animals to establish the science of botany. Theophrastus also began to question the validity of teleology, and proposed to place a limit on its application to biology:

> We must try to set a limit to the assigning of final causes. This is the prerequisite of all scientific inquiry into the universe, that is, into the conditions of existence of real things and their relations with one another.[13]

He went back to the materialist explanations of the pre-Socratic philosophers in order to overcome the contradictions in which Aristotle had found himself in relation to matter and movement.

Strato, who was head of the Lyceum from 287 to 267 BC, can be considered the father of scientific experiment. According to Polybius, he earned the nickname 'The Physicist', which at that time denoted anyone interested in the investigation of nature. Cicero says, in a disapproving tone, that he "abandoned ethics, which is the most necessary part of philosophy, and devoted himself to the investigation of nature".[14] In 1893, Hermann Diels analysed a fragment attributed to Hero of Alexandria, *Pneumatica* (*The Pneumatics*), written in the second half of the first century AD, which clearly lays down the basis of the experimental method worked out by Strato.

The scientists of the Alexandrine period (roughly 330-30 BC) made great advances in all fields of knowledge. In mechanics, for example, they produced mathematical explanations of a whole host of operations: the lever, the balance, the pulley, the potter's wheel, the wedge, the oars of a boat, the problem of inertia, etc. In the field of botany, the work of Theophrastus remained without parallel until modern times, according to Farrington. Strato is now considered to be the author of the document 'Mechanical Problems', originally attributed to Aristotle, which contains the germ of an important principle of mechanics, the principle of virtual velocities (the principle

---

13 Quoted in B. Farrington, *Greek Science*, p. 163.
14 Quoted ibid., p. 171.

of virtual displacements). Eratosthenes calculated the circumference of the earth, using scientific methods, and appears to have come within 0.4 per cent of the correct result.

The great discoveries of the Alexandrine period laid the basis for further scientific achievements under the Roman Empire. Hero of Alexandria (10-70 AD) famously invented a steam engine, although it could not be put to use. Greek scientists even succeeded in building the first ever analogue computer, the 'Antikythera mechanism' in this period, based on the astronomical and mathematical theories of the Alexandrine Period. The question invariably arises in our minds why such extraordinary discoveries did not lead to a technological and industrial revolution 2,000 years ago. The answer to this question lies in the nature of the slave economy itself.

Engels remarked in a letter:

> If, as you say, technique largely depends on the state of science, science depends far more still on the *state* and the *requirements* of technique.[15]

In general, with certain exceptions like mining, war engines and public works, the rulers of Greece and Rome were uninterested in the application of scientific discoveries in production. In the period when slavery became the dominant mode of production, the divorce between science and technology was almost total. Philosophical and scientific speculation was regarded as an intellectual pastime for the wealthy. Philosophers and mathematicians looked with contempt at the men of practical affairs. Euclid, the great geometrician, when asked by an incautious pupil what he would gain by studying geometry, ordered a slave to give him a few coins, "since he must make a gain out of what he learns".[16] In point of fact, no practical use was found for Euclid's theories until the seventeenth century, when Galileo discovered that projectiles move in parabolas and Kepler found that planets move in ellipses.

---

15 F. Engels, 'Letter to H. Starkenburg, 25 January 1894', MESC, p. 517.
16 Quoted in T. Heath, *A History of Greek Mathematics*, Vol. 1, p. 25.

Limits & Slavery

SLAVERY

Despite the existence of a large and sophisticated trade network across the Ancient Mediterranean, production at this time was still overwhelmingly for use, not exchange, and the competitive pressure to produce an ever-expanding mass of commodities as efficiently as possible that we see under capitalism was almost completely absent. Marx comments in *Capital*:

> [I]n any given economic formation of society, where not the exchange value but the use value of the product predominates, surplus labour will be limited by a given set of wants which may be greater or less, and that here no boundless thirst for surplus labour arises from the nature of the production itself.[17]

Further, with an abundance of cheap slave labour, there was no incentive to move towards labour-saving technology. Even in agriculture, which in the later period of Roman history was based on large-scale latifundia, there was a disincentive to introduce machinery. This was firstly because of the abundant supply of slaves, and secondly, because the slaves, unlike free labourers, could not be relied upon to look after delicate and costly machines. In a perceptive footnote in the first volume of *Capital*, Marx explains the reason for the impossibility of introducing advanced technology on the basis of slavery:

> This is one of the circumstances that makes production by slave labour such a costly process. The labourer here is, to use a striking expression of the ancients, distinguishable only as *instrumentum vocale* [instrument with a voice], from an animal as *instrumentum semi-vocale*, and from an implement as *instrumentum mutum*. But he himself takes care to let both beast and implement feel that he is none of them, but is a man. He convinces himself with immense satisfaction, that he is a different being, by treating the one unmercifully and damaging the other *con amore* [with love]. Hence the principle, universally applied in this method of production, only to employ the rudest and heaviest implements and such as are difficult to damage owing to their sheer clumsiness. In the slave-

---

17 K. Marx, *Capital,* Vol. 1, MECW, Vol. 35, pp. 243-4.

states bordering on the Gulf of Mexico, down to the date of the Civil War, ploughs constructed on old Chinese models, which turned up the soil like a hog or a mole, instead of making furrows, were alone to be found. (Conf. J. E. Cairnes, *The Slave Power*, London, 1862, p. 46 sqq.) In his *Sea Board Slave States*, Olmsted tell us: "I am here shown tools that no man in his senses, with us, would allow a labourer, for whom he was paying wages, to be encumbered with; and the excessive weight and clumsiness of which, I would judge, would make work at least ten per cent greater than with those ordinarily used with us. And I am assured that, in the careless and clumsy way they must be used by the slaves, anything lighter or less crude could not be furnished them with good economy, and that such tools as we constantly give our labourers and find our profit in giving them, would not last out a day in a Virginia cornfield – much lighter and more free from stones though it be than ours. So, too, when I ask why mules are so universally substituted for horses on the farm, the first reason given, and confessedly the most conclusive one, is that horses cannot bear the treatment that they always must get from Negroes; horses are always soon foundered or crippled by them, while mules will bear cudgelling, or lose a meal or two now and then, and not be materially injured, and they do not take cold or get sick, if neglected or overworked. But I do not need to go further than to the window of the room in which I am writing, to see at almost any time, treatment of cattle that would ensure the immediate discharge of the driver by almost any farmer owning them in the North."[18]

The rise of the slave mode of production undermined the free peasantry of the Roman Republic, who were crushed by military service, debt, and the competition of slavery. Paradoxically, the productivity of slave labour was lower than that of the small peasants they displaced. But with a huge supply of slaves from foreign wars of conquest, the low level of productivity of the individual slave was compensated for by the cheapness of labour power of a large number of slaves subjected to forced labour. The replacement of small peasant holdings by vast latifundia, worked by armies of slaves, gave rise to huge surpluses, as long as the supply of cheap slaves continued. Where slavery is

18 Ibid., p. 207n.

the main mode of production, the very concept of labour becomes debased, identified in men's minds with all things base and degraded. No wonder Aristotle could not stomach Anaxagoras' theory that human intelligence depended on the hands!

This is not the place to analyse in detail the contradictions of the slave mode of production, which finally led to its demise. Suffice it to note that, despite the common attempt to compare the slave system with modern capitalism, in many ways it was the exact opposite. For example, today, the proletariat, along with nature, produces all the wealth of society. However, in the period of the Roman Empire, it was a parasitic class, which lived on the backs of the slaves and the subject peoples of the empire. On the other hand, whereas the modern capitalist depends on the continual search for avenues of reinvestment, the possibilities for investment open to the Roman capitalist were limited by the nature of slave production itself.

The key to the expansion of the productive forces under capitalism is the reinvestment of the surplus into new means of production, the manufacture of new machines, which leads to a constant increase in capital. In Antiquity, however, the conditions for the development and application of machinery were lacking. The first of these is the existence of a large class of free labourers, who are compelled to sell their labour power to the owners of industry. There was no incentive to invent machines which could not be put to practical use. The relatively small class of craftsmen devoted themselves to the production of luxury articles for the gratification of the wealthy who, unlike the modern capitalists, having no productive outlet for their surpluses, devoted themselves to conspicuous consumption on a grand scale.

The entire system began to break down when the supply of cheap slave labour dried up, as the empire reached its limits. In the absence of a revolutionary overturn, the whole of society entered into a prolonged phase of decline and decay. The barbarian invasions did not cause the collapse, but were an expression of the fact that the system of slavery had exhausted itself. However, the giant, parasitic imperial state continued to survive, choking the progress of new social relations. The all-pervading sense of decay affected the outlook of every class. The feeling of weariness, of moral decadence, of disgust with a world that had outlived itself, finds its expression in the prevailing philosophies of the period – the words for two of them, cynicism and scepticism, have passed into the vocabulary of our own times, although with meanings completely different to the originals.

CYNICS AND SCEPTICS

The cynics were followers of Diogenes of Antisthenes, a pupil of Socrates, who professed his open contempt for all existing morals and customs. His more famous disciple, also named Diogenes, from Sinope, carried this idea to the extreme of wishing to live 'like a dog', hence the word 'cynic', from the Greek word for a dog. It is said that he lived in a barrel. The idea, like that of present-day 'drop-outs', was to reduce one's dependence on material things to a minimum. According to legend, when Alexander the Great offered him anything he wanted, he answered, "step out of my light". The whole idea, in contrast to the modern cynics, was to despise worldly things.

This idea of turning away from the world to seek spiritual salvation in oneself reflected the profound social and cultural crisis caused by the decline of the Greek city-states. Even Pythagoras and Plato, despite their idealist philosophy, did not actually renounce the world entirely. Both tried to influence it by trying to persuade rulers to put their philosophical views into practice. Both appealed to logic and reason. What we see here is something different. A complete renunciation of this world, and a total denial of the possibility of knowing anything.

While Aristotle's Lyceum produced important scientific results, the Academy fell increasingly under the influence of scepticism. The sceptic philosophy, represented by Pyhrro, Sextus Empiricus and others, questioned the possibility of the objective knowledge of reality. We can never know anything, not even that we know nothing: this was their central tenet. It was, to some extent, the logical outcome of the method of deduction, which was held up by the idealists as the only means of arriving at the truth. It was to be discovered, not by reference to the real world of observation and experiment, but by deriving ideas from other ideas, axioms and 'first principles', like those of Euclid in geometry, which are regarded as self-evident, and in no need of proof.

Sceptics like Timon denied the possibility of finding such principles. Everything had to be proved by something else, and that in turn by something else, and so on *ad infinitum*. And therefore, nothing can be known.

This marks a degeneration from objective idealism – which, for all its defects, was capable of reaching some important conclusions – to subjective idealism, the lowest, most primitive and sterile form of idealism. Ultimately, it leads to solipsism, the notion that only 'I' exist. Everything depends on 'my' subjective impressions. There is no objective truth. For example, I cannot assert that honey is sweet, only that it seems sweet to me. To most people this seems absurd. But it is basically no different to the views later put forward by Hume and Kant, which have been widely accepted by modern bourgeois philosophers and scientists. For example, the idea advanced by the sceptics that you cannot say anything for certain about the world, but only that certain things are 'probable', is the philosophical basis for a false interpretation of the results of quantum mechanics put forward by people such as Werner Heisenberg and uncritically assimilated by many scientists.

Ideas like this do not drop from the clouds. They are the indirect and confused reflection in men and women's brains of an existing social reality. Scepticism in all its guises, including the modern ones, is the expression of a period in which a particular society has entered into irreversible decline, when the old ideals are breaking down, but the new ones have not yet asserted themselves. A general mood of uncertainty and malaise spreads through society, beginning with the educated layer, which feels it has lost its bearings. The most common expression of such moods is precisely scepticism: the insistence upon the relativity of all human knowledge, doubt, agnosticism. In the eighteenth century, the period of the revolutionary ascent of the bourgeoisie, the scepticism of Montaigne and others played a progressive role in criticising the religious dogmas of the theologians. However, the scepticism of Hume and Kant, which attempted to place a limit on the possibilities of human understanding, opened the door to the re-entry of religious faith. Not accidentally, it is this latter variant which has been taken over by modern bourgeois philosophy, in the guise of logical positivism.

The common feature of all these philosophies of the period of decline of slave society is the idea of a retreat from the world. It is the philosophy of despair. The world is seen as a vale of tears, from which it is necessary to escape, seeking individual salvation by various means. In the period of decline of the Roman Empire, the philosophies of Epicureanism and Stoicism, dominant from the first century AD, displayed the same tendency, although, as often happens, there was frequently a discrepancy between theory and practice. For example, Seneca, the stern moral philosopher of stoicism, who taught ethics to the emperor Nero, made a fortune out of lending money at exorbitant rates of interest, which provoked the rebellion of Boudica against the Romans in Britain. This prophet of poverty left behind one of the biggest fortunes of the time – 300 million sesterces.

In his masterly study of Antiquity, *The Foundations of Christianity*, Karl Kautsky describes the intellectual and moral climate in which these ideas took root:

> Epicurus called philosophy an activity that brings about a happy life by means of concepts and proofs. He believed this would be achieved by striving for pleasure, but only for rational lasting enjoyment, not for transitory sensual dissipations, which lead to the loss of health and wealth, and hence to pain.

> This was a philosophy very well suited to a class of exploiters that found no other employment for their wealth than to consume it. What they needed was a rational regulation of the life of enjoyment. But this theory gave no consolation to those, and their number kept growing, who had already suffered bodily, spiritual or financial shipwreck; nor to the poor and wretched, nor to the satiated, those who were revolted by pleasures.

And not to those who still had an interest in the traditional forms of the community and still followed goals beyond their own personality, those patriots who grieved to see the decline of state and society, without being able to prevent it. For all these groups the pleasures of this world seemed stale and vain. They turned to the Stoic doctrine, which valued not pleasure but virtue as the highest good, as the only blessedness, and held external goods, health, wealth, etc., to be matters just as indifferent as external evils.

This ended by leading many people to turn away from the world altogether, to despise life, even to long for death. Suicide became common in Imperial Rome; it actually became fashionable.[19]

Here we stand on the threshold between philosophy and religion. A society which has exhausted itself economically, morally and intellectually finds its expression in a general mood of pessimism and despair. Logic and reason provide no answers, when the existing order of things is itself shot through with irrationality. Such circumstances are not conducive to the growth of scientific thought and bold philosophical generalisations. They are much more likely to produce an inward-looking tendency, reflecting social atomisation, mysticism and irrationality. From this world we can expect nothing, and even understand nothing. Far better to turn our backs on it, and prepare ourselves for a better life to come. In place of philosophy, we have religion, in place of reason, mysticism.

We already see this phenomenon in the period of decline of the Greek city-states when, in the words of Professor Gilbert Murray: "Astrology fell upon the Hellenistic mind as a new disease falls upon some remote island people."[20] The same phenomenon was multiplied a thousandfold in the long drawn-out decline of the Roman Empire. The epidemic of Oriental religions and cults which afflicted Roman society at this time is well documented – not just Christianity and Judaism, but the cult of Mithras, the cult of Isis and Osiris, and a

---

19 K. Kautsky, *Foundations of Christianity*, p. 89.
20 Quoted in B. Russell, *History of Western Philosophy*, p. 237.

thousand other exotic sects proliferated at the expense of the official religion.

Many of these cults had similar ceremonies and rituals. The sacrament of Mithras included a sacred meal, in which consecrated bread and a chalice of wine were served to the faithful in anticipation of the future life. In fact, many elements of Christianity were taken over from other religions, and most of its doctrines from pagan philosophers.

A special role was played by Plotinus (205-270 AD), the Greek mystic and founder of the neoplatonist school. Here we have the final decadence of classical idealism. The world is supposed to consist of the One, which is unknowable and inexpressible. We can only know it by mystical means, ecstatic communion, trances, and the like. This, in turn, is achieved through the mortification of the flesh, and the emancipation of our better self from the bondage of matter. Plotinus sets out from the idea of a Holy Trinity. Matter has no independent reality, but is the creation of the soul. The only question is, why the soul bothered to create such stuff in the first place. But one is not supposed to ask such questions here, only to accept it as a 'mystery'. All this was taken over, bag and baggage, by the Christian apologists, who produced a theology which is the bastard child of Oriental religion and Greek idealism in the period of its decadence. Such was to become the staple diet of European culture for 2,000 years, with the most negative results for science.

4. THE RISE OF CHRISTIANITY

THE DARKENING AGE

The rise of Christianity is one of the most extraordinary phenomena in history. It occurred at a time of upheaval and change associated with the dissolution of slave society, which found its reflection in a crisis of the old morality, philosophy and religion. The Roman Empire in the phase of its decline was a fertile ground for the spread of mystical ideas. This partly explains the rapid spread of new religions from the East. The old religion and morality represented a world that had outlived its usefulness and was already on the point of passing into history.

The temples stood empty and people sought a religion that would offer them some consolation for their endless suffering, and some prospect of salvation. In this context, the idea of a Saviour, a Redeemer, had an obvious attraction. The only real hope for a revolutionary overthrow of slavery would have been to unite the slaves with the Roman proletariat – the mass of propertyless, free citizens in Rome. But the Roman proletariat, unlike the modern working class, was a non-productive, parasitic class that lived off the state. The real productive class was the slaves, on whose backs the whole oppressive edifice rested.

In *The Eighteenth Brumaire*, Karl Marx quoted Sismondi's statement: "The Roman proletariat lived at the expense of society, while modern society lives at the expense of the proletariat."[1] In its psychology, the Roman proletariat resembled the poor whites of the southern states of the USA at the time of the Civil War. Although they were the lowest of the low, regarded contemptuously by the wealthy slave owners as 'white trash', in the last analysis, they sided with the slave owners against the slaves. As a result, the numerous slave uprisings that characterised the late Roman Republic, despite some spectacular victories under the great revolutionary leader Spartacus, inevitably ended in defeat.

THE EARLY CHRISTIANS

The early Christians were a revolutionary movement based on the poor and oppressed layers of society. The class nature of early Christianity is faithfully reflected in the gospels. The Acts of the Apostles show that the early Christians believed in equality. The communion of believers was expressed in the form of primitive communism.

All who joined this communion had first to relinquish all their worldly goods. Tertullian (c. 155-220 AD) wrote:

> … our brotherhood is upheld by the family substance, which among you as a rule dissolves the fraternal tie.
>
> So we, who are united in mind and soul, have no hesitation about sharing property. All is common among us – except our wives. At that point we dissolve our partnership, which is the one place where the rest of men make it effective.[2]

John Allegro notes:

> The early Church also observed a form of communism, was at loggerheads with established Jewry as represented by the Jerusalem cultus, practised a ritual meal of some kind, baptised its initiates, and paid special regard to

---

1 K. Marx, 'Preface to the 2nd Edition of *The Eighteenth Brumaire*', MECW, Vol. 21, p. 57.
2 Tertullian, *Apologeticus*, XXXIX. 10-12, pp. 177-179.

the teachings of the biblical prophets, whose every word was thought to offer insight into the future of mankind.[3]

The early Christians were convinced that the profound crisis of society heralded the imminent end of the world, the second coming of Christ and the emergence of the New Jerusalem. For them this was not a kingdom in the clouds, but a very real kingdom of God on earth. They were committed to an unrelenting struggle against the existing order, which the *Book of Revelation* – the earliest and most authentic of surviving Christian texts – describes as the 'Whore of Babylon'. They adopted a proud and obstinate revolutionary standpoint.

They remained stubbornly steadfast before the heathen judges, refusing to renounce their faith and willingly embracing martyrdom, confident in their final victory. They impatiently awaited the imminent return of Christ and the thousand-year kingdom, which was shortly to dawn. Originally, Christianity had been a Jewish sect. It was Paul who developed the idea of converting non-Jews, eliminating circumcision and the dietary prohibitions that were serious obstacles to winning over the latter. It proved to be extremely successful.

Friedrich Engels explained:

What kind of people were the first Christians recruited from? Mainly from the 'labouring and burdened', the members of the lowest strata, as becomes a revolutionary element. And what did they consist of? In the towns of impoverished free men, all sorts of people, like the 'mean whites' of the southern slave states and the European beachcombers and adventurers in colonial and Chinese seaports, then of freedmen and, above all, slaves; on the large estates in Italy, Sicily, and Africa of slaves, and in the rural districts of the provinces of small peasants who had fallen more and more into bondage through debt. There was absolutely no common road to emancipation for all these elements. For all of them paradise lay lost behind them; for the ruined free men it was the former *polis*, the

3 J. M. Allegro, *The Dead Sea Scrolls and the Christian Myth*, p. 4.

town and the state at the same time, of which their forefathers had been free citizens; for the war-captive slaves the time of freedom before their subjugation and captivity; for the small peasants the abolished gentile social system and communal landownership. All that had been smitten down by the levelling iron fist of conquering Rome...

The pressure of taxation and the need for money which it caused in regions with a purely or predominant natural economy plunged the peasants into ever deeper bondage to the usurers, gave rise to great differences in fortune, making the rich richer and the poor completely destitute. Any resistance by isolated small tribes or towns to the gigantic Roman world power was without prospect. Where was the way out, salvation, for the enslaved, oppressed and impoverished, a way out common to all these diverse groups of people whose interests were mutually alien or even opposed? And yet it had to be found if a great revolutionary movement was to embrace them all.

This way out was found. But not in this world. As things were, it could only be a religious way out. Then a new world was embraced. The continued life of the soul after the death of the body had gradually become a recognised article of faith through-out the Roman world. A kind of recompense or punishment of the deceased souls for their actions while on earth also received more and more general recognition. As far as recompense was concerned, admittedly, the prospects were not so good: antiquity was too primitively materialistic not to attribute infinitely greater value to life on earth than to life in the shades; to live on after death was considered by the Greeks rather as a misfortune. Then came Christianity, which took seriously recompense and punishment in the world beyond and created heaven and hell, and a way out was found which would lead the labouring and burdened from this vale of woe to eternal paradise. And in fact only with the prospect of a reward in the world beyond could the stoico-philonic renunciation of the world and ascetics be exalted to the basic moral principle of a new world religion which would enthuse the oppressed masses.[4]

---

4   F. Engels, 'On the Early History of Christianity', MECW, Vol. 27, pp. 460-61.

The Church had an obvious appeal: in a troubled and anxious age, it offered every individual the hope of salvation and the promise of life after death. By contrast, the old gods seemed cold and aloof. But when the new religion broke out of its original Jewish context, it was mangled, changed beyond recognition and turned into something quite different. This led to new contradictions. Although the new religion found its first and most enthusiastic adepts in the most oppressed and marginalised elements of society (slaves and women), it gradually attracted the attention of a layer of the educated and privileged classes, who were increasingly alienated by the spiritual emptiness of a decadent society. Over a period, the early Church changed and regulated its doctrines to suit its new position in society.

All the attempts to crush the Christian movement by state repression failed. Despite the most ferocious persecution, the Christians won mass support. Therefore, the ruling class did what they always do in such circumstances. If they cannot defeat a movement by force, the oppressor classes resort to cunning. They corrupt the leaders. The unprincipled cynic Constantine (306-337 AD) realised that the Christians could not be crushed by repression and decided that the best tactic was to neuter them by bribing their leaders, the bishops, and co-opting them.

In the period of approximately 100-300 AD we see a gradual consolidation of the power of the bishops, the crystallisation of a privileged bureaucratic stratum. Gradually, the Christian Church acquired a bureaucratic apparatus, which fused with the Roman state.

The bishops were originally the treasurers. They began to concentrate considerable wealth and authority in their hands. In a biting footnote, the English historian Edward Gibbon, in his monumental work *The Decline and Fall of the Roman Empire*, writes:

> I have somewhere heard or read the frank confession of a Benedictine abbot: "My vow of poverty has given me an hundred thousand crowns a year; my vow of obedience has raised me to the rank of a sovereign prince."[5]

---

5   E. Gibbon, *The Decline and Fall of the Roman Empire*, Vol. 2, p. 13n.

With his characteristic irony, Gibbon wonders to what excesses the abbot's vows of chastity had led him.

CONSTANTINE

When the new religion was eventually recognised by the Emperor Constantine, it changed into its opposite. From being a revolutionary movement of the poor and oppressed, the Church was absorbed into the state to become a formidable weapon in the hands of the rich and powerful. Constantine calculated correctly that any disadvantages that might flow from the abandonment of the old religion would be outweighed by the advantages of having the Church, with its powerful apparatus and control over the masses, as an ally.

This opportunist used religion to strengthen his grip on power. The earlier doctrines of the Christians, with their strong revolutionary and communist overtones, were persecuted as heresy and stamped out once Christianity became accepted as the state religion. To do this the Church had to be centralised as part of the imperial state. As a result, the bishop of Rome, who originally had no special status (and would have been subordinate to the bishop of Jerusalem), was now elevated to the Supreme Head of the Church – the Pope.

It was Constantine who built the church of the Holy Sepulchre and other 'Holy Places' in Jerusalem, although there was absolutely no basis for claiming that these places were what they were supposed to be. Constantine's mother, Helena, who is said to have been the daughter of a fishmonger, went to Jerusalem to obtain the nails that were supposed to have been used in the crucifixion of Christ, together with pieces of wood from the original cross, and even some milk from his mother's breasts!

The Catholic Church still has possession of these 'Holy Places', which every year bring in a handsome profit. The Church and its ruling elite began to amass vast amounts of wealth. In fact, the introduction of the rule of celibacy was actually a measure to protect Church property and prevent it being lost to children through inheritance.

ORTHODOXY

In the first decades of the second century there were a large number of rival Christian sects, each with their own gospels and rites, that were in bitter conflict. This presented a problem. There had to be one emperor, one state, one religion, one god and one Church. Deny one of these things and you must deny them all. In order to consolidate his power, Constantine had to eliminate all competing versions of Christianity and introduce orthodoxy. It took a series of bloody wars to extirpate these 'heresies'. Constantine imposed order by state violence, backed up by the even greater threat of eternal punishment wielded by the authorities of a Church that had become merely an arm of the state power.

The scriptures were repeatedly purged to wipe out all traces of the original revolutionary and communist message of early Christianity, with only a few remnants in the version of the New Testament available today. But it was impossible to remove the revolutionary content completely. Later, in western Europe, the Church got round this difficulty very simply: the Bible was only made available in Latin, which the overwhelming majority did not understand. The only ones allowed to interpret the scriptures were the priests, who were gradually separated from society as a special privileged caste.

From the very beginning, the authority of the gospels was gradually acquired by *tradition*. The gospels do not even claim to have been written by the Disciples of Christ, but gradually, people have accepted that they were – from force of tradition, and nothing else. By the end of the third century there were at least twenty gospels in circulation, as well as numerous letters, lives and sayings of Jesus Christ etc., amounting to more than eighty in total. This situation was intolerable to Constantine, who decided to put an end to it once and for all.

THE COUNCIL OF NICAEA

It was the Council of Nicaea (325 AD), organised by Constantine, that formally settled all the disputed issues, such as the divinity of Jesus. But few people nowadays are aware of the methods whereby this result was achieved. For many days, in the Bithynian city of

Nicaea, a delegation of Christian bishops and their retinues, overseen by Constantine himself, pondered the problematic question of the nature of Christ and the Trinity. How could the Son be also the Father, and what about God the Holy Ghost? These questions were not satisfactorily resolved even when the Council ended. There was still no agreed text, which probably did not matter to most of them, since they could not read.

Very little is known about this celebrated meeting because it has been erased from the historical record by the Church, who wished to hide the truth about what went on. The Council was packed by Constantine's henchmen, who were willing to carry out the will of the emperor. The bishops were a motley crew: some were ex-slaves or ex-convicts from as far afield as the border with India, Egypt, the Sahara Desert, Persia, England, Africa, Greece and other exotic places. Many were supporters of an array of heretical sects: Arians, Donatists, Gnostics, etc.

Such men were in no position to compete in debate with the educated intriguers who supported Constantine. There were a number of problems that irked the Emperor such as the refusal of Christians to serve in the army or worship the Emperor. But these could be managed with intelligent tactics. And in any case, all attempts to destroy the Church through repression had failed. The presence of the emperor was in itself enough to make those present shake in their sandals. Many probably had never seen him before, and certainly not this close. And if psychological intimidation was not enough, other more direct methods were available.

Some of those present had already suffered torture at his command. These tortures included having an eye extracted with a hot iron, or having one's leg ligaments cut, and other pleasant methods of persuasion that left one blind or crippled. These men would not be eager to repeat the experience. But, just to make sure of the vote, before the meeting ended, some delegates had been murdered or disappeared, never to be seen again, for having expressed their thoughts with excessive frankness.

In the end, there remained a small handful of accepted works that have come down to us as the Bible. What people could or could not read was decided by an endless series of religious wars, purges, persecution and martyrdom. The struggle to suppress heresy was long, bitter and bloody, and it lasted for hundreds of years. It was far more vicious than any of the persecutions launched by the pagans against Christianity.

PERSECUTION AND DESTRUCTION

The persecution of other religions commenced almost immediately. In 386 AD, a law was passed declaring that those "who contend about religion ... shall pay the penalty of high treason with their lives and blood."[6] Books were systematically burned. The military colony of Aelia Capitolina in Jerusalem destroyed a pagan temple for the purpose of constructing a Christian church. This was only the beginning of a long campaign that lasted centuries and led to the wholesale eradication of many brilliant cultures in all parts of the world.

The Spanish Conquistadores slaughtered millions of men, women and children in their American colonies under the banners of Christ. They melted down priceless objects of art for gold and they built Christian churches and cathedrals over the ruined temples of the Mayas and Aztecs. Christians went on to destroy thousands of ancient religions and cultures in Europe, the Middle East, Africa, Australia and elsewhere. The persecution of pagans in the late Roman Empire began during the reign of Constantine. The Christians were bitterly hostile to anything remotely resembling rational thought and philosophy. They were hell-bent on tearing up the old world, root and branch. Gibbon remarks:

> The Christians, who, by the interposition of evil spirits, could so readily explain every præternatural appearance, were disposed and even desirous to admit the most extravagant fictions of the Pagan mythology. But the belief of the Christian was accompanied with horror. The most trifling

---

6   *The Corpus of Roman Law,* Vol. 1, *The Theodosian Code,* 16.4.1, p. 449.

mark of respect to the national worship he considered as a direct homage yielded to the dæmon, and as an act of rebellion against the majesty of God.[7]

This hatred of the old religions was openly admitted by the Christians themselves. Take the following words of St. Augustine: "That all superstition of pagans and heathens should be annihilated is what God wants, God commands, God proclaims!"[8]

This was a superstitious time, when people believed it possible to conjure up supernatural powers by the use of magic signs, formulas and rites. They believed in miracles. To win popularity, the Church had to provide a plentiful supply of miracles. Eusebius of Caesarea, a Christian biblical scholar and historian who wrote the first biography of Constantine, portrayed the cross as a magical sign, the effectiveness of which was said to be proved by the following story, which he clearly invented for his own purposes.

The usurper Constantine won a great victory on 28 October 312 AD. The Battle of the Milvian Bridge was the final battle of the civil war, by which he became Emperor. Eusebius claims that, before the battle, Constantine and his army saw a cross of light in the sky above the sun with words in Greek that are generally translated into Latin as "*In hoc signo vinces*" – "In this sign thou shalt conquer". That night Constantine had a dream in which Christ told him he should use the sign of the cross against his enemies. He then ordered his soldiers to mark the Christian symbol on their shields, which naturally gave him overwhelming victory.

The truth of this story – like everything else Eusebius writes – is open to doubt. The earliest account of the battle, dating from 313 AD, mentions nothing about a vision or a dream. But it is in any case self-evident that the battle was won, not by the sign of the cross, but by sharp steel blades and the strong arms of the men that wielded them.

---

7   E. Gibbon, *The Decline and Fall of the Roman Empire*, Vol. 1, pp. 395-96.

8   Quoted in C. Nixey, *The Darkening Age: The Christian Destruction of the Classical World*, p. xxv.

In 315 AD the Senate dedicated a triumphal arch in Rome to Constantine with an inscription praising him because 'with divine instigation' he and his army had won the victory. It tactfully refrained from saying which god had provided the 'instigation' and citizens could credit it to Sol Invictus or the Christian deity or whichever god they chose. Actually, there is not a shred of historical evidence that Constantine was ever converted to Christianity. He never actually claimed to be a Christian during his lifetime and it is said that he only converted on his deathbed. But we only have Eusebius' word for that, and he lied about practically everything. Early Christianity was thoroughly impregnated with such superstition.

In place of reason, the Church Fathers preached blind faith, summed up in the celebrated phrase attributed to Tertullian, "*Credo, quia absurdum est*" – "I believe because it is absurd". Science was looked on as suspicious, a heritage of paganism. In the period under consideration, pagan priests and philosophers were the primary target of the early Christians, who knew they were the spiritual and intellectual elite of the pagan society and culture. Once they were destroyed, it would be a simpler task to convert the pagans. And this is what they did.

Their attitude to the Jews is shown by a statement of one of the most celebrated early Church Fathers, St. John Chrysostom – he of the Golden Mouth: "… the synagogue … is a den of robbers and a lodging for wild beasts … a dwelling of demons …"[9] These words were quoted with approval in Nazi Germany 1,500 years later.

Today, as we walk through the marvellous national museums of Athens, admiring the miraculous artistry of its ancient statues, our admiration is tinged with a profound sense of sorrow at the loss of so much of the art of classical Greece. All over Greece, the evidence of wanton destruction is plain to see: ruined temples, headless statues of gods and goddesses bear mute witness to an orgy of vandalism. One might suppose that this deliberate destruction of culture was the work of the barbarians. But this supposition

---

9 Quoted ibid., p. 133.

would be fundamentally mistaken. This crime was perpetrated by Christians at the instigation of Emperor Theodosius (392-395 AD).

Up to that time, Rome was still more pagan than Christian. In Gaul, Spain and northern Italy, all but the urban areas remained stubbornly loyal to the old gods. Even Milan remained half pagan. But all that was about to change. In the year 392 AD, Theodosius became Emperor of both the eastern and western part of the Roman Empire; the last emperor to rule over both. In the same year he authorised the destruction of pagan temples throughout the empire. He issued a comprehensive law that prohibited the performance of any type of pagan sacrifice or worship. Paganism was proscribed as a "*religio illicita*".

Theodosius dedicated himself steadfastly to the work of establishing a single brand of faith, Nicene Christianity, as the only accepted religion of the state, repressing dissident Christians (heretics) and enacting explicit legal measures to abolish paganism. In order to complete his work, he enlisted the services of mobs of fanatical monks, who set about the work of destruction with ferocious zeal. In her book, *The Darkening Age: The Christian Destruction of the Classical World*, Catherine Nixey delivers a hard-hitting and truthful account of the savage war of extermination waged by the Church against the religion and culture of the ancient world.

She opens her book with a description of black-robed zealots taking iron bars to the beautiful statue of Athena in the sanctuary of Palmyra in Syria. Their vandalism was completed by ISIS not long ago. Athena was the deity of wisdom. But it was not just statues embodying this virtue that were mutilated and beheaded. Intellectuals in Antioch and elsewhere were tortured and beheaded by the Christians. Nixey writes:

> Damascius's [a Greek philosopher] own brother had been arrested and tortured to make him reveal the names of other philosophers...
>
> Others in Damascius's circle of philosophers had been tortured; hung up by the wrists until they gave away the names of their fellow scholars. A

fellow philosopher had, some years before, been flayed alive. Another had
been beaten before a judge until the blood flowed down his back.[10]

THE MURDER OF HYPATIA

In the history of philosophy, we do not find the names of many
women. But there is at least one notable exception to the rule. Hypatia
of Alexandria was one of the most remarkable women who has ever
lived.

This extraordinary woman was the leading mathematician and
astronomer in the world at the time. She is probably the only woman
for whom such a claim can be made. One of the last of the pagan
philosophers, she was born around the year 355 AD, though the
precise date is not known. However her death occurred in March
415 AD, and the circumstances are known only too well. Hypatia
was a product of the brilliant scientific school of Alexandria – the
intellectual hub of the Roman Empire – where the precious heritage of
the knowledge of antiquity was preserved in its world-famous library.

Her father, who had also been a mathematician and astronomer,
is best known for the part he played in the preservation of Euclid's
Elements, and he also wrote extensively, commenting on Ptolemy's
Almagest and *Handy Tables*. His life's work was devoted to the
preservation of the Greek mathematical and astronomical heritage.
Hypatia continued his work. Her philosophical views led her to
adopt a life of dedicated virginity. She was also a popular teacher,
whose lectures on philosophical topics attracted huge audiences and
a numerous following of dedicated students. But these were very
dangerous times, and dark clouds were gathering over Hypatia and
her world. Her successes aroused the suspicions of the Christians. It
was precisely her popularity that sealed her fate.

Hypatia was an adherent to the philosophical trend known as
Neoplatonism – a trend that was actually the main source of the
early Christian dogma. But this fact was completely unknown to
the fanatical Christian mob in Alexandria, for whom anything that

---

10 Ibid., p. xxvii.

smelled even remotely of pagan philosophy came straight from the mouth of the Devil. Alexandria, like many other cities at that time, was the scene of bitter religious conflicts in which Christians vented their blind hatred, now against Jews, then against 'heretical' Christians and, naturally, against all pagans.

An early warning was the razing of the Serapeum, the temple of the Greco-Egyptian god Seraphis by Alexandria's bishop Theophilus. This event marked the final end of the great Library of Alexandria, since the Serapeum seems to have contained some of the Library's books. Theophilus, however, was friendly with Synesius, an admirer and pupil of Hypatia, so she was not herself affected by this development and was permitted to pursue her endeavours unimpeded. But she was living on borrowed time. Her life was hanging by a slender thread, which could break at any moment.

This fragile equilibrium was suddenly destroyed by the death of Theophilus and the accession of Cyril, a vicious bigot, to the bishopric of Alexandria. The uneasy climate of tolerance lapsed and, shortly afterward, Hypatia became the victim of a particularly brutal murder.

She was butchered with indescribable cruelty by a Christian mob, fired up by blind hatred and blood lust. Soraya Field Fiorio describes the scene:

> One early spring day during the year 415 in the city of Alexandria – the intellectual heart of the waning Roman Empire – the pagan philosopher Hypatia was murdered by a mob of Christian men. These men, the *parabalani*, were a volunteer militia of monks serving as henchmen to the archbishop. Their conscripted purpose was to aid the dead and dying but they could be more readily found terrorising opposing Christian groups and levelling pagan temples. At the urging of Cyril, bishop of Alexandria, they had already destroyed the remains of the Library of Alexandria. The *parabalani* razed pagan temples, attacked the Jewish quarters, and defiled masterpieces of ancient art they considered demonic by mutilating statues and melting them down for gold. They now set their gaze on the city's beloved teacher of mathematics and philosophy, whose social ranking was on par with Alexandria's most important men. Understanding nothing of

her philosophy, they called her a witch. They pulled the elderly teacher from her chariot as she rode through the city and dragged her to a temple. She was stripped naked, her skin flayed with jagged pieces of oyster shells, her limbs pulled from her body and paraded through the streets. Her remains were burned in a mockery of pagan sacrifice. Hypatia's death marked the end of paganism and the triumph of Christianity, the final act of a one-hundred-year-old feud waged by the new religion against the ancient world.[11]

Thus perished the last notable philosopher of antiquity. With her an entire world of light and culture passed away. Europe was plunged into a world of darkness, ignorance and superstition that lasted a thousand years. To quote the words of William Manchester, it was a world lit only by fire.

---

11 S. F. Fiorio, 'The Killing of Hypatia', *Lapham's Quarterly*, 16 January 2019.

5. ISLAMIC PHILOSOPHY

In the absence of a revolutionary alternative, the breakdown of slave society produced a frightful collapse of culture in Europe, the effects of which lasted for centuries. In the period known as the Dark Ages, the scientific and artistic achievements of Antiquity were largely lost. The flame of learning was kept alight in Byzantium, Ireland and, above all, in the Islamic world. The majority of Europe remained sunk in barbarism for a long time.

The religion of Islam arose in the seventh century in Arabia, in the period of the transition of the Arab people from the primitive communal system to class society. It signified the unification of the Arabs in a common state (the Caliphate). The advent of Islam radically transformed the lives of millions of people. At the time of the Hegira (Mohammed's departure to Medina in 622 AD), the Eastern Roman Empire and Sassanid Persia were in crisis, exhausted by centuries of conflict, and their downtrodden subjects were crushed under the weight of taxation. With its simple, levelling message, it struck a responsive note especially among the poorest and most downtrodden layers of the population, who greeted the Arab invaders more as liberators than oppressors. In its origins, Islam represented a revolutionary movement and the awakening of the Arab nation. One of Mohammed's last speeches ends with the following words: "Ye people! hearken to my speech and comprehend the same. Know that every Moslem is the brother of every other Moslem. All of you are of the same equality."[1]

Not unlike the Gothic invasions of the fourth and fifth centuries, the early Arab conquests swept away the rotten edifice of the imperial state. But unlike the Goths, who conquered a disintegrating and overwhelmingly rural economy, the Arabs took possession of the richest provinces of the Roman Empire, including the magnificent metropolises of Alexandria and Antioch. This produced a profound spiritual and intellectual awakening across this newly-formed empire, not least among the Muslim conquerors themselves. Despite frequent attempts by later so-called fundamentalists to interpret Islam in a narrow and fanatical spirit that denies independent thought and cultural inquiry, in its early period, the Islamic revolution gave a powerful impulse to culture, art and philosophy. In his classic *Short History of the Saracens*, Syed Ameer Ali has this to say about Ali, the nephew of the Prophet and head of the first Arab Republic:

> While Islam was … extending its sway in distant parts, Ali was endeavouring in Medina to give a turn to the new-developed energy of the Saracen race. In the public mosque at Medina, Ali and his cousin, Abdullah the son of Abbais, delivered lectures on philosophy and logic, the traditions (history), rhetoric and law, whilst others dealt with other subjects. Thus was formed the nucleus of that intellectual movement which displayed itself in such great force in later times in Baghdad.[2]

This was already the state of affairs in the seventh century. Contrary to the opinions of the modern fundamentalists, Islam, in its origins, was not equivalent to the worship of ignorance and narrow-minded fanaticism. In complete contrast to what passed for philosophy in the universities of medieval Europe, where it was utterly subservient to the Catholic Church, Islamic philosophy was not a handmaid of theology. The formative period of Islamic philosophy dates from

---

1   Quoted in A. C. Bouquet, *Comparative Religion*, p. 274.
2   S. A. Ali, *Short History of the Saracens*, p. 47.

the late eighth century to the mid-ninth century. Supported by the Caliphs, notably Ma'mun, it was known for its tolerance and freedom of scientific inquiry. Scholars from nations conquered by the Arabs were welcomed by state-endowed institutions. Free-ranging rationalist debate was encouraged. An important feature was the study of Greek texts in translation. At a time when Europe languished in the dark ages, the flame of culture and civilisation was kept shining brightly in the Islamic countries. Baghdad was the centre of a vast civilisation that extended from Cordoba in Spain to India.

This was a truly universal civilisation. Islamic thinkers such as Ibn Sina (known in the West by his Latin name Avicenna), who lived in Central Asia, in the important university town of Bokhara, was not only a philosopher but also a physician and natural scientist. Although faithful to Islam, he did much to spread the knowledge of the scientific and philosophical knowledge of Greek antiquity throughout the Arab world, and thence to Europe, which, for all its fear of Islam, looked to the Arabs as a source of knowledge and education. There were many other great thinkers, like Al-Farabi (who flourished in the late ninth and early tenth centuries), the author of the first works of political philosophy within the context of the religion of Islam (*The Attainment of Happiness and The Political Regime*). Ibn Sina and others like him helped to consolidate rationalist thinking and propagate natural science and mathematics – both fields in which the Arabs made great discoveries.

SPAIN AND THE ARABS

The conquest of Spain which began in 711 AD marked a turning-point in world history. The Arabs who made the first incursions from North Africa had only intended to make a plundering raid, but the inner rottenness of the Visigoth kingdom led to its speedy collapse. The Arabs – or Moors, as the Spaniards called them – conquered almost the whole peninsula and advanced deep into France. The speed of the conquest was mainly because the oppressed Spanish masses rallied to the invaders, who certainly treated them better than their fellow Christian landlords.

The Arabs appeared before the Spanish serfs as social emancipators, not foreign conquerors. They abolished the oppressive rights of the possessing classes – the feudal landlords and clergy – and replaced the crushing burden of taxes by a single tax which, as well as being relatively light, was not levied on women, children, the sick, the blind, beggars or slaves. Even the Christian monasteries were exempt. Most Spanish cities were granted favourable terms which were honourably kept by the conquerors. The only land that was confiscated was that of the nobles and clergy who had fled to join the enemy.

In essence, Islam contains a democratic and levelling idea which asserts the equality of all men, irrespective of race or colour. This was remarkably advanced for the period under consideration. Far from persecuting other faiths, the Arabs in Spain were far more tolerant than the Christians either before or after Arab rule. They protected all religions and immediately allowed the persecuted Jews to worship freely. Let us recall that the Spanish Inquisition later brutally expelled the Jews from Spain. Like the Mogul rulers of India, they encouraged intermarriage between the conquerors and the conquered in order to bring about the fusion of the two peoples. They advanced agriculture and created the architectural wonders of Granada, Cordoba and Seville. No wonder a large part of the Spanish population became converts to Islam, and demonstrated their loyalty by fighting to defend their homeland and freedoms against the armies of Christian-feudal reaction in the North.

W. C. Atkinson describes the impact of Islamic culture on the minds of the Spaniards in the words of the famous lament of Alvaro of Cordoba:

> Alas, all the Christian youths who become famous for their talent know only the language and the literature of the Arabs; they read and study zealously Arabic books, of which by dint of great expenditure they form extensive libraries, and proclaim aloud on all sides that this literature is worthy of admiration.[3]

---

3   W. C. Atkinson, *A History of Spain and Portugal*, p. 60.

The same author outlines the economic advance achieved by the Arabs in Spain:

> Irrigation works, of which traces still survive today, made fertile wide areas of irregular or inadequate rainfall; rice, the sugar-cane, and other exotic crops were introduced; and although the Koran forbade the drinking of wine, the vine was cultivated on a large scale.

> Industry enjoyed a parallel prosperity, that ranged through gold and silver mining, the weaving of wool and silk, the manufacture of paper, introduced into Europe by the Arabs, and of glass, invented in Cordoba in the ninth century, metalwork, ceramics, and leatherware. The fame of these products travelled far, and to handle the flourishing commerce that resulted there grew up a great trading fleet based chiefly in Seville, Malaga, and Almeria.[4]

Thus began a period of economic and social advance that lasted for centuries, and with it a brilliant chapter in the history of human culture, art and science. One commentator writes:

> The Moors organised that wonderful kingdom of Cordova, which was the marvel of the Middle Ages, and, when all Europe was plunged in barbaric ignorance and strife, alone held the torch of learning and civilisation bright and shining before the Western world.[5]

Anyone who today visits the Alhambra in Granada or the Mosque at Cordoba will instantly understand that the Arabs of Spain were far in advance of medieval Europe, over which they excelled, not only in science and technology, but also in the fine arts, sculpture and painting. The Arabs' cultural tradition was broad: it included the study of logic, the sciences of nature (including psychology and biology), the mathematical sciences (including music and astronomy), metaphysics, ethics, and politics. No town, however small, was without a school or college, while every principal town had its own university, including Cordoba (renowned throughout Europe), Seville (Ishbilia), Malaga, Zaragoza, Lisbon (Alishbuna), Jaen and Salamanca, which

---

4   Ibid., p. 58.
5   Quoted in S. A. Ali, *Short History of the Saracens*, p. 115.

subsequently became the most prestigious of all Spanish universities. There were a galaxy of writers, poets, historians and philosophers.

Contrary to what one might expect, there were many famous women intellectuals. At a time when the notion of the equality of women would have been anathema in Christian Europe, many distinguished women poets and cultured ladies were held in esteem in Cordoba and Granada. Hassana at-Tamimiyeh, daughter of Abu'l Hussain the poet, and Umm ul-Ula, both natives of Guadalajara, flourished in the sixth century of the Hegira. Ammat ul-Aziz (a descendant of the Prophet, and therefore styled ash-Sharifa) and al-Ghusanieh, from the province of Almeria, were both women who were in the front rank of scholars at the time. There were many others. Mariam, daughter of Abu Yakub al-Ansari, was a native of Seville, where she taught rhetoric, poetry and literature, "which, joined to her piety, her good morals, her virtues, and amiable disposition, gained her the affection of her sex, and gave her many pupils."[6]

BACKWARD EUROPE AND ADVANCED ASIA

So, far from Islamic thought being limited to mysticism and religious fanaticism, it showed a natural inclination to rationalism and science, in which, for centuries, the Arabs led the world. Great advances were made, especially in mathematics and astronomy, but also in many other spheres of science and technology. This point is made by Alfred Hooper in his history of mathematics:

> We have much for which to thank the Moors. They introduced new ideas about medicine and medical knowledge; they taught improved methods of working in metal and leather; they built waterworks, sluices and canals in Spain; in all, they brought the wisdom of India and the East to a Europe which had sunk back into ignorance and savage ways.

> The Arabs were familiar with the work of the great Greek mathematicians who had built up the 'Golden age of Greek mathematics' before the fragile and wonderful civilisation of Greece was absorbed by the intensely practical and utilitarian Romans; *they also introduced into Spain the new*

---

6 Ibid., p. 578.

and revolutionary method of writing numbers that they had learned from
the Hindus, a method that was to pave the way for our modern world of
science and engineering and aeronautics.[7]

Throughout the Middle Ages the only real advances in mathematics
were made by the Indians and Arabs. It was they who discovered
trigonometry. It was the Arabs who discovered algebra. The very word
is Arabic – *al-jabr* – which, like so many other things, found its way
into Europe from Spain. The Arab mathematician al-Khowarizmi,
as well as writing a book on Hindu-Arab number systems (the
Indians also played a vital role in developing mathematics, and the
Arabs learned from them), wrote another book on the treatment of
equations which he called *al jabr w'al muquabalah* – the reunion and
the opposition. This was later translated into Latin and hence became
accessible to Europeans.

Alfred Hooper comments:

> The years from about 800 to about 1450, known as the Middle Ages,
> were marked by an almost complete stagnation of independent thought,
> which paralysed mathematical progress and cast its gloom over European
> mathematicians as over all other thinkers.[8]

The same author adds:

> Centuries after the Arabs had introduced the new number-symbols into
> Europe many people still clung to the old familiar Roman numerals and
> would have nothing to do with the new system, which they associated with
> traders and heathens. By the thirteenth century, however, the new system
> of writing numbers had become established in various parts of Europe.
> *It was not until then that any real development in the number-reckoning we*
> *now call elementary arithmetic could take place.*[9]

The Medieval world gained access to the ideas of Aristotle and Plato
mainly from Arab sources. Out of a host of brilliant thinkers who

---

7   A. Hooper, *Makers of Mathematics*, pp. 24-5.

8   Ibid., p. 84.

9   Ibid., p. 26, my emphasis.

influenced medieval Europe, the most outstanding was Ibn Rushd
Muhammed, known in the West by his Latin name Averroes. He
was a scientist, a polymath and a courageous radical rationalist. This
great Arab philosopher lived between 1126 and 1198 in Spain during
the Caliphate of Cordoba. In his writings, we see the elements of
a materialist philosophy, derived from a careful reading of Aristotle.
Although he remained a devout Muslim, Ibn Rushd attempted to
prove that matter and motion could neither be created nor destroyed,
thus anticipating the conservation theories of modern physics. He
likewise denied the immortality of the soul.

Averroes denied that the world had been created. Rather, he held
that the world had existed eternally and, contrary to the myth of
genesis, that there had never been a first human. He struck blow after
blow against the teachings of official religion, arguing that human acts
are not ruled by divine providence.

Following Aristotle, Averroes maintained that knowledge is derived
from sense experience; a belief he openly contrasted to blind faith in
religious institutions and scripture:

> So we affirm definitely that whenever the conclusion of a demonstration is
> in conflict with the apparent meaning of Scripture, that apparent meaning
> admits of allegorical interpretation according to the rules for such
> interpretation in Arabic. This proposition is questioned by no Muslim
> and doubted by no believer.[10]

By taking this position, Averroes relegated religious scripture to
mere metaphors which should not be taken literally. This was an
open attack on the religious officialdom who looked at Averroes
with suspicion. So radical were these ideas, that his theories were
persecuted by orthodox Muslims, and, as we shall see later, also by the
Catholic church. The influence and importance of Averroes' works
cannot be underestimated. It was primarily through the work of this
remarkable philosopher, particularly his commentaries on Aristotle,

10 Averroes, 'The Decisive Treatise', *On the Harmony of Religion and
Philosophy*, p. 51.

that Europeans initially became acquainted with the long-forgotten world of classical Greek philosophy.

The main fountainhead of this knowledge was Islamic Spain, which, until it was destroyed by the Christians, was a flourishing, prosperous and cultured nation. Granada, Seville and Cordoba were important and internationally renowned centres of learning. All religions were treated with enlightened tolerance – until the Spaniards, led by those narrow-minded and fanatical bigots Fernando of Castille and Isabelle of Aragon, set about reducing the flower of Al-Andalus to a heap of bloody ashes.

The so-called Crusades, about which so much romantic rubbish has been written, were just so many destructive and bloodthirsty raids of barbarians against people who were, in every respect, their superiors. One of the Christian chroniclers of the siege of Granada, Father Agapito, writes in contemptuous terms about the Arab habit of washing themselves:

> [W]ater is more necessary to these infidels than bread, making use of it in repeated daily ablutions enjoyed by their damnable religion, and employing it in baths and in a thousand other idle and extravagant modes, of which we Spaniards and Christians make but little account.[11]

The reactionary and barbarous nature of the Crusades has been sufficiently demonstrated by modern historians like Stephen Runciman. Here is a typical extract by another writer:

> In each captured city the Tafurs [poor crusaders] looted everything they could lay their hands on, raped the Moslem women and carried out indiscriminate massacres. The official leaders of the Crusade had no authority over them at all. When the Emir of Antioch protested about the cannibalism of the Tafurs, the princes could only admit apologetically: "All of us together cannot tame King Tafur".[12]

And again:

---

11 Quoted in W. Irving, *The Conquest of Granada*, p. 269.
12 N. Cohn, *The Pursuit of the Millennium*, pp. 66-7.

The fall of Jerusalem was followed by a great massacre; except for the governor and his bodyguard … every Moslem – man, woman and child – was killed. In and around the Temple of Solomon "the horses waded in blood up to their knees, nay up to the bridle. It was a just and wonderful judgement of God that the same place should receive the blood of those whose blasphemies it had so long carried up to God." As for the Jews of Jerusalem, when they took refuge in their chief synagogue the building was set on fire and they were all burnt alive. Weeping with joy and singing songs of praise the crusaders marched in procession to the church of the Holy Sepulchre. "O new day, new day and exultation, new and everlasting gladness... That day, famed through all centuries to come, turned all our sufferings and hardships into joy and exultation; that day, the confirmation of Christianity, the annihilation of paganism, the renewal of our faith!"[13]

It is ironic that, to this day, Europeans still see themselves as the exclusive bearers of human culture when for the whole of the Middle Ages they acted as the grave-diggers of culture in the East. In reality the roles were opposite to the myths created by the West. It was in the Islamic world that the flame of art, science and philosophy were kept alive and slowly found their way into Europe as it began to emerge out of the Dark Ages.

---

13 Ibid., p. 68.

6. PHILOSOPHY IN THE MIDDLE AGES

Following the collapse of the Western Roman Empire in the fifth century, most of Europe entered a stage of barbarism known as the Dark Ages which was characterised by a tragic decline of culture. All the enormous advances made by the Greeks and the Romans in the spheres of art, science and philosophy were lost for hundreds of years. Humanity would have to go through a painful path lasting almost 1,000 years to recover them again.

Gradually, a new form of society emerged from the wreckage of the old system, based on the exploitation of a peasantry who were no longer slaves, but were tied to the land under the domination of temporal and spiritual lords. The pyramidal structure of society reflected this domination, with a rigid system of alleged duties and rights to one's 'natural superiors'. The fundamental duty, however, upon which everything else depended, was the duty of the serf to provide free labour service for his lord and master. This is what distinguishes this form of society from both chattel slavery, which came before it, and capitalism, which followed it. The whole system was sanctified by the Church, which wielded immense power, and was organised along similar hierarchical lines.

The rigid social hierarchy that characterised the feudal system found an ideological expression in the fixed dogmas of the Church, which demanded unquestioning obedience based on the official interpretation of the sacred texts. In place of reason, the Church Fathers preached blind faith, summed up in the celebrated phrase attributed to Tertullian, "*Credo, quia absurdum est*" – "I believe because it is absurd". Science was looked on as suspicious, a heritage of paganism.

The heritage of classical Greek philosophy was lost, and only partially revived in Western Europe in the twelfth century. Such a situation was not conducive to the development of thought and science. J. D. Bernal writes:

> The conditions of feudal production reduced the demand for useful science to a minimum. It was not to increase again till trade and navigation created new needs in the later Middle Ages. Intellectual effort was to go in other directions and largely in the service of a radically new feature of civilisation – *organised religious faiths.*[1]

According to Forbes and Dijksterhuis:

> Generally speaking it may be said that during the first centuries of its existence Christianity was not conducive to scientific pursuits. Science was regarded with suspicion because of its pagan origin; moreover, the ideal prevailed that it was not advisable for the spiritual welfare of Christians to penetrate more deeply into the secrets of nature than was made possible by the Holy Scriptures and than was required to understand these.[2]

When the remnants of classical culture eventually reached Western Europe, it was in translations from Arabic. As we have seen in the previous chapter, the great energy shown by the Arabs in conquering North Africa and Spain right up to the Pyrenees was matched by their intelligent and flexible attitude to the culture

---

1   J. D. Bernal, *Science in History*, p. 254.
2   R. J. Forbes, and E. J. Dijksterhuis, *A History of Science and Technology*, Vol. 1, pp. 101-2.

of the conquered peoples, in marked contrast to the ignorant barbarism displayed by the Christians after the reconquest of Al-Andalus. For centuries, the Islamic universities in Spain, especially the one at Córdoba, were the only real centres of learning in Western Europe, if we exclude Ireland, which, because of its remoteness, remained outside the mainstream. The Arabs made great advances in a whole number of fields – mathematics, astronomy, geography, medicine, optics and chemistry, as well as important technological advances, shown by the vast irrigation schemes which were wantonly destroyed by the Christians. But it took hundreds of years for this knowledge to percolate through to Western Europe.

Because of the Church's monopoly on culture, all intellectual life had to be channelled through it. For centuries, education was confined to the monasteries under the strict control of the Church officialdom. For the medieval Schoolmen – or Scholastics, as the official intelligentsia were called – philosophy was the "handmaiden of theology." Science was reduced to a bare minimum: "Arithmetic was numeration; geometry the first three books of Euclid; astronomy hardly got past the calendar and how to compute the date of Easter; and the physics were very remote and Platonic."[3] No interest was shown in scientific research and experiment.

REALISM AND NOMINALISM: THE QUESTION OF UNIVERSALS

The ideological pillar of mediaeval theocracy was the ideas of St Augustine of Hippo (354-430 AD), the most influential philosopher of the Dark Ages. Augustine based himself on the most reactionary elements of neoplatonist thought. His philosophy was a mix of Christian mysticism and a crude and impoverished form of Platonic idealism. As the main ideology of the Roman Catholic Church, any and all opposition to Augustinian thought was deemed inherently heretical and persecuted.

---

3   Ibid., p. 218.

Following Plato, Augustine believed that all beings were formed in accordance to universal archetypes, which are real entities existing beyond our physical world. In Plato's system, these archetypes – or 'forms', as he called them – exist in a different realm which can only be accessed by humans by way of pure philosophical thought. For Augustine, however, the archetypes – or 'reasons', as he called them – exist in the divine mind and are only accessible to humans by way of faith.

Augustine's theory of universals lay at the base of the trend in mediaeval philosophy confusingly called Realism. The Realists, following Augustine and Plato, believed that the general concepts that we have, such as 'man', 'animal', 'tree', 'rock' etc., are based on *real* existing and unchanging archetypal things. These universals in turn form the basis of the singular and changing men, animals, trees and rocks that we experience in life. But how do we get to know these universals? According to Augustine, it is in God's mind that the true essence of things can be found. Hence, there is no point in looking for them on earth: rather, we should direct our gaze to the heavens where God resides.

Augustine's world view leaves no room for science or investigation, and ultimately not even for rational thought. Here the intellect is passive and merely receives knowledge on grounds of its faith. In accordance with Christian doctrine, Augustine considered all material and earthly things to be inherently inferior, and even sinful. The bodies of men and women (particularly women) were objects of sin, to be regarded with abhorrence. Real life began at the moment of death, when the soul was finally freed from its material prison. From this point of view, it was quite natural that truth was not to be found in the material world: "… truth in any genuine sense is not something to be expected from the bodily senses."[4]

Accordingly, the objective world is, at best, of a secondary importance, and our senses are useless in leading us to the truth. "*Crede, ut intelligas*" – "Believe so that you may understand" – Augustine

---

4 St Augustine, *Eighty-Three Different Questions*, p. 41.

famously said. Truth is only to be found in the static and immutable mind of God, who in turn illuminates our minds with his truth – that is, if we are 'pure' and 'holy' enough. Thus, the ultimate judgement of all truth is placed in the hands of the holiest of holies: the clerical elite of the Catholic Church. This theory of knowledge was known as the theory of Divine Illumination and, along with Augustinian Realism, it laid the philosophical foundation of mediaeval reaction.

This school of thought reigned supreme in Europe for hundreds of years, when all hope for science and culture appeared to be lost. However, underneath the surface, the mole of history was still burrowing away. The productive forces were developing – albeit very slowly – and along with them science and technology.

In the twelfth and thirteenth centuries, feudal society in Europe was reaching its peak. Almost all arable land was in use and the productivity of the land, as well as the total yield of agriculture, was at its highest. On this basis, the population increased and the sparsely populated continent of the early mediaeval period gave way to a vast network of small towns, and even a few cities. Paris, Florence, Venice and Genoa reached populations of around 100,000, while London, Ghent and Cologne reached around 50,000. The state apparatus and urban institutions swelled, and with them the need for professionals. The old monastic education institutions were no longer sufficient. Hence, we witness the rise of the universities, where law and medical science developed separately from theology.

In the monastic educational tradition, students were not allowed to speak, not even to ask questions. But in the universities matters were quite different. Here, one of the main methods of learning was through 'disputations', which were open public debates about theological topics. Another important discipline, which developed in conjunction with the disputations, was dialectics, the discipline of rational argument. The topics in question in these debates were still highly mystical and religious. Departure from Christian authority was not allowed. The exceptions were Plato and Aristotle, along with commentaries on these, which the Church reluctantly had to accept.

Nevertheless, this partial liberation of ideas gave philosophy a new lease on life. Underneath debates on such things as whether angels are individuals or a species, whether God is simple or complex, and the question of the Universals in the divine mind, the mediaeval Schoolmen were slowly rediscovering philosophy.

Meanwhile, another important event gave a major impulse to this development. To fill the curriculums in the universities, in particular for the arts faculties and the medical sciences, a serious endeavour was made to translate scientific and philosophical texts from Arabic into Latin. Almost all of the classical Greek works had been lost during the Dark Ages, but now they started finding their way back into Europe, along with works by Arabic scientists and philosophers.

This was the early beginning of the process of separation of philosophy and science from religion. For the first time in hundreds of years, a glimmer of light could be seen in the darkness that had covered Europe. In philosophy, contradictions began to pile up that the old Augustinian paradigm could not account for.

The first break with the old way – *via antiqua*, as it was called – came from the French scholastic, Peter Abelard (1079-1142). Abelard is known for his tragic love life with another prominent thinker of the time, Heloïse. This often distracts from the fact that he was an innovative and courageous thinker, renowned across Europe for being the most formidable debater and dialectician of his time.

Abelard was also the father of Nominalism, the school of thought that, as opposed to Realism, claimed that universals do not exist as real things in the mind of God or anywhere else. Basing himself on Aristotle and a meticulous logic, he rejected Augustinian Realism and proved that universals are not really existing archetypes in which singular things in the world participate or otherwise reflect. Rather, he maintained that all beings are singular: a man is just that man, and a rock is just that, a particular rock.

He held that concepts such as man, animal, etc., are just words that humans have evolved by convention to signify things in the real world, but which have no reality beyond human consciousness. According to Abelard, the form of material objects – apart from God, angels and human beings – is merely the result of different combinations of the four elements: earth, air, fire and water. Universals do not figure as a separate compound in this equation.

But this does not mean that Abelard thought that our general universal concepts do not correspond to anything at all. According to him, singular things have similar natures. It is in the nature of birds, for instance, to lay eggs and to have wings – something we can deduce from our experience of them. Our universal words, he said, correspond to what he calls the 'statuses' of things – a term we can broadly interpret to mean their mode of existence or their inner lawfulness. Hence, the shared features of say, animals, are not arbitrary. They reflect the similar natural processes that lead to the creation of animals.

This is a radical departure from conventional Church beliefs and leaves little room for the supernatural. The only role God has in this process, according to Abelard, is to define these laws of nature at the inception of time. It also means that no divine illumination is needed for humans to acquire knowledge. Rather, our knowledge is acquired by way of our sense experiences, as well as our ability to abstract and generalise the phenomena that we meet in the real world.

This deviation from the official doctrines caused a lot of anger among the Catholic officialdom, but Abelard stubbornly stood his ground. In spite of all the attempts of his enemies to shut him up, he dealt a mortal blow to the theory of knowledge via divine illumination. After his time, it was almost universally accepted that knowledge is acquired via sense experience and abstraction. Later on, this would lead to the complete unravelling of Augustinian thought.

Abelard was a devout Christian, but he was more dedicated to his convictions and rational thought, something which time and time again brought him into conflict with the Church. For his many deviations from the official doctrines, Abelard was persecuted, excommunicated and condemned as a heretic on several occasions by ecclesiastic authorities. At one point, his books were ordered to be burned, and only narrowly escaped that fate thanks to the intervention of a wealthy patron. Nevertheless, Abelard remained hugely popular with young students, who flocked to his lectures in their thousands.

While Abelard was by no means a revolutionary, his ideas were seen as an existential threat to the ideological stranglehold of the Catholic Church on medieval society. But the Church was fighting a losing battle. Abelard anticipated the developments of the thirteenth century, where the *old way* of Augustinian thought entered a period of definitive decline. The final element in this development was the recovery of Aristotle's works, which had long been forgotten in the monastic educational tradition.

Prior to the twelfth century, only Aristotle's *Categories* and *On Interpretation* were available in Latin, and these were some of Aristotle's poorest works. By the middle of the thirteenth century, however, almost all of his existing books were translated from Arabic into Latin along with commentaries from Islamic thinkers like Avicenna and, most importantly, Averroes. In fact, Averroes became the primary guide to Aristotle to the degree that where Aristotle was spoken of as 'The Philosopher', Averroes was known as 'The Commentator'. On the basis of Averroes' writings, a trend of radical Aristotelianism began to develop amongst the Schoolmen.

This newly unearthed material revolutionised all of philosophy and religious thought, and led to a full-blown crisis within the prevailing ideology. The scientific and inquisitive method of Aristotle stood in sharp contrast to Augustine's Platonic dogmas. The Church attempted to censor its way out of this. In the condemnations of 1210, 1270 and 1277, lists of forbidden books and theses were drawn up, mainly as an attempt to censor Aristotle's natural philosophy and the radical interpretation of Aristotle by Averroes.

But the Church could not stop the march of history. Abelard's theory of knowledge was now universally accepted and backed up by the rediscovery of Aristotle. Along with the slow advance of science, bigger and bigger gaps were beginning to appear in the Augustinian approach. In this context, Averroism was rapidly gaining ground. Therefore, a trend emerged trying to merge the Platonic and

Aristotelian world views, in order to combat the radical Averroist interpretation of Aristotle.

The most prominent representative of this trend was Thomas Aquinas (1225-1274), perhaps the most famous mediaeval scholastic. Aquinas had to admit that knowledge of universal concepts is acquired via sense experience, which the mind then abstracts. However, he maintained that this ability to abstract is a function of the soul, which has been provided with intelligible light by God in order to be able to understand universals. In this manner, Aquinas believed that the contradiction between Aristotle's materialism and Plato's idealism could be reconciled. In reality of course, he was bastardising Aristotle's ideas and using them to save the Platonism of the Church.

He also admitted that the world is only inhabited by singular beings, but that these are composed of a combination of matter, as well as a separate universal essence, which only reason – without recourse to experience – is able to understand. Again, Aquinas believed that this would reconcile the scientific approach, which was gaining traction in Europe with the old tradition. But in effect, Aquinas remained a Realist and his ideas were merely an attempt at propping up the ruling ideas of the time.

At first, Aquinas was met with hostility by many of the ecclesiastic elite. Later on, however, as the advances of science increasingly exposed the old views, the Church had to concede and incorporate Thomism – as Aquinas' philosophy was called – into its canon. Augustinian thought was doomed to perish. Aquinas' ideas thus became the best way to sell the old dogma in a quasi-scientific guise. To this day in fact, neo-Thomism remains a basic position of the Roman Catholic Church.

In opposing Aquinas, Scottish philosopher John Duns Scotus (1265-1308) developed the theory of the Univocity of Being. Univocity means the quality of only possessing one meaning, which maintains that the same propositions that we use about the natural world can also be used to speak about God. This went against the official doctrine, which claimed that God and the propositions we apply to him belong to an entirely different realm. Essentially, what

Scotus' view was hinting at was that the difference between God and other creatures is merely a matter of degree. Marx said of Scotus:

> Materialism is the born son of Britain. Even one of his great schoolmen, Duns Scotus, asked himself "whether matter cannot think." In performing this wonder, Duns had recourse to God's omnipotence, that is, he made theology itself preach materialism.[5]

This outlook is in many ways an early anticipation of the Pantheism later developed by Spinoza.

The last of the important Schoolmen was William of Ockham (1287-1347), who developed Nominalism – the school of thought inaugurated by Abelard – to its fullest. Like other Nominalists, he maintained that the world is only populated by singular elements, and that there is no room in it for universal entities. In fact, he went as far as to denounce Realism's position on universals as "the worst error in philosophy".[6] Instead, Ockham held that universals were merely concepts of the human mind solely based on our experiences. Thus, when I say 'man', according to Ockham, I am merely speaking about the concept I have developed through all of my experiences of men. It is on the basis of such experiences that science can establish universal truths.

Ockham also maintained that the existence of God and other religious dogmas could not be proven by reason, and was thus founded solely upon faith. This was a dangerous doctrine, since it would mean separating philosophy from religion, enabling it to develop separately, freed from the dead hand of the Church. Ockham was excommunicated in 1328, but escaped from the Pope's territory in Avignon and fled to the protection of Louis, King of France, who was also excommunicated. Louis then appealed to a general Council, and the Pope found himself accused of heresy. It is said that when

5   K. Marx, 'England and Materialist Philosophy', *The Revolutionary Philosophy of Marxism*, p. 252.

6   Quoted in R. Pasnau, *Theories of Cognition in the Later Middle Ages*, p. 280.

Ockham met the Holy Roman Emperor, he said to him: "Do you defend me with the sword, and I will defend you with the pen?". At bottom, this was not an abstract debate about philosophy, but the reflection of a life and death struggle between the Church and Emperor, and between France, England and Germany. The struggle over seemingly abstract ideas was itself part of the general crisis of the feudal order that had emerged in the thirteenth century, even prior to the Black Death.

While containing the germ of a correct materialist idea, the philosophy of Nominalism went too far in assuming that general concepts ('universals') are only names, and nothing else. In fact, they reflect real qualities of objectively existing things, which, apart from their particular features, also embody within themselves elements of the general, which identify them as belonging to a specific genus or species. These are not supernatural general features, but features reflecting the general lawfulness of nature itself. This denial of the general and insistence on particulars is a peculiar feature of the empirical cast of mind, which has characterised the Anglo-Saxon philosophical tradition ever since. As a reaction against the sterile idealist doctrines of the medieval Church, it represented an important advance – a step in the direction of scientific experiment.

Nominalism contained the germ of materialism, but a one-sided and superficial materialism which later led to a philosophical dead-end with Berkeley, Hume and the modern semantic philosophers. At the time, however, it represented a huge advance. Ockham was the last of the great Schoolmen, but his approach encouraged a new generation of thinkers who would make important discoveries in science. In reality, Ockham's Nominalism represented the last nail in the coffin of scholasticism as such. From this point, science and philosophy embarked upon a distinctly separate path from theology.

While the medieval Schoolmen did have among them brilliant thinkers, they were limited in what they could achieve due to the official dogma imposed by the Church. Even the works of the greatest minds of the time were clouded by religious mysticism. Hence, in the main, scholastic philosophy did not go beyond the achievements of classical Greek philosophy. Nevertheless, it played an important role in recovering the advances of the past, setting the stage for the advances made during the Renaissance.

SCIENCE VS. RELIGION

For hundreds of years prior to this, the progress of science had been stifled by the spiritual police of the Church. Most of the (not inconsiderable) intellectual energies of the Schoolmen were dissipated in endless and complicated debates on such subjects as the sex of angels. Nobody was permitted to go beyond the limits laid down by Church dogma, and those who attempted to do so left themselves open to harsh reprisals. But that was beginning to come to an end. People like Roberte Grosseteste, Albert the Great and, later on, Jean Buridan also made important contributions to the proliferation of science and the scientific method of observation and experimentation.

Nevertheless, it called for great courage when the English scholastic Roger Bacon (c. 1214-92) went so far as to challenge the Schoolmen's dogmatism and veneration of authority. Going against the spirit of the times, and anticipating the scientific method, he advocated the experimental study of nature. Given the fact that science had still not separated itself from alchemy and astrology, it is not surprising that elements of these were present in Bacon's writings. Nor is it surprising that he was rewarded for his boldness by being dismissed from teaching at Oxford and confined to a monastery for his heretical views. Given the circumstances, he got off lightly.

Nicholas of Oresme, a pupil of Ockham's, anticipated Copernicus by considering the geocentric theory of the universe, which places the Earth at the centre of the universe. Comparing this idea with the heliocentric theory, which states that the sun is at the centre, he concluded that either theory would serve to explain all the known facts, and that, therefore, it was impossible to choose between them. This apparently cautious conclusion was, in fact, quite a bold step, since it put a question mark over the orthodox position of the Church, and thereby challenged its whole world outlook.

The cosmology of the medieval Church formed an important part of its general world outlook. It was not a secondary issue. The picture of the universe was supposed to be a mirror image of the world, with the same kind of static, unchanging character, the same rigid hierarchy. It was not derived from observation, but taken over from the cosmology of Aristotle and the Alexandrines, and accepted dogmatically. Bernal comments:

> The hierarchy of society was reproduced in the hierarchy of the universe itself; just as there was the pope, bishops, and archbishops, the emperor, kings, and nobles, so there was a celestial hierarchy of the nine choirs of angels: seraphim, cherubim, thrones; dominations, virtues, and powers; principalities, archangels, and angels (all fruits of the imagination of the pseudo Dionysius). Each of these had a definite function to perform in the running of the universe, and they were attached in due rank to the planetary spheres to keep them in appropriate motion. The lowest order of mere angels that belonged to the sphere of the moon had naturally most to do with the order of human beings just below them. In general there was a cosmic order, a social order, an order inside the human body, all representing states to which Nature tended to return when it was disturbed. There was a place for everything and everything knew its place.[7]

This view of the universe could not be challenged without calling into question the entire world outlook of the Church, and the type of society it defended. The conflict around the ideas of Copernicus and Galileo was not an abstract intellectual debate, but a life-and-death battle between opposing views of the world, which ultimately reflected a desperate struggle between two mutually exclusive social orders.

THE RISE OF THE BOURGEOISIE

In the later Middle Ages, the rise of the towns and trade saw the emergence of a new and vigorous element in the social equation. This development had an uneven character. Some regions grew faster than

---

7 J. D. Bernal, *Science in History*, p. 227.

others. Tawney shows how the embryo of a new society was growing within the womb of the old:

> In spite of the ubiquity of manor and gild, there was as much difference between the life of a centre of capitalist industry, like fifteenth-century Flanders, or a centre of capitalist finance, like fifteenth-century Florence, and a pastoral society exporting raw materials and a little food, like medieval England, as there is between modern Lancashire or London and modern Denmark.[8]

In this context, the rising class of wealthy merchants began to flex its muscles, demanding rights. The expansion of commerce, the opening up of new trade routes, the rise of a money economy, the creation of new needs and the means of satisfying them, the development of arts and crafts, the rise of a new national literature: all these developments heralded the birth of a revolutionary force in society, the bourgeoisie, whose interests laid in breaking down the artificial feudal barriers which impeded its development, and also, to an ever-increasing extent, in developing and exploiting technical innovations.

The development of open-sea navigation, for example, demanded the production of new and better charts, based on accurate astronomical observations, and also of more advanced navigational instruments. The introduction of paper and printing had a revolutionary effect on the accessibility of ideas, which had earlier been limited to a tiny minority of ecclesiastics. The production of literature written in the vernacular for the first time had the same effect, with the emergence of great recognisable national writers like Boccaccio, Dante, Rabelais, Chaucer and, finally, Luther. The introduction of gunpowder not only revolutionised warfare and helped undermine the power of the nobles, but also gave a new impetus to the study of physics and chemistry.

First in Italy, then in the Low Countries, Britain, Bohemia, Germany and France, this new class began to challenge the old order, which, after nearly a thousand years, had exhausted itself and entered a phase of decline. The endless wars and civil wars of the

---

8 R. H. Tawney, *Religion and the Rise of Capitalism*, p. 29.

period bore witness to the impasse of feudalism. The Black Death, which decimated the population of Europe in the fourteenth century, hastened the dissolution of feudal relations on the land. The peasant jacqueries in France and the Peasant Rising in England in 1381 were a warning of the approaching dissolution of the feudal order. To many people, it seemed that the end of the world was approaching. The sensation of impending doom gave rise to phenomena like the flagellant sects, groups of religious fanatics who travelled the country, whipping and otherwise inflicting pain on themselves in anticipation of the impending Day of Wrath. This was merely a confused reflection in the popular imagination of the impending break-up of the existing social order.

CRISIS OF IDEOLOGY

The breakdown of a social system is anticipated by a crisis of the official morality and ideology, which increasingly enters into conflict with the changed social relations. A critical spirit arises among a layer of the intellectuals, a barometer of the tensions building up within the depths of society. The moral and ideological basis for the feudal system was the teaching of the Church. Any serious challenge to the existing order meant an assault on the Church, which defended its power and privileges with all the means at its disposal, including excommunication, torture and burning at the stake.

The Middle Ages are usually depicted as a time of extreme religious devotion and piety. But that description certainly does not apply to the period under consideration. The Church, a wealthy and powerful institution which weighed heavily on the back of society, was widely discredited. Huizinga writes:

> Of all the contradictions which religious life of the period presents, perhaps the most insoluble is that of an avowed contempt of the clergy, a contempt seen as an undercurrent throughout the Middle Ages, side by side with the very great respect shown for the sanctity of the sacerdotal office ... Hence it was that nobles, burghers and villeins had for a long time past been feeding their hatred with spiteful jests at the expense of

the incontinent monk and the guzzling priest. Hatred is the right word to use in this context, for hatred it was, latent, but general and persistent. The people never wearied of hearing the vices of the clergy arraigned. A preacher who inveighed against the ecclesiastical state was sure of being applauded. As soon as a homilist broaches this subject, says Bernardino of Siena, his hearers forget all the rest; there is no more effective means of reviving attention when the congregation is dropping off to sleep, or suffering from heat or cold. Everybody instantly becomes attentive and cheerful.[9]

The undercurrents of dissent were felt even within the Church itself, reflecting the pressures of society. Heretical movements like the Albigenses were put down in blood. But new oppositional trends appeared, sometimes disguised in the garb of mysticism. A nineteenth century Italian historian relates:

> The same spirit of reformation which animated the Albigenses had spread throughout Europe: many Christians, disgusted with the corruption and vices of the clergy, or whose minds revolted against the violence on their reason exercised by the church, devoted themselves to a contemplative life, renounced all ambition and the pleasures of the world, and sought a new road to salvation in the alliance of faith with reason. They called themselves *cathari*, or the purified; *paterini*, or the resigned.[10]

The Dominican and Franciscan orders were founded in the early twelfth century to combat heresies, anti-clericalism and new philosophical ideas. Sismondi says of Pope Innocent the Third:

> He founded the two mendicant orders of Franciscans and Dominicans; new champions of the church, who were charged to repress all activity of mind, to combat growing intelligence, and to extirpate heresy. He confided to the Dominicans the fearful powers of the inquisition, which he instituted: he charged them to discover and pursue to destruction the

---

9   J. Huizinga, *The Waning of the Middle Ages*, pp. 172-3.
10 J. S. Sismondi, *A History of the Italian Republics*, p. 66.

new reformers, who, under the name of *paterini*, multiplied rapidly in Italy.[11]

Violent repression of opposition of any kind was a constant feature of the conduct of the ecclesiastical authorities from the highest level, as the history of the papacy shows. Pope Urban the Sixth, when he could not get the support of his cardinals, resolved the problem by the simple expedient of accusing them of conspiracy against him. He had many cardinals put to the torture in his presence, while he calmly recited his rosary. Others he ordered to be put in sacks and drowned in the sea. The reforming monk Girolamo Savonarola, an Italian precursor of Luther, was tortured until he confessed all the crimes attributed to him, and burnt alive with two other monks. Examples can be multiplied at will.

But no amount of repression can preserve an idea whose time has passed. An ideology and morality which no longer reflects reality is one that has outlived itself and is destined to be overthrown. The ground was prepared for one of the greatest revolutions in history. When, on 31 October 1517, an obscure monk called Martin Luther nailed his ninety-five theses to the door of All Saints' Church in Wittenberg, he lit a fuse that blew the old feudal order sky-high, opening the door to a new epoch – the age of the bourgeois revolution.

---

11 Ibid. p. 60.

7. THE RENAISSANCE

Then felt I like some watcher of the skies
When a new planet swims into his ken;
Or like stout Cortez when with eagle eyes
He stared at the Pacific – and all his men
Look'd at each other with a wild surmise –
Silent, upon a peak in Darien.
(John Keats, *On First Looking into Chapman's Homer*)

Eppur si muove.
[But it does move.]
(Galileo)

Modern science takes its starting point from the Renaissance, that marvellous period of spiritual and intellectual rebirth, which put an end to the 1,000 year reign of ignorance and superstition. Humanity once again looked to nature with eyes unblinkered by dogma. They rediscovered the wonders of classical Greek philosophy, directly translated from reliable versions which reached Italy after Constantinople was taken by the Turks. The materialist world outlook of the old Ionians and the atomists pointed science onto the right path.

This was a revolutionary period in every sense of the word. Luther not only started the Reformation in religion, but also reformed the

German language. At the same time, the Peasants' War in Germany, with its communistic overtones, pointed the way to future class struggles. To quote Engels:

> The dictatorship of the Church over men's minds was shattered; it was directly cast off by the majority of the Germanic peoples, who adopted Protestantism, while among the Latins a cheerful spirit of free thought, taken over from the Arabs and nourished by the newly-discovered Greek philosophy, took root more and more and prepared the way for the materialism of the eighteenth century.[1]

The discovery of America and the sea route to the East Indies opened up new horizons for trade and exploration. But even vaster horizons came into view in the field of the intellect. The old narrow one-sidedness became impossible. It was necessary to break down all the old barriers in order to get at the truth. As in all revolutionary epochs, there was a burning desire to know.

The development of science is closely linked to the growth of technology, which, in turn, is connected to the development of the productive forces. Take astronomy. The cosmological speculations of the ancient Greeks were limited by the lack of telescopes which could aid their observations. In the year 137 AD, observers had tabled the existence of 1,025 planetary bodies. By 1580, the number was exactly the same, and was arrived at using the same instrument – the naked eye.

Today's astronomers, using powerful radio telescopes, can observe a vast array of stars and galaxies. This fact has transformed astronomy. Unfortunately, the advances of technology have proceeded far more rapidly than the development of the ideas in the minds of men and women. In many respects, the world outlook of some scientists today has more in common with that of the mediaeval Church than the heroes of the Renaissance whose struggles against philosophical obscurantism made modern science possible.

Anaximander and Anaxagoras held that the universe was infinite – it had no beginning and no end. Matter could not be created or

---

1   F. Engels, *Dialectics of Nature*, p. 21.

destroyed. This idea found acceptance with many other philosophers of Antiquity, and was summed up by the famous aphorism: "*Ex nihilo nihil fit*" – "out of nothing comes nothing". It is therefore futile to look for a beginning or a creation of the universe, because it has always existed.

For the Church, such a view was anathema because it left the Creator out of the picture. In an infinite material world there is no room for God, the Devil, the angels, heaven or hell. Therefore, they seized avidly upon the weakest and most puerile of Plato's writings, the *Timaeus*, which is really a creation-myth. On the other hand, they had the Ptolemaic system of the cosmos, which, in addition, corresponded to the cosmological scheme of Aristotle, whose authority was absolute at the time. This was the picture of a closed universe. The earth stood at the centre, enclosed by seven crystal spheres, on which the sun, the moon and the planets traced perfect circular orbits around the earth. This concept seems strange to modern minds. But it actually was sufficient to explain many observable phenomena. In fact, from the standpoint of simple 'common sense', it would seem that the sun goes round the earth and not vice-versa.

Despite this, the geocentric view was challenged even in Ptolemy's day. The alternative heliocentric theory was defended by Aristarchus of Samos (c. 310-230 BC), who put forward the complete hypothesis of Copernicus, that all planets, including the earth, go round the sun in circles, and that the earth revolves on its axis every twenty-four hours. This brilliant theory was discarded in favour of the Ptolemaic view, because it fitted in with the Church's outlook. The earth stood at the centre of the universe, and the Church stood at the centre of the world.

Copernicus, the great Polish astronomer (1473-1543), had travelled to Italy in his youth, and was infected with the new spirit of inquiry and free thinking abroad. He soon came to accept that the sun was at the centre of the universe, but kept his ideas to himself for fear of the reaction of the Church. Only on his deathbed did he decide to publish his book, *De Revolutionibus Orbium Coelestium* (*On the Revolutions of the Heavenly Bodies*), which he dedicated to the Pope in the hope of escaping censure. He succeeded temporarily. The book was not condemned until Galileo's time, when the Inquisition and the Jesuits, the shock-troops of the Counter-Reformation, were in full swing.

Tycho Brache, the Danish astronomer (1546-1601), took an intermediate position, arguing that, while the sun and moon go round the earth, the planets go round the sun. Far more important was the role of the German, Johannes Kepler (1571-1630), who made use of Brache's calculations to correct some inaccuracies in Copernicus' model, and put forward his three laws: that planets move, not in circles, but in ellipses; that the line joining a planet to the sun sweeps out equal areas in equal times; and that the square of the period of revolution of a planet is proportional to the cube of its average distance from the sun.

These propositions struck a heavy blow against the orthodox positions of the Church. The planets had to move in circles because the circle was the perfect form. That had been the accepted view of all idealists since Pythagoras. Kepler's first law now meant that they moved in an ellipse – a far from perfect form! His second law was still more monstrous from the 'official' point of view. Instead of a nice smooth movement, the speed of the planets in orbit varied, being faster when nearer the sun, and slower when furthest away from it. How could this be compatible with the notion of the divine harmony of the universe?

The point is that, whereas Kepler's theories were based upon Brache's scrupulous observations, the position of the Church was based on an idealist theory which was simply assumed to be true. To the modern observer the position of the opponents of Copernicus and Kepler seem absurd. Yet echoes of this idealist method are still heard today, when serious physicists and mathematicians defend their equations, not on their correspondence with the known facts of observation, but on their alleged aesthetic value.

GALILEO

The greatest Renaissance scientist of them all was probably Galileo (1564-1642). Having already made great discoveries in the field of

projectiles and falling objects, Galileo, a convinced supporter of the
Copernican position, was the first astronomer to make use of the
recently invented telescope to investigate the heavens. His observations
left not a single stone standing of the old view of the universe. The
moon, far from being a perfect sphere, was an irregular surface,
with mountains and seas. Venus had phases like the sun, and, most
important of all, Jupiter had four moons. The Church maintained
that there were seven planets, because seven was a mystical number.
How could there be eleven? The image of the professor refusing
to look through Galileo's telescope has passed into the folklore of
scientific history, summing up the clash of two antagonistic world
outlooks.

In the recent past, attempts have been made to minimise the Church's
persecution of science. Pope John Paul II launched an investigation
into the 'Galileo Affair'. That enquiry, published in 1992, revealed
"grave reciprocal misunderstandings", and errors on both sides. But
it all happened in "a cultural context very different from ours."[2]
In October 1993, the Pope delivered a message to a conference at
Copernicus' alma mater, the University of Ferrara, commemorating
the 450th anniversary of the publication of the Polish astronomer's
book, *De Revolutionibus Orbium Coelestium*. He was, says the Pope, a
man both of science and of faith. In fact, the only reason Copernicus
escaped persecution by the Church was to make sure his book saw the
light of day when he was in a very safe place – the cemetery!

Galileo was put on trial twice by the Inquisition, once in private
(1616) and once in public (1633). The second time he was forced
to recant his views. He promised never again to claim that the earth
goes round the sun or rotates on its axis. In this way, the Church
silenced the greatest scientist of the age, and in the process killed off
science in Italy for a long time. A worse fate befell others. Giordano
Bruno (1548-1600) was burnt at the stake in Rome after eight years
of imprisonment.

---

2   Quoted in A. P. Balk, *Saints and Sinners: An Account of Western Civilization*,
    p. 587.

Bruno was an uncompromising materialist. He had been influenced by Nicholas of Cusa, who argued that the universe has no beginning or end in space or time. Bruno's materialism was coloured by a kind of pantheism, the idea that God is everywhere and nowhere – that is, that God and nature are one and the same. In a concept similar to that of the old Ionian hylozoism, he held that matter was an active, self-moving substance, and that man and his consciousness was part of nature, which was a single whole. Arguing that the universe is infinite, he deduced that the universe also consisted of an infinite number of worlds, some of them possibly inhabited. It is easy to see why the Church saw these startlingly modern ideas as subversive. Bruno did not shrink from paying for them with his life.

The Roman Church did not have a monopoly of the persecution of new ideas. The Protestant Luther denounced Copernicus as "an upstart astrologer who strove to show that the earth revolves, not the heavens or the firmament, the sun and the moon."[3] As Engels observes:

> At that time natural science also developed in the midst of the general revolution and was itself thoroughly revolutionary; it had indeed to win in struggle its right of existence. Side by side with the great Italians from whom modern philosophy dates, it provided its martyrs for the stake and the dungeons of the Inquisition. And it is characteristic that Protestants outdid Catholics in persecuting the free investigation of nature. Calvin had Servetus burnt at the stake when the latter was on the point of discovering the circulation of the blood, and indeed he kept him roasting alive during two hours; for the Inquisition at least it sufficed to have Giordano Bruno simply burnt alive.[4]

Despite all reverses, the new mode of thinking steadily gained ground, until, by the late seventeenth century, it had won a decisive victory. The same scientists who, in the name of orthodoxy had condemned the

---

3   Quoted in A.D. White, *A History of the Warfare of Science With Theology in Christendom*, Vol. 1, p. 126.

4   F. Engels, *Dialectics of Nature*, p. 22.

ideas of Galileo, in practice quietly dropped the discredited Ptolemaic cosmology. The discovery of the circulation of the blood by William Harvey (1578-1657) revolutionised the study of the human body, destroying the old myths. The discoveries of science, more than the logical disputation of the philosophers, made the old views untenable.

Although the traditional methods of the Schoolmen remained in place for a long time, they were increasingly seen as out of step with reality. The growth of science proceeded on other lines and with other methods – observation and experiment. Once again, England was in the vanguard in advocating the empirical method. The most prominent proponent of this was Francis Bacon (1561-1626). For some time Lord Chancellor of England under King James I, he eventually lost this position as a result of being too successful in enriching himself by accepting gifts from litigants. Thereafter, he put his talents to better use writing books.

Bacon's writings are full of sound, practical common sense, and are materialist in the English – that is, empirical – sense of the word. The general spirit of his works is that of a good natured and witty man of the world. Unlike Sir Thomas More, Bacon was not the stuff that martyrs are made of. He accepted the orthodox religion, just because he attached little importance to general principles. But religion played no role in his philosophy, which was inspired by the idea of developing learning as a means of increasing man's power over nature.

He reacted against the dogmatism of the Schoolmen, with their "unwholesome" and "vermiculate"[5] disputes which end in "monstrous altercations and barking questions."[6] The only times he displays real indignation is when he touches on this subject:

> This kind of degenerate learning did chiefly reign amongst the Schoolmen: who having sharp and strong wits, and abundance of leisure, and small variety of reading, but their wits being shut up in the cells of a few authors (chiefly Aristotle their dictator) as their persons were shut up in the cells

---

5 F. Bacon, *The Advancement of Learning*, p. 26.

6 Ibid., p. 55.

of monasteries and colleges, and knowing little history, either of nature or time, did out of no great quantity of matter and infinite agitation of wit spin out unto those laborious webs of learning which are extant in their books. For the wit and mind of man, if it work upon matter, which is the contemplation of the creatures of God, worketh according to the stuff, and is limited thereby; but if it work upon itself, as the spider worketh his web, then it is endless, and brings forth indeed cobwebs of learning, admirable for the fineness of thread and work, but of no substance or profit.[7]

Here we have the healthy reaction against the sterile method of idealism. In turning its back upon the real world, idealism spins fancies out of its own head and takes them for the truth just because they correspond to a set of preconceived prejudices which are taken as axioms. Instead of this, Bacon urges us to "imitate nature, which doth nothing in vain."[8] Significantly, he prefers Democritus the atomist to Plato and Aristotle. Speaking ironically of the Supreme Craftsman who was supposed to have created the world from nothing, he asks a pertinent question:

For if that great Workmaster had been of a human disposition, he would have cast the stars into some pleasant and beautiful works and orders, like the frets in the roofs of houses; whereas one can scarce find a posture in square, or triangle, or straight line, amongst such an infinite number; so differing a harmony there is between the spirit of man and the spirit of nature.[9]

This is a very important point, and one that is too often forgotten by scientists and mathematicians, who imagine that their equations represent the ultimate truth. In nature there are no such perfect forms, no triangles, no circles, no planes, only real material objects and processes, of which these ideal representations are only rough approximations. Bacon understood this very well, when he wrote:

---

7 Ibid., p. 26.
8 Ibid., p. 201.
9 Ibid., p. 133.

Hence it cometh, that the mathematicians cannot satisfy themselves except they reduce the motions of the celestial bodies to perfect circles, rejecting spiral lines, and labouring to be discharged of eccentrics. Hence it cometh, that whereas there are many things in nature as it were *monodica, sui juris*; yet the cogitations of man do feign unto them *relatives, parallels*, and *conjugates*, whereas no such thing is.[10]

The abstract generalisations of science, including those of mathematics, are only of use insofar as they correspond to the real world and can be applied to it. Even the most fruitful and ingenious generalisation will necessarily only reflect reality in an imperfect and one-sided way. The problem arises when idealists make exaggerated claims for theories which they elevate to absolute principles to which reality is expected to conform.

Modern day chaos theory is returning, on a much higher level, to the fruitful line of argument of Bacon and the materialists of the Renaissance, who, in turn, represented the rediscovery of a much older tradition – that of the Greek materialism of the Ionic and atomic schools. Bacon evolved his own materialist conception of nature, based on the idea that matter was made up of particles endowed with manifold properties, one of which was motion, which he did not limit to mechanical motion. He advanced the brilliant hypothesis that heat itself is a form of motion. Motion is here regarded not merely as an external impulse – as a mechanical force – but as an inherent quality of matter, a kind of vital spirit or inner tension. Marx likens it to the term used by the German philosopher Jakob Böhme, 'Qual', which cannot be easily translated, but which signifies extreme inner tension, or 'torment', as with a living thing. Thus, the primary forms of matter are endowed with movement and energy, almost like a living force. Nowadays we would use the word energy. Compared with the lifeless, wooden mechanistic conceptions of the following century, this view of matter is strikingly modern and comes close to the position of dialectical materialism.

---

10 Ibid., p. 133.

This last observation brings us close to the heart of the matter. The real significance of Bacon's philosophy was that it pointed the way forward. Although incomplete in itself, it contained the seeds of future development, as Marx explains in *The Holy Family*:

> In *Bacon*, its first creator, materialism still holds back within itself in a naive way the germs of a many-sided development. On the one hand, matter, surrounded by a sensuous, poetic glamour, seems to attract man's whole entity by winning smiles. On the other, the aphoristically formulated doctrine pullulates with inconsistencies imported from theology.[11]

Bacon's theory of knowledge was strictly empirical. Like Duns Scotus, he emphatically denied the existence of 'universals'. He developed the method of reasoning known as induction which is already present in the works of Aristotle. This is a way of studying things experimentally, in which we proceed from a series of single facts to general propositions. As an antidote to the arid idealism of the Schoolmen, this was an important advance, but it had serious limitations, which later became an obstacle to the development of thought. Here we see the beginning of that peculiarly Anglo-Saxon aversion to theory, the tendency towards narrow empiricism, the slavish worship of the 'facts', and a stubborn refusal to accept generalisations which has dominated educated thought in Britain and, by extension, the United States, ever since.

The limitations of a strictly inductive method are self-evident. No matter how many facts are examined, it only takes a single exception to undermine whatever general conclusion we have drawn from them. If we have seen a thousand white swans, and draw the conclusion that all swans are white, and then see a black swan, our conclusion no longer holds good. These conclusions are hypothetical, demanding further proof. Induction, in the last analysis, is the basis of all knowledge, since all we know is ultimately derived from observation of the objective world and experience. Over a long period of observation, combined with practical activity which enables us

---

11 K. Marx and F. Engels, *The Holy Family*, MECW, Vol. 4, p. 128.

to test the correctness or otherwise of our ideas, we discover a series of essential connections between phenomena, which show that they possess common features and belong to a particular genus or species.

The generalisations arrived at over a lengthy period of human development, some of which are considered as axioms, play an important role in the development of thought and cannot be so easily dispensed with. The thought-forms of traditional logic play an important role, establishing elementary rules for avoiding absurd contradictions and following an internally consistent line of argument. Dialectical materialism does not regard induction and deduction as mutually incompatible, but as different aspects of the dialectical process of cognition, which are inseparably connected, and condition one another. The process of human cognition proceeds from the particular to the universal, but also from the universal to the particular. It is therefore incorrect and one-sided to counterpose one to the other.

Despite claims made to the contrary, it is impossible to proceed from the 'facts' without any preconceptions. Such supposed objectivity has never existed and will never exist. In approaching the facts, we bring our own conceptions and categories with us. These can either be conscious or unconscious. But they are always present. Those who imagine that they can get along quite happily without a philosophy, as is the case with many scientists, merely repeat unconsciously the existing 'official' philosophy of the day and the current prejudices of the society in which they live. It is therefore indispensable that scientists, and thinking people in general, should strive to work out a consistent way of looking at the world, a coherent philosophy which can serve as an adequate tool for analysing things and processes.

In his introduction to *The Philosophy of History*, Hegel rightly ridicules those historians (all too common in Britain) who pretend to limit themselves to the facts, presenting a spurious facade of 'academic objectivity', while giving free reign to their prejudices:

> We must proceed historically – empirically. Among other precautions we must take care not to be misled by professed historians who … are

chargeable with the very procedure of which they accuse the Philosopher
– introducing a priori inventions of their own into the records of the
Past ... We might then announce it as the first condition to be observed,
that we should faithfully adopt all that is historical. But in such general
expressions themselves, as 'faithfully' and 'adopt,' lies the ambiguity. Even
the ordinary, the 'impartial' historiographer, who believes and professes
that he maintains a simply receptive attitude; surrendering himself only
to the data supplied him – is by no means passive as regard the exercise
of his thinking powers. He brings his categories with him, and sees the
phenomena presented to his mental vision, exclusively through these
media. And, especially in all that pretends to the name of science it is
indispensable that Reason should not sleep – that reflection should be in
full play. To him who looks upon the world rationally, the world in its turn
presents a rational aspect. The relation is mutual. But the various exercises
of reflection – the different points of view – the modes of deciding the
simple question of the relative importance of events (the first category
that occupies the attention of the historian), do not belong to this place.[12]

Bertrand Russell, whose views are diametrically opposed to dialectical
materialism, makes a valid criticism of the limitations of empiricism,
which follows in the same line as Hegel's remarks:

As a rule, the framing of hypotheses is the most difficult part of scientific
work, and the part where great ability is indispensable. So far, no method
has been found which would make it possible to invent hypotheses by
rule. Usually some hypothesis is a necessary preliminary to the collection
of facts, since the selection of facts demands some way of determining
relevance. Without something of this kind, the mere multiplicity of facts
is baffling.[13]

Thus, the Baconian school of thought exercised a contradictory
influence upon subsequent developments. On the one hand, by
stressing the need for observation and experiment, it gave a stimulus to
scientific investigation. On the other hand, it gave rise to the narrow

12 G. W. F. Hegel, *The Philosophy of History*, pp. 10-11.
13 B. Russell, *History of Western Philosophy*, p. 529.

empiricist outlook that has had a negative effect on the development of philosophical thought, above all in Britain. In *The Dialectics of Nature*, Engels points out the paradox that this same empirical school, which imagined that it had disposed of metaphysics once and for all, actually ended up accepting all kinds of mystical ideas, and that this trend "which, exalting mere experience, treats thought with sovereign disdain and really has gone to the furthest extreme in emptiness of thought."[14]

The immediate battle against religion had been won. Science was set free from the bonds of theology which had kept it in thrall for so long. This was the prior condition for the giant leap forward of the next period, when more was achieved in a century than in the whole of the previous 1,000 years. But the new world outlook was still insufficiently developed, characterised in general by a shallow and naive empiricism that was far from sufficient to get rid of religion and idealism once and for all.

> The emancipation of natural science from theology dates from this, although the fighting out of particular mutual claims has dragged on down to our day and in many minds is still far from completion.[15]

Today, over 100 years later, despite the undreamed-of advances of science and human knowledge, the war has still not been decisively won.

THE AGE OF IMMUTABILITY

During the Renaissance, as in ancient times, philosophy and science, which were mainly the same thing, looked upon nature as a single, interdependent whole. A series of brilliant hypotheses were advanced as to the nature of the universe, but could not be verified or developed further because of the existing state of technology and production. Only with the birth of capitalism, and particularly with the beginnings of the industrial revolution, did it become possible to investigate in detail the workings of nature in their different manifestations. This profoundly altered the way men and women looked at the world:

---

14 F. Engels, *Dialectics of Nature*, p. 51.
15 Ibid., p. 22.

Real natural science dates from the second half of the fifteenth century, and thence onward it has advanced with constantly increasing rapidity. The analysis of nature into its individual parts, the grouping of the different natural processes and objects in definite classes, the study of the internal anatomy of organic bodies in their manifold forms – these were the fundamental conditions of the gigantic strides in our knowledge of nature that have been made during the last 400 years. But this method of work has also left us as legacy the habit of observing natural objects and processes in isolation, apart from their connection with the vast whole; of observing them in repose, not in motion; as constants, not as essentially variables; in their death, not in their life. And when this way of looking at things was transferred by Bacon and Locke from natural science to philosophy, it begot the narrow, metaphysical mode of thought peculiar to the last century.[16]

In the writings of Thomas Hobbes (1588-1679) the materialism of Bacon is developed in a more systematic way. Hobbes lived in a period of revolution. A convinced monarchist, he experienced at first hand the storm and stress of the English Civil War. The impending victory of Parliament forced him to flee to France, where he met and clashed with Descartes. His royalist convictions should have endeared him to the monarchist exiles in whose midst he lived (for a while he taught mathematics to Prince Charles). But, like Hegel, whose conservative politics did not prevent his philosophy from attracting the suspicions of the authorities, Hobbes' ideas proved too radical for his contemporaries. The materialist tone of his *Leviathan*, which appeared in 1651, provoked the wrath of the Church and government of France, while his theories of society offended the English exiles by their rationalism. By a supreme irony, Hobbes was forced to flee to England, where he was welcomed by Cromwell on condition he abstained from political activity.

The Restoration of the monarchy after the death of Cromwell led to the imposition of severe restrictions on intellectual freedom. Baconians

16 F. Engels, *Anti-Dühring*, p. 31.

were expelled from Oxford and Cambridge, effectively undermining them as centres of science. Under the Licensing Acts (1662-95) an iron censorship was re-imposed. Hobbes was afraid that the bishops would attempt to have him burnt. He was suspected of atheism, and even mentioned in a parliamentary report on the subject. His book *Behemoth* was withheld from publication until 1679. After that, he could get nothing of importance published in England for fear of ecclesiastical repression.

It is not hard to see why he attracted such a reputation. Right from the first page of *Leviathan*, he proclaims the materialist doctrine in the most intransigent spirit. For him, there is absolutely nothing in the human mind which does not originate in the senses:

> Concerning the Thoughts of man, I will consider them first *Singly*, and afterwards in *Trayne*, or dependance upon one another. *Singly*, they are every one a *Representation* or *Apparence*, of some quality, or other Accident of a body without us; which is commonly called an *Object*. Which Object worketh on the Eyes, Eares, and other parts of mans body; and by diversity of working, produceth diversity of Apparences.

> The Originall of them all, is that which we call SENSE; (For there is no conception in a mans mind, which hath not at first, totally, or by parts, been begotten upon the organs of Sense.) The rest are derived of that originall.[17]

Elsewhere, he comes close to attributing the origins of religion to primitive superstitions arising from phenomena such as dreams, although, for obvious reasons, he limits the application of this idea to non-Christian religions!

> From this ignorance of how to distinguish Dreams, and other strong Fancies, from Vision and Sense, did arise the greatest part of the Religion of the Gentiles in time past, that worshipped Satyres, Fawnes, Nymphs, and the like; and now adayes the opinion that rude people have of Fayries, Ghosts, and Goblins; and of the power of Witches.[18]

---

17 T. Hobbes, *Leviathan*, p. 3.
18 Ibid., p. 7.

Following in Bacon's footsteps, Hobbes appeals directly to nature, as the source of all knowledge:

> Nature it selfe cannot erre: and as men abound in copiousnesse of language; so they become more wise, or more mad than ordinary. Nor is it possible without Letters for any man to become either excellently wise, or (unless his memory be hurt by disease, or ill constitution of organs) excellently foolish. For words are wise mens counters, they do but reckon by them: but they are the mony of fooles, that value them by the authority of an *Aristotle*, a *Cicero*, or a *Thomas*, or any other Doctor whatsoever, if but a man.[19]

And, like Bacon and Duns Scotus, he follows in the tradition of nominalism, denying the existence of universals, except in language:

> Of Names, some are *Proper*, and singular to one onely thing; as *Peter, John, This man, this Tree*: and some are *Common* to many things; as *Man, Horse, Tree*; every of which though but one Name, is nevertheless the name of divers particular things; in respect of all which together, it is called an *Universall*; there being nothing in the world Universall but Names; for the things named, are every one of them Individuall and Singular.[20]

In comparison to Bacon, the method of Hobbes is much more worked-out, but at the same time becomes increasingly more one-sided, rigid, soulless, in a word, mechanistic. This was not accidental, since the science which was advancing most rapidly at the time was mechanics. Increasingly, the entire workings of the world came to be seen in terms borrowed from mechanics. Thus, for Hobbes, society was like a human body, which, in turn, was just a machine:

> Nature (the Art whereby God hath made and governes the World) is by the *Art* of man, as in many other things, so in this also imitated, that it can make an Artificial Animal. For seeing life is but a motion of Limbs, the begining whereof is in some principall part within; why may we not say, that all *Automata* (Engines that move themselves by springs and wheeles

---

19 Ibid., pp. 15-6.
20 Ibid., p. 13.

as doth a watch) have an artificiall life? For what is the *Heart*, but a *Spring*; and the *Nerves*, but so many *Strings*; and the *Joynts*, but so many *Wheeles*, giving motion to the whole Body, such as was intended by the Artificer? *Art* goes yet further, imitating that Rationall and most excellent worke of Nature, *Man*. For by Art is created that great LEVIATHAN called a COMMON-WEALTH, or STATE, (in latine CIVITAS) which is but an Artificiall Man.[21]

Marx and Engels sum up Hobbes' contribution in the following passage from *The Holy Family*:

Hobbes, as Bacon's continuator, argues thus: if all human knowledge is furnished by the senses, then our concepts, notions, and ideas are but the phantoms of the real world, more or less divested of its sensual form. Philosophy can but give names to these phantoms.

One name may be applied to more than one of them. There may even be names of names. But it would imply a contradiction if, on the one hand, we maintained that all ideas had their origin in the world of sensation, and, on the other, that a word was more than a word; that besides the beings known to us by our senses, beings which are one and all individuals, there existed also beings of a general, not individual, nature. An *unbodily substance* is the same absurdity as an *unbodily body*. *Body, being, substance*, are but different terms for the same *reality*. It is impossible to separate thought from matter *that* thinks. This matter is the substratum of all changes going on in the world. The word *infinite* is *meaningless*, unless it states that our mind is capable of performing an endless process of addition. Only material things being perceptible, knowable to us, we cannot know *anything* about the existence of God. My own existence alone is certain. Every human passion is a mechanical movement which has a beginning and an end. The objects of impulse are what we call good. Man is subject to the same laws as nature. Power and freedom are identical.[22]

This mechanistic view of the world, in a sense, represents a step back in relation to Bacon.

---

21 Ibid., p. 1.
22 K. Marx and F. Engels, *The Holy Family*, MECW, Vol. 4, pp. 128-9.

Knowledge based upon the senses loses its poetic blossom, it passes into the abstract experience of the *geometrician*. *Physical* motion is sacrificed to *mechanical* or *mathematical* motion; *geometry* is proclaimed as the queen of sciences. Materialism takes to *misanthropy*. If it is to overcome its opponent, *misanthropic, fleshless* spiritualism, and that on the latter's own ground, materialism has to chastise its own flesh and turn *ascetic*. Thus it passes into an *intellectual entity*; but thus, too, it involves all the consistency, regardless of consequences, characteristic of the intellect.[23]

Yet this type of mechanical materialism was to predominate for the next century-and-a-half in Britain and France.

John Locke (1632-1704) continued in the same direction as Hobbes, declaring that experience is the sole source of ideas. To him belongs the celebrated maxim "*nihil est in intellectu, quod non prius fuit in sensu*" – "nothing is in the intellect which was not first in sense". It was Locke, with his *Essay on the Human Understanding*, who supplied the proof for Bacon's fundamental principle, that the origin of all human knowledge and ideas was the material world given to us in sense-perception. He is the philosopher of sound common sense, who "said indirectly that there cannot be any philosophy at variance with healthy human senses and the reason based on them."[24] "Reason", he said, "must be our judge and guide in everything." Locke's work was translated into French, and inspired Condillac and others to launch the French school of materialist philosophy, which prepared the ground intellectually for the Revolution of 1789-93.

THE ADVANCE OF SCIENCE

The period from the end of the seventeenth and beginning of the eighteenth centuries saw a complete transformation of the world of science rooted in the conquests of the previous period. In England, the victory of the bourgeoisie in the Civil War, and the subsequent compromise of a constitutional monarchy after 1688, provided relatively freer conditions for the development of scientific research and

---

23 Ibid., p. 128.
24 Ibid., p. 129.

investigation. At the same time, the growth of trade and, increasingly, manufacture, created a need for more advanced technology and the capital necessary to pay for it. It was a period of unprecedented innovation and scientific advance.

Improvements in optics made possible the invention of the microscope. In France, Gassendi resurrected the atomic theories of Democritus and Epicurus. In Germany, Von Guericke invented the air-pump. Robert Boyle made significant progress in chemistry. The discoveries of Copernicus, Tycho Brache, Kepler, Galileo and Huygens prepared the ground for Newton's revolution in astronomy, which were made necessary by the demand for more accurate navigation. The predominant method of science at the time was mechanistic: that is, that natural phenomena were to be interpreted in terms of form, size, position, arrangement, and motion of corpuscles, and their behaviour was to be explained exclusively in terms of contact with other particles.

The chief exponent of the new science was Sir Isaac Newton (1643-1727). Newton, who became President of the Royal Society in 1703, exercised a colossal influence, not just in science, but in philosophy and the general mode of thinking of the period in which he lived and later. The poet Alexander Pope sums up the adulatory attitude of contemporary Englishmen with his verse:

> Nature and Nature's laws lay hid in night:
> God said 'Let Newton be!' and all was light.[25]

Newton was born on Christmas day 1642, the year when Galileo died and the Civil War broke out between Charles I and Parliament. In 1687, he published his famous *Principia Mathematica*, which set forth three laws of motion – the law of inertia, law of proportionality of force and velocity, law of equality of action and counteraction, from which the basic principles of classical physics and mechanics were deduced. Here he set out and proved his theory of universal gravitation. This marks the definitive break with the old Aristotelian-

---

25 A. Pope, *Epitaph: Intended for Sir Isaac Newton.*

Ptolemaic world-picture. Instead of celestial spheres operated by angels, Newton put forward a scheme of a universe functioning according to the laws of mechanics without the need for any divine intervention whatsoever, except for an initial impulse needed to set the whole thing in motion.

A typical product of the English empirical school, Newton was not much bothered about this, preferring to ask no questions about the role of the Almighty in his mechanical universe. For their part, the religious Establishment, personified by Bishop Sprat, bowing to the inevitable, advocated a compromise with science (much like the compromise between King William and Parliament). This held in place for about a century, until it was overthrown by Darwin's discoveries. The demands of capitalism ensured that science was left in peace to get on with the job.

Like the great thinkers of the Renaissance, the scientists of Newton's age were mostly men with a broad vision of science. Newton himself was not only an astronomer, but also a mathematician, optician, mechanic, and even a chemist. His contemporary and friend, Robert Hook, was not only the greatest experimental physicist before Faraday, but was also a chemist, mathematician, biologist and inventor, who shares with Papin the credit of preparing the way to the steam engine.

THE INVENTION OF CALCULUS

The discovery of the infinitesimal calculus, which revolutionised mathematics, has been variously ascribed to Newton and Leibniz. It is possible that both came to the same conclusion independently. In his *Method of Fluxions*, Newton sets out from the conception of a line as a 'flowing quantity' (the 'fluent'), and the velocity by which the line 'flows' is described as its 'fluxion'. Newton refers to a 'moment' as an infinitely small length by which the fluent increased in an infinitely small time. This represented a complete break with the traditional method of mathematics, which totally excluded the concept of infinity and infinitesimals, which were not supposed to exist. The colossal advantage of this method was that it allowed mathematics for the first time to deal with motion. Indeed, Newton refers to it as the "mathematics of motion and growth." It was this instrument that permitted him to formulate the laws of planetary motion discovered by Kepler as general laws of motion and matter.

The discovery of the infinitesimal calculus was fundamental for the whole development of science. Yet it involves a contradiction which immediately caused a controversy and which lasted for a long time. The first detractor of calculus was none other than Bishop Berkeley, who objected to the use of infinitesimally small quantities. This, he argued, was in contradiction to logic, and therefore unacceptable.

> What are these fluxions? The velocities of evanescent increments. And what are these same evanescent increments? They are neither finite quantities, nor quantities infinitely small, nor yet nothing. May we not call them the ghosts of departed quantities?[26]

Here again, we see the fundamental limitation of the method of formal logic. Its basic premise is the elimination of contradiction. Yet motion is a contradiction – that of being and not being in the same place at the same time. In the first volume of his *Science of Logic*, Hegel deals in detail with the differential and integral calculus, and shows that it deals with magnitudes that are in the process of disappearing, neither before, when they are finite magnitudes, nor after, when they are nothing, but in a state which is and is not. This is in clear contradiction to the laws of formal logic, and hence provoked the indignant assaults of orthodox mathematicians and logicians. Despite all objections, the new mathematics achieved brilliant results in solving problems which could not be solved by the traditional methods. Yet when Newton published his *Principia*, he felt obliged to recast it in the form of classical Greek geometry, so as to cover up the fact that he had used the new method in all his calculations.

Newton also advanced the theory that light was composed of particles, tiny corpuscles projected through space by luminous bodies. In the early nineteenth century, this theory was abandoned in favour of Huygens' wave theory, which was linked to the idea of the 'ether',

---

26 Quoted in A. Hooper, *Makers of Mathematics*, pp. 321-22.

a hypothetical weightless, invisible medium, which, rather like the 'dark matter' of modern astronomers, could not be detected by our senses, but which supposedly permeated space and filled the gaps between the air and other matter.

This theory seemed to explain all the known phenomena of light until 1900, when Max Planck put forward the idea that light was transmitted in small packets of energy or 'quanta'. Thus, the old Newtonian particle theory was revived, but with a striking difference. It was discovered that subatomic particles behave both like waves and particles. Such a contradictory and 'illogical' concept shocked the formal logicians as much as the differential and integral calculus had done. Eventually, they were compelled reluctantly to accept it, purely because, as with the calculus, the theory was backed up by practical results. But at every decisive turn, we see the same clash between the real advances of science and the obstacles placed in its way by outmoded ways of thinking.

The revolutionary contribution of Newton to science is not in doubt. Yet his legacy was not an unmixed blessing. The uncritical adulation which he received in his lifetime in England obscured the important role of his contemporaries, like Hooke, who anticipated his *Principia* by seven years, though without the necessary mathematical backing, and Leibniz, the German philosopher who was probably the real discoverer of the calculus. Several of his most important theories were in fact put forward much earlier by Galileo and Kepler. His major role was to systematise and sum up the discoveries of the past period, and give them a general form, backed up by mathematical calculations.

On the negative side, Newton's enormous authority gave rise to a new orthodoxy that was to inhibit scientific thinking for a long time. Bernal writes:

> His abilities were so great, his system so apparently perfect, that they positively discouraged scientific advance for the next century, or allowed it only in regions he had not touched.[27]

27 J. D. Bernal, *Science in History*, p. 343.

The limitations of the English school of empiricism was summed up in his celebrated phrase: "*hypothesis non fingo*" – "I make no hypotheses". This slogan became the battle cry of empiricism, yet bore absolutely no relation to the actual method of science, including that of Newton, who, for example, in the field of optics, made:

> [N]umerous conjectures as to the physical causes of optical and other phenomena and even partly propounding them as facts. Thus, in his explanation of what were afterwards called Newton's rings, he treated the alternate fits of easy transmission and easy reflection along a ray of light as experimentally established facts, which he then made use of.[28]

The advances of science were enormous. Yet the general world view bequeathed by the period was conservative. The static and mechanical outlook coloured men's minds for generations, as Engels points out:

> But what especially characterises this period is the elaboration of a peculiar general outlook, the central point of which is the view of the *absolute immutability of nature*. In whatever way nature itself might have come into being, once present it remained as it was as long as it continued to exist. The planets and their satellites, once set in motion by the mysterious 'first impulse', circled on and on in their predestined ellipses for all eternity, or at any rate until the end of all things. The stars remained for ever fixed and immovable in their places, keeping one another therein by 'universal gravitation'. The earth had remained the same without alteration from all eternity or, alternatively, from the first day of its creation. The 'five continents' of the present day had always existed, and they had always had the same mountains, valleys, and rivers, the same climate, and the same flora and fauna, except in so far as change or transplantation had taken place at the hand of man. The species of plants and animals had been established once for all when they came into existence; like continually produced like, and it was already a good deal for Linnaeus to have conceded that possibly here and there new species could have arisen by crossing. In contrast to the history of mankind, which develops in time,

28 R. J. Forbes and E. J. Dijksterhuis, *A History of Science and Technology*, Vol. 1, p. 247.

there was ascribed to the history of nature only an unfolding in space. All change, all development in nature, was denied. Natural science, so revolutionary at the outset, suddenly found itself confronted by an out-and-out conservative nature, in which even today everything was as it had been from the beginning and in which – to the end of the world or for all eternity – everything would remain as it had been since the beginning.[29]

THE DECADENCE OF EMPIRICISM

Whereas the materialism of Bacon reflected the hopeful, forward-looking outlook of the Renaissance and the reformation, the philosophy of the late seventeenth and early eighteenth centuries took shape in an altogether different climate. In England, the rich and powerful had received a shock in the period of the Civil War, with its 'excesses'. Having effectively broken the power of the absolute monarchy, the bourgeoisie no longer needed the services of the revolutionary petty-bourgeoisie and the lower orders of society, the shock troops of Cromwell's Model Army, who had begun to give voice to their independent demands, not only in the field of religion, but by calling into question the existence of private property.

Cromwell himself had crushed the left wing represented by the Levellers and Diggers, but the wealthy Presbyterian merchants of the City of London did not feel safe until, after Cromwell's death, they had invited Charles back from France. The compromise with the Stuarts did not last long, and the bourgeoisie was forced to eject Charles' successor James from the throne. But this time there was no question of appealing to the masses for support. Instead, they called on the services of the Dutch Protestant, William of Orange, to take possession of the English throne, on condition of accepting the power of Parliament. This compromise, known as the 'Glorious Revolution' (although it was neither), established once and for all the power of the bourgeoisie in England.

The stage was set for a rapid growth of trade and industry, accompanied by giant advances of science. In the realm of philosophy, however, it did not produce great results. Such periods are not

---

29 F. Engels, *The Dialectics of Nature*, pp. 24-25.

conducive to broad philosophical generalisations. "New times", wrote Plekhanov, "produce new aspirations, the latter producing new philosophies."[30] The heroic revolutionary age was past. The new ruling class wanted to hear no more of such things. They even baptised the real revolution, which had broken the power of their enemies, 'The Great Rebellion'. The men of money were guided by narrow practical considerations, and looked with distrust at theory, although they encouraged scientific research which had practical consequences, translatable into pounds, shillings and pence. This mean-spirited egotism permeates the philosophical thinking of the period – at least in England – where it was only enlivened by the writings of satirists like Swift and Sheridan.

The further evolution of the empiricist trend revealed its limited character, which ended up by leading Anglo-Saxon philosophy into a cul-de-sac out of which it has still not emerged. This negative side of 'sensationalism' was already evident in the writings of David Hume (1711-76) and George Berkeley. The latter was the bishop of Cloyne in Ireland, who lived just at the end of a stormy period when Ireland had been drawn into the maelstrom of England's Civil War and subsequent dynastic and religious upheavals. This ended in the 'Glorious Revolution' and the Battle of the Boyne, where the interests of the Irish people were betrayed in a struggle between an English and a Dutch Pretender, neither of whom had anything to do with them.

Reflecting the prevailing mood of philosophical conservatism, Berkeley was obsessed with the need to oppose what he saw as the subversive trends in contemporary science, which he interpreted as a threat to religion. An astute, if not original thinker, he soon realised that it was possible to seize upon the weak side of the existing materialism, in order to turn it into its exact opposite. This he did quite effectively in his most important work, *A Treatise Concerning the Principles of Human Knowledge* (1734).

---

30 G. V. Plekhanov, 'Essays on the History of Materialism', *Selected Philosophical Works*, Vol. 2, p. 78.

Taking as his starting point Locke's philosophical premises, he attempted to prove that the material world did not exist. Locke's empiricist theory of knowledge begins with the self-evident proposition: "I interpret the world through my senses." However, it is necessary to add the equally self-evident statement that the world exists independent of my senses, and that the impressions I obtain through my senses come from the material world outside me. Unless this is accepted, we very quickly land up in the most grotesque mysticism and subjective idealism.

Berkeley was well aware that a consistent materialist position would lead to the complete overthrow of religion. He was, for instance, deeply suspicious of the new science, which seemed to leave no room for the Creator. Newton professed himself a believer. But his explanation of the universe as a vast system of moving bodies, all acting in accordance with the laws of mechanics, shocked the bishop. Where did God come into all this? he asked. True, Newton assigned to the Almighty the task of getting it all started with a push, but after that, God did not seem to have been left very much to do!

Locke, like Newton, never renounced religion, but the bare declaration that God exists (deism), while giving Him no real role in the affairs of man or nature was merely a convenient fig leaf to conceal unbelief. As Marx and Engels put it, "for materialism, deism is but an easy-going way of getting rid of religion."[31] Following Newton, Locke was happy to take for granted the existence of an obliging Deity who, after giving the universe a bit of a shove, then retired to the celestial sidelines for the rest of eternity to allow men of science to get on with their work. It was the philosophical equivalent of the constitutional monarchy established as a compromise between parliament and William III after the 'Glorious Revolution' of 1688, which, incidentally, was Locke's political ideal.

The deist disguise, however, did not fool Berkeley for a moment. There was an evident weak link. What if the universe did not start in

---

31 K. Marx and F. Engels, *The Holy Family*, MECW, Vol. 4, p. 129.

this way? What if it had always existed? Locke and Newton assumed that, following the laws of elementary mechanics, a clockwork universe must have commenced with an external impulse. But there was no way they could disprove the contrary assertion, that the universe had existed eternally. In that case, the last vestige of a role for the Creator vanished altogether. Locke also supposed that, in addition to matter, the universe contained 'immaterial' substances, minds and souls. But, as he himself confessed, this conclusion did not flow necessarily from his system. Consciousness might just be another property of matter – which is just what it is in fact: the property of matter organised in a certain way. Here too, Locke's concessions to religion hung uneasily from his materialist premises, as if they had been tacked on as an afterthought.

Berkeley's philosophy, like that of Hume, is the expression of a reaction against the revolutionary storm and stress of the previous period, identified in his mind with materialism, the root cause of atheism. Berkeley consciously set out to eradicate materialism once and for all, by the most radical means – by denying the existence of matter itself. Beginning with the undeniable assertion that "I interpret the world through my sense," he draws the conclusion that the world only exists when I perceive it: "*esse is percipi*" – "to be is to be perceived".

> The table I write on I say exists, that is, I see and feel it; and if I were out of my study I should say it existed – meaning thereby that if I was in my study I might perceive it, or that some other spirit actually does perceive it…
>
> For, what are the aforementioned objects but the things we perceive by sense? and what do we perceive besides our own ideas or sensations? and is it not plainly repugnant that any one of these, or any combination of them, should exist unperceived?[32]

This, then, is where empiricism – inconsistent materialism – gets us when carried to its logical, or, rather, illogical, conclusions. The world

32 G. Berkeley, *Principles of Human Knowledge*, pp. 66-7.

cannot exist unless I observe it. For this is exactly what Berkeley says. In fact, he considers it strange that anyone should believe otherwise:

> It is indeed an opinion strangely prevailing amongst men, that houses, mountains, rivers, and in a word all sensible objects, have an existence, natural or real, distinct from their being perceived by the understanding.[33]

The question arises as to what it is that makes the world real by the mere act of perceiving it. Berkeley replies: "This perceiving, active being is what I call *mind, spirit, soul,* or *myself.*"[34]

All this is admirably clear and unambiguous. It is the doctrine of subjective idealism, with no 'ifs' or 'buts'. The modern philosophers of the different schools of logical positivism follow in just the same line, but lack both Berkeley's style and his honesty. The consequence of this line of argument is extreme mysticism and irrationality. Ultimately, it results in the notion that only I exist, and that the world only exists insofar as I am present to observe it. If I walk out of the room, it no longer exists, and the like. How did Berkeley deal with this objection? Very easily. There may be objects that are not perceived by my mind, but they are perceived by the 'cosmic mind' of God, and exist in it. Thus, at a single stroke, the Almighty, who was reduced to a precarious existence on the margins of a mechanical universe, has been reintroduced as the "choir of Heaven and furniture of the earth",[35] in a world entirely free of matter. In this way, Berkeley believed that he had scored the "most cheap and easy triumph in the world" over "every wretched sect of *atheists.*"[36]

In purely philosophical terms, Berkeley's philosophy is open to many objections. In the first place, his main criticism of Locke was that he duplicated the world, that is, he supposed that behind the sense-perceptions – which, according to empiricism, are the only things we can know – there was an external world of material

---

33 Ibid., p. 66.
34 Ibid., p. 65.
35 Ibid., p. 67.
36 Ibid., pp. 111-2.

things. To remove this duality, Berkeley simply denied the existence of the objective world. But this does not solve the problem at all. We are still left with something outside our sense-perceptions. The only difference is that this 'something' is not the real, material world, but, according to Berkeley, the immaterial world of spirits created by the 'cosmic mind' of God. In other words, by taking our sense-impressions as something independent, separate and apart from the objective material world outside us, we quickly land in the realm of spiritualism, the worst kind of mysticism.

Berkeley's arguments only retain a degree of consistency if one accepts his initial premise, that we can only know sense-impressions, but never the real world outside ourselves. This is put forward dogmatically at the beginning, and all the rest is derived from this proposition. In other words, he presupposes what has to be proved, namely that our sensations and ideas are not the reflection of the world outside us, but things existing in their own right. They are not a property of matter that thinks, of a human brain and nervous system, capable of being investigated and understood scientifically, but mysterious things of the spirit world, emanating from the mind of God. They do not serve to connect us with the world, but constitute an impenetrable barrier, beyond which we cannot know anything for sure.

By pushing the arguments of empiricism to the limit, Berkeley succeeded in turning it into its opposite. Engels points out that even Bacon in his natural history gives recipes for making gold, and:

> Similarly Isaac Newton in his old age greatly busied himself with expounding the Revelation of St. John. So it is not to be wondered at if in recent years English empiricism in the person of some of its representatives – and not the worst of them – should seem to have fallen a hopeless victim to the spirit-rapping and spirit-seeing imported from America.[37]

As we shall see, the propensity for mystical thinking does not disappear, but rather appears to grow in geometrical proportion to

---

37 F. Engels, *Dialectics of Nature*, p. 51.

the advance of science. This is the price we have to pay for the cavalier attitude of scientists who wrongly imagine that they can get along without any general philosophical principles. Expelled by the front door, philosophy immediately flies back in through the window, and invariably in its most retrograde and mystifying form.

Just as all ideas ultimately are derived from this objective material world, which is said not to exist by Berkeley, so, in the last analysis, their truth or otherwise is decided in practice, through experiment, by countless observations, and, above all, through the practical activity of human beings in society. Berkeley lived at a time when science had largely succeeded in freeing itself from the deadly embrace of religion, and had thereby made possible the greatest advances. How did Berkeley's ideas fit in with all this? What kind of explanation do Berkeley's ideas give of the material world? How do they relate to the discoveries of Galileo, Newton and Boyle? For example, the corpuscular theory of matter cannot be true, according to Berkeley, because there is nothing for it to be true of.

Berkeley rejected Newton's theory of gravity, because it attempted to explain things by "corporeal causes." Naturally enough, since, while the sun and moon, being material, have mass, my sense-impressions of these have none whatsoever and can exercise a gravitational pull only on my imagination. He likewise disapproved of the most important mathematical discovery of all – the differential and integral calculus, without which the achievements of modern science would not have been possible. But no matter. Since the concept of infinite divisibility of "real space" ran counter to the basic postulates of his philosophy, he opposed it vehemently. Having set his face against the major scientific discoveries of his day, Berkeley spent his later years extolling the properties of tar-water as an elixir to cure all ills. One could be excused for thinking that such an eccentric philosophy as this would vanish without trace. Not so. The ideas of Bishop Berkeley have continued to exercise a strange fascination on bourgeois philosophers down to the present day, being the true origin and basis of the theory of knowledge ('epistemology') of logical positivism and linguistic philosophy. This was dealt with brilliantly by Lenin in his book *Materialism and Empirio-Criticism*, to which we shall return later.

Incredible as it may seem, this thoroughly irrational and anti-scientific philosophy has penetrated the thinking of many scientists, through the agency of logical positivism in different guises. In Berkeley's lifetime his ideas did not get much of an echo. They had to wait for the intellectual climate of our own contradictory times, when the greatest advances of human knowledge rub shoulders with the most primitive cultural throwbacks to get accepted in polite society. As G. J. Warnock points out, in the introduction to *The Principles of Human Knowledge*, Berkeley's philosophy "in our own day has won far more general support than ever before." Thus, "today some physicists…are inclined to argue exactly as he did, that physical theory is not a matter of factual truth, but essentially of mathematical and predictive convenience."[38] The scientist and idealist philosopher Eddington claimed that we:

> [H]ave a right to believe that there are, for instance, colours seen by other people but not by ourselves, toothaches felt by other people, pleasures enjoyed and pains endured by other people, and so on, but that we have no right to infer events experienced by no one and not forming part of any 'mind'.[39]

Logical positivists like A. J. Ayer accept the argument that we can only know "sense-contents" and, therefore, the question as to the existence of the material world is 'meaningless'. And so on and so forth. Old Berkeley must be laughing in his grave!

The value of any theory or hypothesis is ultimately determined by whether it can be applied successfully to reality, whether it enhances our knowledge of the world and our control over our lives. A hypothesis which does none of these things is good for nothing, the product of idle speculation, like the disputations of the mediaeval Schoolmen about how many angels can dance on the head of a pin. A colossal amount of

---

38 G. Berkeley, *The Principles of Human Knowledge*, p. 25.
39 B. Russell, *History of Western Philosophy*, p. 631.

198 THE HISTORY OF PHILOSOPHY: A MARXIST PERSPECTIVE

time has been wasted in universities on endlessly debating this kind of
thing. Even Bertrand Russell is compelled to admit that a theory like
Berkeley's – "would forbid us to speak about anything that we have
not ourselves explicitly noticed. If so, it is a view that no one can hold
in practice, which is a defect in a theory that is advocated on practical
grounds." Yet in the very next sentence he feels obliged to add that "The
whole question of verification, and its connection with knowledge,
is difficult and complex; I will, therefore, leave it on one side for the
present."[40] These questions are only "difficult and complex" for someone
who accepts the premise that all we can know are sense-data, separate
and apart from the material world. Since this is the starting point of a
great deal of modern philosophers, no matter how they twist and turn,
they cannot dig themselves out of the trap set by Bishop Berkeley.

THE END OF THE ROAD

The philosophy of empiricism, which began its life with such great
expectations, finally comes to a dead stop with David Hume (1711-
76). An arch-Tory, Hume followed faithfully in the path laid down by
Berkeley, albeit more cautiously. His most famous work, the *Treatise on
Human Nature* was published in 1739 in France where it went down
like a lead balloon. For Hume, reality is only a string of impressions,
the causes of which are unknown and unknowable. He regarded
the question of the existence or non-existence of the world to be an
insoluble problem, and was one of the first of those philosophers to
translate their ignorance into Greek and call it agnosticism. In essence,
what we have here is a throwback to the idea of the Greek sceptics that
the world is unknowable.

His main claim to fame rests on the section of his work entitled *Of
Knowledge and Probability*. Here also he was not original, but merely
developed an idea already present in Berkeley, namely the non-
existence of causation. Arguing against the discoveries of the newly
developed science of mechanics, he tried to show that mechanical
causation did not exist, that we cannot say that a particular event

---

40 Ibid., p. 632.

causes another event, but only that one event follows another. Thus, if we boil a kettle of water to 100 degrees centigrade, we cannot say that this action has caused it to boil, but only that the water boiled after we heated it. Or if a man is knocked over by a ten-ton truck, we have no right to affirm that his death was caused by this. It just succeeded it in time. That is all.

Does this seem incredible? But it is the inevitable result of the strict application of this kind of narrow empiricism, which demands of us that we stick to 'the facts, and nothing but the facts.' All we can say is that one fact follows another. We have no right to assert that one thing actually causes another, since this would be to go beyond the single fact registered by our eyes and ears at a given moment in time. All of which forcibly brings to mind the warning of old Heraclitus: "Eyes and ears are bad witnesses to men if they have souls that understand not their language."[41]

Once again, it is astonishing to note that, of all the marvellous philosophical ideas produced in the last two centuries or so, modern philosophers and scientists choose to take as their starting-point and inspiration the writings of…Hume! His denial of causality has been eagerly seized upon in order to provide some ideological support for certain incorrect philosophical conclusions which Heisenberg and others have attempted to draw from quantum mechanics. We shall speak of that later. In essence, Hume asserts that, when we say 'A' causes 'B', we only mean that these two acts have been seen together many times in the past, and that, therefore, we believe they may be repeated in the future. This, however, is not a certainty but only a belief. It is not necessity, but only probability. Thus, "necessity is something that exists in the mind, not in objects."

First of all, to deny causation leads us to the denial of scientific and rational thought in general. The whole basis and *raison d'être* of science is the attempt to provide a rational explanation for the observed phenomena of nature. From the observation of a large number of facts, we draw general conclusions, which, if they have been sufficiently tested and shown to have a wide application,

---

41 Quoted in J. Burnet, *Early Greek Philosophy*, p. 133.

acquire the status of scientific laws. Naturally, all such laws reflect the state of our knowledge at a given stage of human development, and, consequently, are subsequently overtaken by other theories and hypotheses, which explain things better. In the process, we gradually arrive at a deeper understanding both of nature and ourselves. This process is as limitless as nature itself. Thus, to look for an Absolute Truth, which would explain everything, or, to use a fashionable expression, a Grand Universal Theory (GUT) is about as profitable as looking for the philosopher's stone.

The fact that a particular generalisation may be falsified at a given moment does not entitle us to dispense with generalisations altogether. Nor does it mean that we have to renounce the search for objective truth, taking refuge in a sceptical attitude like that of Hume, which, because of its complete and utter irrelevance to our actual practice, whether in science or in everyday life, is really just a pretentious pose. It is an idiotic posing, like that of those who deny the existence of the material world, but who do not, on that account, refrain from eating and drinking, and who, while firmly maintaining the non-existence of causality, are very careful to avoid untimely physical encounters with ten-ton trucks.

All natural laws are based on causality. The ocean tides are caused by the gravitational pull of the sun and moon. The splitting of the atom causes a nuclear explosion. Deprivation of food and drink over a long period causes death, and being run over by a lorry causes the same result by other means. The existence of causality is as certain as anything can be in this sinful material world of ours. But it is not certain enough for the disciples of Hume. Accepting his line of argument, all future prediction becomes irrational, because there is always the possibility that things will turn out differently. Bertrand Russell, supposedly with a straight face, explains:

> I mean that, taking even our firmest expectations, such as that the sun will rise tomorrow, there is not a shadow of reason for supposing them more likely to be verified than not.[42]

---

42 B. Russell, *History of Western Philosophy*, p. 641.

Further on he says:

> For example: when (to repeat a former illustration) I see an apple, past experience makes me expect that it will taste like an apple, and not like roast beef; but there is no rational justification for this expectation.[43]

Since we cannot know anything, according to Hume, he concludes that "*all our reasonings concerning causes and effects, are derived from nothing but custom; and that belief is more properly an act of the sensitive, than of the cogitative part of our natures.*"[44] In other words, knowledge is abandoned in favour of belief.

It should be borne in mind that the declared intention of all this is to eliminate metaphysics from thought, which will thus be limited to a bare and, hopefully, scientific enumeration of the 'facts'. Some wit once defined metaphysics as "a blind man, in a dark room, looking for a black hat which isn't there." This phrase adequately describes the metaphysical fumbling of those who, by denying causation, immediately open the door to irrationality. With Hume, empirical philosophy comes full circle. As Russell correctly says:

> The ultimate outcome of Hume's investigation of what passes for knowledge is not what we must suppose him to have desired. The sub-title of his book is: 'An attempt to introduce the experimental method of reasoning into moral subjects.' It is evident that he started out with a belief that scientific method yields the truth, the whole truth, and nothing but the truth; he ended, however, with the conviction that belief is never rational, since we know nothing. After setting forth the arguments for scepticism (Book I, part IV, sec. I), he goes on, not to refute the arguments, but to fall back on natural credulity.[45]

One may be tempted to ask what the practical worth of such a philosophy is. On this point no answer is forthcoming from Hume, who comments with the utmost frivolity, tinged with cynicism:

---

43 Ibid., p. 643.
44 D. Hume, *A Treatise of Human Nature*, Vol. 1, p. 179.
45 B. Russell, *History of Western Philosophy*, p. 644.

This sceptical doubt, both with respect to reason and the senses, is a malady, which can never be radically cured, but must return upon us every moment, however we may chase it away, and sometimes may seem entirely free from it ... Carelessness and inattention alone can afford us any remedy. For this reason I rely entirely upon them; and take it for granted, whatever may be the reader's opinion at this present moment, that an hour hence he will be persuaded there is both an external and internal world.[46]

This is not real philosophy but precisely a metaphysical dead end. It tells us nothing about the world and leads nowhere. Just what one would expect from a man who thought that there was no reason to study philosophy except as a pleasant way of passing the time. And indeed, there is certainly no reason to study Hume's philosophy except as a pointless way of wasting time.

On one thing we can agree with Bertrand Russell: the philosophy of Hume "represents the bankruptcy of eighteenth-century reasonableness."[47] Hume's ideas, like Berkeley's, represent a move in the direction of subjective idealism. It is empiricism turned inside out. From the starting point that everything was learnt from experience, we arrive at the conclusion that nothing can be learnt from experience and observation. This is the antithesis of the progressive scientific spirit with which the period opened. Nothing positive can be obtained from such an outlook. We may therefore safely leave those who cannot be sure that the sun will rise tomorrow where we found them – in the dark, where they can find some consolation for their difficulties by looking forward one day to eating an apple which tastes like roast beef.

THE BIRTH OF FRENCH MATERIALISM

From this point on the road to further development of philosophy in Britain was blocked, but not before it had given a powerful impulse to the movement which became known as the Enlightenment in France.

---

46 Ibid., p. 645.
47 Ibid., p. 718.

The difference between English empiricism and French materialism is sometimes ascribed to difference of national temperament. For instance:

> To carry out the empiricism of Locke into its ultimate consequence, into sensualism and materialism – this is the task which has been assumed by the French. Though grown on a soil of English principles, and very soon universally prevalent there, empiricism could not possibly be developed amongst the English into the extreme form which presently declared itself among the French – that is, into the complete destruction of all the foundations of the moral and religious life. This last consequence was not congenial to the national character of the English.[48]

The existence of different national temperaments and traditions undoubtedly played a major role, as Marx and Engels pointed out in *The Holy Family*:

> The difference between *French* and *English* materialism reflects the difference between the two nations. The French imparted to English materialism wit, flesh and blood, and eloquence. They gave it the temperament and grace that it lacked. They *civilised* it.[49]

Nonetheless, to explain great historical movements it is not sufficient to appeal to national characteristics alone. The character of the French and English were also different 100 years before, without producing either Hume or Voltaire, who were products of their own time, or, more accurately, products of a particular concatenation of circumstances – social, economic and cultural. The philosophy of Berkeley and Hume emerged in a period when the bourgeoisie had already triumphed, and was trying to lay revolution to rest. Concordet, Diderot and Voltaire belong to an entirely different period – the period of social and intellectual ferment leading up to the revolution of 1789-93. In an important sense the struggle of the 'philosophers' against religion and orthodoxy was a preparation for the storming of the Bastille.

---

48 A. Schwegler, *History of Philosophy*, p. 184.
49 K. Marx and F. Engels, *The Holy Family*, MECW, Vol. 4, pp. 129-30.

Before the old order was overthrown in fact, it first had to be shown to be redundant in the minds of men and women.

In his excellent essay on Holbach and Helvétius, Plekhanov has this to say about eighteenth-century French philosophy:

> Eighteenth-century materialist philosophy was a revolutionary philosophy. It was merely the ideological expression of the revolutionary bourgeoisie's struggle against the clergy, the nobility, and the absolute monarchy. It goes without saying that, in its struggle against an obsolete system, the bourgeoisie could have no respect for a world-outlook that was inherited from the past and hallowed that despised system. "Different times, different circumstances, a different philosophy", as Diderot so excellently put it in his article on Hobbes in the *Encyclopédie*.[50]

The ideas of Locke had a great impact on the Abbe de Condillac (1715-80). Condillac accepted Locke's teaching that all knowledge comes from the senses, but went even further, claiming that all mental processes, even the will, are only modified sensations. He never actually denied the existence of God, but nevertheless maintained that only matter existed; a very remarkable conclusion for someone who was a priest. Another disciple of Locke, Claude Adrien Helvétius (1715-71), with whom, said Marx, "materialism assumed a really French character."[51] Helvétius was so outspoken that even his fellow materialists were taken aback, and did not dare follow him in his bold conclusions.

Baron Holbach (1723-89), although a German, spent most of his life in France, where he played a major role in the materialist movement. Like Helvétius, he was persecuted by the Church, and his book *Le Système de la Nature* was publicly burnt by order of the Paris Parliament. A determined materialist, Holbach attacked religion and idealism, especially the ideas of Berkeley. Locke already thought it possible that matter could possess the faculty of thinking, and

---

50 G. V. Plekhanov, 'Essays on the History of Materialism', *Selected Philosophical Works*, Vol. 2, p. 45.

51 K. Marx and F. Engels, *The Holy Family*, MECW, Vol. 4, p. 130.

Holbach enthusiastically agreed, but, unlike Locke, was prepared to draw all the conclusions, throwing religion and the Church out of the window:

> If we consult experience, we shall see that it is in religious illusions and opinions that we should seek for the real source of the host of evils that we everywhere see overwhelming mankind. Ignorance of natural causes has led it to create its Gods; deception has made the latter terrible; a baneful concept of them has pursued man without making him any better, made him tremble uselessly, filled his mind with chimeras, opposing the progress of reason, and hindering the search for happiness. These fears have made him the slave of those who deceived him under the pretext of caring for his good; he did evil when he was told that his Gods called for crimes; he lived in adversity because he was made to hear that his Gods had condemned him to misery; he never dared to resist his Gods or to cast off his fetters, because it was drummed into him that stupidity, the renunciation of reason, spiritual torpor and abasement of the soul were the best means of winning eternal bliss.[52]

La Mettrie (1709-51) went still further in recognising that all forms of life, plant and animal (including man), consisted of matter organised in different ways. His main works were the famous *L'Homme Machine* (*Man, a Machine*), and *Le Système d'Epicure* (*The System of Epicurus*). La Mettrie was partly a follower of Descartes, who said that animals were machines in the sense that they could not think. Taking this literally, La Mettrie said that man also must be a machine, then, because there was no qualitative difference between man and the animals. This merely reflects the predominant influence of mechanics on the scientific thinking of the period.

The intention of La Mettrie was to oppose the idea that man was a special creation of God, something entirely set aside from the rest of nature, by the special privilege of an immortal soul. This argument, in effect, was already disposed of by the English materialist and

---

52 Quoted in G. V. Plekhanov, 'Essays on the History of Materialism', *Selected Philosophical Works*, Vol. 2, p. 72.

scientist Joseph Priestley, remembered today mainly as the discoverer of oxygen:

> The power of *cutting*, in a razor, depends upon a certain cohesion, and arrangement of the parts of which it consists. If we suppose this razor to be wholly dissolved in any acid liquor, its power of cutting will certainly be *lost*, or *cease to be*, though no particle of the metal that constituted the razor be annihilated by the process; and its *former shape, and power of cutting*, etc., may be restored to it after the metal has been precipitated. Thus when the body is dissolved by putrefaction, its power of thinking entirely ceases.[53]

La Mettrie considered that thought was one of the properties of matter:

> I believe thinking to be so little incompatible with organised matter that it seems to be a property of the latter in the same way as electricity, the faculty of movement, impenetrability, extent, etc.[54]

From the radical materialism and rationalism of the Enlightenment it was easy to draw revolutionary conclusions, and this was done. Voltaire (1694-1778), although not really a philosopher, played a prominent role in this movement as a writer, historian and pamphleteer. He was arrested twice for his political satires, and had to spend most of his life outside France. Voltaire's greatest contribution was his collaboration with Diderot in the great *Encyclopédie* (1751-80), a massive undertaking which gave a systematic summary of all the scientific knowledge of the time. A galaxy of the greatest French thinkers participated in this unique task: Montesquieu, Rousseau, Voltaire, Holbach, Helvétius, and other progressive and materialist philosophers combined to produce a militant work directed against the basis of the existing social order, its philosophy and morality.

Compared to the writings of the French materialists, the philosophical views of Jean-Jacques Rousseau represent a step

---

53 Quoted ibid., p. 82n.
54 Quoted ibid., p. 333.

backwards. Nevertheless, in the field of social criticism, he produced a number of masterpieces, and Engels specifically singled out for praise his work *Discourse of the Origins of Inequality Among Men*. Still, as he is also not really a philosopher in the strict sense, we will not enter into his ideas more fully here.

In general, these writers were preparing the ground for the bourgeois revolution of 1789-93. Their fierce denunciations are directed against the evils of feudalism and the Church. The ideal for most of them was a constitutional monarchy. Nevertheless, it is easy to see how, later on, people began to draw socialist and communist conclusions from their writings:

> There is no need for any great penetration to see from the teaching of materialism on the original goodness and equal intellectual endowment of men, the omnipotence of experience, habit and education, and the influence of environment on man, the great significance of industry, the justification of enjoyment, etc., how necessarily materialism is connected with communism and socialism. If man draws all his knowledge, sensation, etc., from the world of the senses and the experience gained in it, then what has to be done is to arrange the empirical world in such a way that man experiences and becomes accustomed to what is truly human in it and that he becomes aware of himself as man.

> If correctly understood interest is the principle of all morality, man's private interest must be made to coincide with the interest of humanity. If man is unfree in the materialistic sense, i.e., is free not through the negative power to avoid this or that, but through the positive power to assert his true individuality, crime must not be punished in the individual, but the anti-social sources of crime must be destroyed, and each man must be given social scope for the vital manifestation of his being. If man is shaped by environment, his environment must be made human. If man is shaped by nature, he will develop his true nature only in society, and the power of his nature must be measured not by the power of the separate individual but by the power of society.[55]

---

55 K. Marx and F. Engels, *The Holy Family*, MECW, Vol. 4, pp. 130-1.

8. DESCARTES, SPINOZA AND LEIBNIZ

In one of his comedies, Richard Sheridan, the great Irish dramatist of the eighteenth century, makes one of his characters, an inveterate gambler, say: "I never lose at cards – or, at least, I never feel that I am losing, which is the same thing." Of course, we know that it is not the same thing, just as it is not the same thing to *think* one has a million pounds, compared to actually possessing that amount of money. That thought and being are two different things is self-evident to most people. But what is the precise nature of thought? And what exactly is its relation to being? These were difficult philosophical questions, which exercised some of the most brilliant brains of the period.

Thought itself is immaterial, despite the efforts of some mechanical materialists to prove that it is a material substance, secreted by the brain, as bile is secreted from the liver. Thought is the property of matter organised in a particular way, but it is not itself matter. Once thought begins to develop, it takes on a certain life of its own, which proceeds more rapidly with the development of the division of labour and the growth of civilisation, which coincides with the division of society into classes. Thought itself becomes an object of study. Its material origins are lost sight of. It appears as something mystical, separate and apart from matter, a divine substance, linked to God, an immortal soul, independent of our body, which will not perish when we die.

The question arises, if thought and material reality are completely different, how does it happen that they are so often found to be in agreement? The exact relation between thought and being was the source of all the main philosophical disputes for two-and-a-half years, and was only resolved satisfactorily by dialectical materialism. The rise of a new kind of materialism in the period of the Renaissance was the prior condition for the rebirth of science on a qualitatively higher level. But, as we have seen, it suffered from a one-sidedness, in the form of empiricism, which had extremely negative consequences. Man was seen as a mere observer, and his thoughts as isolated from his life as well as the external world.

The denial of the validity of anything which did not come from immediate observation, the rejection of theory and broad generalisations ("I do not make hypotheses", as Newton said) doomed this kind of materialism to sterility. The main result was that the representatives of this school could not rise above the limitations of the outlook of the science of the day, which was fundamentally mechanical and static in character. This defect applies not only to the English empiricists, but even to the French materialists, despite their far broader outlook and occasionally brilliant forays into dialectics.

To the old materialism, human thought appeared one-sided and was considered in a static, passive and contemplative way. Man was merely observing nature, taking note of 'the facts'. Setting out from a correct idea, this narrow conception of materialism ended up in a blind alley, incapable of further development. In fact, until the revolution effected by Marx and Engels, with their theory of materialist dialectics, no further development of materialism took place. Even Feuerbach really went no further than the French materialists of the eighteenth century.

We therefore come face to face with one of the greatest paradoxes in the history of philosophy – that the really significant advances in thought in the period after Locke were made, not by the materialists, but by the idealists. Unrestricted by the self-imposed limits of empiricism, they arrived at a whole series of brilliant theoretical generalisations, although, setting out from false hypotheses, they invariably had a fantastic character to them. This peculiar phenomenon reached its most extreme expression in the philosophy of Hegel, the most "colossal miscarriage"[1] in history, where all the main elements of dialectics appear in a systematic form, but standing on their head, as Marx put it.

The question of the relation of thought to being was posed by the French philosopher Descartes (1596-1650) in a different way to the English empiricists. Born into a moderately wealthy family, he had studied with the Jesuits. This taste of arid orthodoxy produced in him a lifetime's aversion for dogmatism of any kind, and an impatience with received ideas. His scepticism, in contrast with the jaundiced pessimism of Hume, had a lively and positive character. He began to doubt, not the possibility of knowledge in general, but only the existing opinions put forward as infallible truths. From an early age, his motto was: 'Doubt everything'.

> ...and, as I made it my business in each matter to reflect particularly upon what might fairly be doubted and prove a source of error, I gradually rooted out from my mind all the errors which had hitherto crept into it. Not that in this I imitated the sceptics who doubt only that they may doubt, and seek nothing beyond uncertainty itself; for, on the contrary, my design was singly to find ground of assurance, and cast aside the loose earth and sand, that I might reach the rock or the clay.[2]

> For these reasons, as soon as my age permitted me to pass from under the control of my instructors, I entirely abandoned the study of letters, and resolved no longer to seek any other science than the knowledge of myself, or of the great book of the world.[3]

In order to gain knowledge and expand his horizons he enlisted, first in the Dutch, and then the Bavarian army, at the start of the Thirty

---

1 F. Engels, *Anti-Dühring*, p. 35.
2 R. Descartes, *A Discourse on Method*, p. 23.
3 Ibid., p. 8.

Years War. While still in the army, he wrote a book on philosophy, but, on hearing of the trial of Galileo, he decided to withhold publication for fear of provoking the anger of the Church. Later on, his writings appear liberally sprinkled with references aimed at placating the religious authorities and averting the dreadful charge of godlessness. Even so, like Locke, he felt obliged to move to the Netherlands, the only country in Europe where there existed a relatively free atmosphere to speak and write. Even here he faced the attacks of religious bigots (in this case, Protestants), who accused him of atheism. Only the personal intervention of the Prince of Orange saved him from prosecution. Even then, the authorities of the University of Leiden placed him under a total ban, forbidding the very mention of his name. Eventually, he had to move to Sweden, where he died, partly because of the effects of the climate on his weak constitution.

While in all probability Descartes was a believer, when reading his works, one has the impression of a man all the time looking over his shoulder. In order to get round the Church, Descartes accepts the existence of God, but then says that religion is too lofty a subject to be "submitted to the impotency of our reason." When dealing with natural history, he accepts that God created the world, but then adds, as if hypothetically:

[I]t may be believed, without discredit to the miracle of creation, that, in this way alone, things purely material might, in course of time, have become such as we observe them at present; and their nature is much more easily conceived when they are beheld coming in this manner gradually into existence, than when they are only considered as produced at once in a finished and perfect state.[4]

To such subterfuges did the greatest French philosopher have to resort in order to publish his ideas.

DESCARTES AND SCIENCE

Descartes is one of the main protagonists in the struggle between rationalism and empiricism, between the method of deduction as

4 Ibid., p. 36.

opposed to that of induction. The Englishman Roger Bacon was the father of empiricism and the method of inductive reasoning, which attempts to derive theories from observed facts alone. In Bacon's case, the obsession with observation proved fatal; he died of bronchitis as a result of an early experiment in refrigeration, involving stuffing a chicken with snow.

The rationalists approached science from a diametrically opposite standpoint, and Descartes was more concerned with general principles than the detailed work of observation. Taking Euclid's geometry as his model, he attempted to develop consistent and coherent theorems derived from pure reason, without recourse to the unreliable evidence of the senses. Rationalism became the main tradition in France, whereas Bacon's empiricism triumphed on the other side of the Channel. Both men, in different ways, advanced the cause of science, and both made important discoveries.

Descartes' contribution to science was outstanding, especially in the field of mathematics, where he may be considered one of the founders of analytical geometry. His great contribution was the invention of 'coordinate geometry', which determines the position of a point in a plane by its distance from two fixed lines. In physics, he was a materialist, as Marx and Engels point out:

> *Descartes* in his *physics* endowed *matter* with self-creative power and conceived mechanical motion as the manifestation of its life. He completely separated his *physics* from his *metaphysics*. *Within* his physics, *matter* is the sole *substance*, the sole basis of being and of knowledge.[5]

Yet Descartes was unable to resolve the fundamental question of the relation between thought and being. In his celebrated *Discourse on Method*, he searches for a truth which everyone can accept as unquestionable. He comes up with the famous phrase: "*I think, therefore I am.*"[6] This is the cornerstone of his philosophy. And yet, it does not follow. At most he could assert, "I think, therefore

---

5   K. Marx and F. Engels, *The Holy Family*, MECW, Vol. 4, p. 125.
6   R. Descartes, *A Discourse on Method*, p. 167.

thought exists." What is this 'I'? Evidently, a human nervous system, a brain, a body, and so on. Gassendi, the French materialist, objected that existence may equally well be inferred from every other human function. Idealists replied that none of these functions can be perceived without thought. But it is also necessary to say what thought is.

Thought, from a consistent materialist position, is matter that thinks. It does not and cannot exist by itself, separate from matter. On this decisive question, Descartes adopted an unsatisfactory and inconsistent position, which ended up in all kinds of contradictions. The fundamental difference between thought and matter, he said, was that matter had extension, whereas thought, spirit and soul had none. This leads us straight to a dualist position. According to Descartes, there is nothing in common between thought and matter. They are not only different, but diametrically opposed. The union of soul and body is, therefore, an entirely mechanical one. The soul inhabits the body as an alien thing, a mechanical and entirely artificial relationship. Without the soul, the body is like a lifeless machine or automaton. Even the best-constructed robot cannot acquire a human consciousness, even if it is programmed to speak (this was written in 1637, but the subject matter is very modern).

For example, a machine may be taught to speak and even express 'feelings':

[B]ut not that it should arrange them variously so as appositely to reply to what is said in its presence, as men of the lowest grade of intellect can do. The second test is, that although such machines might execute many things with equal or perhaps greater perfection than any of us, they would, without doubt, fail in certain others from which it could be discovered that they did not act from knowledge, but solely from the disposition of their organs: for while reason is an universal instrument that is alike available on every occasion, these organs, on the contrary, need a particular arrangement for each particular action; whence it must be morally impossible that there should exist in any machine a diversity of organs sufficient to enable it to act in all the occurrences of like, in the way in which our reason enables us to act.[7]

The lower animals are classed as "automata" for the same reason. It is worth quoting this passage at some length because it shows a markedly materialist line of argument, and certainly is vastly superior to the mystical nonsense talked by some scientists today:

> For it is highly deserving of remark, that there are no men so dull and stupid, not even idiots, as to be incapable of joining together different words, and thereby constructing a declaration by which to make their thoughts understood; and that on the other hand, there is no other animal, however perfect or happily circumstanced, which can do the like. Nor does this inability arise from want of organs: for we observe that magpies and parrots can utter words like ourselves, and are yet unable to speak as we do, that is, so as to show that they understand what they say: in place of which men born deaf and dumb, and thus not less, but rather more than the brutes, destitute of the organs which others use in speaking, are in the habit of spontaneously inventing certain signs by which they discover their thoughts to those who, being usually in their company, have leisure to learn their language.

> And this proves not only that the brutes have less reason than man, but that they have none at all: for we see that very little is required to enable a person to speak; and since a certain inequality of capacity is observable among animals of the same species, as well as among men, and since some are more capable of being instructed than others, it is incredible that the most perfect ape or parrot of its species, should not in this be equal to the most stupid infant of its kind, or at least to one that was crack-brained, unless the soul of brutes were of a nature wholly different from ours.[8]

Descartes' idealism led him into the trap of dividing mind from body, and regarding the body as a mere automaton, inside which the soul dwelt. This became a source of considerable confusion, and had a harmful effect on the scientific understanding of the real nature of

7   Ibid., pp. 44-5.
8   Ibid., pp. 45-6.

the mind and its relation to the body, the brain and the nervous system.

Despite the generally idealist thrust of the *Discourse*, Descartes' materialist physics and biology keep on intruding. He cannot, for example, conceal his enthusiasm for Harvey's discovery of the circulation of the blood, to which he dedicates no fewer than six pages. Yet when he comes to the vexed question of the relationship of mind and body, he takes refuge in unscientific and metaphysical concepts. He locates the soul in the so-called 'pineal gland' in the centre of the brain, purely because all the other parts of the brain are double, and therefore disqualified from acting as the organ of the soul, which would thereby presumably end up with a bad case of double-vision!

The problem with all this is that, if thought and matter are considered as completely separate, by what means are they united and kept together? The only option open to Descartes was to bring in an external agent – divine intervention. Even so, it is impossible to see how they can have any effect upon each other. By what mechanism could they interpenetrate? For example, the mind can will that I lift my arm, but how can it actually lift it? Descartes' disciple, Geulinx, answered with admirable frankness that it could not, that the fact that my arm rises at the same time as I will it to was mere coincidence. This brings out the contradiction of the Cartesian (referring to Descartes) philosophy, the unresolved dualism, which was its Achilles' heel.

Despite its weaknesses, Descartes' philosophy had a notably progressive side. Its advances in science stimulated the growth of natural science in France. Philosophically, Descartes' idealism was overthrown by the prevailing materialist trend of the Enlightenment, though he influenced people like La Mettrie. But outside France his ideas were the starting point for two of the greatest philosophers of all, Spinoza and Leibniz.

SPINOZA

Benedictus (Baruch) Spinoza was born in Amsterdam in 1632, the son of a Jewish merchant, one of many who had fled from Portugal and Spain to escape from religious persecution. From his youth,

Spinoza showed himself to be a fearless searcher after truth, prepared to defend his views regardless of the consequences to himself. It was intended that he should carry on the family business, but in 1656, despite having been a diligent student of the Bible and the Talmud, he fell foul of the orthodox rabbis. He was offered 1,000 florins a year to keep silent, but refused and was cursed and expelled from the Jewish community for his "wrong opinions" and "horrible heresies". Fearing an attempt on his life, he had to flee from Amsterdam. He took up residence at Rijnsburg near Leiden, where he earned his living polishing lenses, while dedicating his spare time to his philosophical writings.

As an outcast himself, Spinoza became friendly with the members of some of the smaller Protestant sects, related to the Anabaptists, who were themselves the victims of persecution and who were open to discussions of new ideas. At this time, the ideas of Descartes were the subject of a raging controversy in the Netherlands. In 1656, university professors were required to take an oath that they would not propound Cartesian ideas which caused offence. To the little circle around Spinoza, Descartes was seen as a source of inspiration, as a brave soul who refused to base his opinions on mere tradition, and affirmed that all we know is known by the 'natural light' of reason. Descartes was an inspiration to Spinoza, but the latter had too keen an intellect to accept him uncritically.

This was an age of great discoveries. Science was beginning to stretch its wings, and the old Aristotelian world view was being replaced by the new scientific-mechanistic view of nature. Galileo himself had written that he believed that the book of nature was written in the language of mathematics. Spinoza's whole outlook was dominated by a passionate interest in nature and science. He conducted a correspondence with the English chemist Robert Boyle, discussed comets with Henry Oldenburg, the secretary of the Royal Society, and commented on Descartes' laws of motion and the theories of Huygens.

The Republic of the Netherlands was the freest country in Europe at this time. The Dutch bourgeoisie had succeeded in throwing off the yoke of Spanish domination by a revolutionary struggle in which it leaned for support on the lower middle class and semi-proletarian masses. In 1579, the Northern provinces of the Protestant Netherlands came together to form the Union of Utrecht, out of which the Dutch Republic emerged. Article Three of the Union proclaimed religious toleration as a basic principle. However, from the outset this was opposed by the powerful sect of 'strict' or 'precise' Calvinists, who wanted only one official Church in Holland – their own.

At the Synod of Dordrecht (1618-19) they succeeded in getting Calvinism recognised as the official religion. But the liberal Johan de Witt, who was the leader of the Netherlands from 1653 to 1672, stood firm against religious intolerance. Spinoza did not stand aloof from the political struggle. He set aside work on his *Ethics* in order to publish a book in defence of the freedom of speech and thought, the *Treatise on Theology and Politics*, which appeared in 1670. This earned him the bitter enmity of the strict Calvinists, who were scandalised by his attempts to show that the Bible is not to be seen as containing philosophical or scientific truths.

In July 1670, the Synod declared the *Treatise* an "evil and blasphemous book." An anonymous pamphlet attacking de Witt described the book as "spawned in Hell by a renegade Jew and the Devil", and that it was published "with the knowledge of Mr. Johan de Witt".[9] In 1672, a French army invaded the Dutch Republic and de Witt was murdered by a mob in The Hague. For opportunist reasons, the stadtholder, William III of Orange, sided with the Calvinists. Two years later the *Treatise* was banned. For the rest of his short life, Spinoza was forced to keep his head down. Tragically, his masterpiece, the *Ethics*, was never published in his lifetime, for fear of the reaction of the Church. It only appeared in 1677, the year the great man died of consumption.

Spinoza was one of those true geniuses who carried out a real revolution in philosophy. Taking as his starting point the philosophy of Descartes, he completely transformed it, and in so doing, laid the basis for a genuinely scientific approach to nature. "It is therefore

---

9 R. Scruton, *Spinoza*, p. 14.

worthy of note", wrote Hegel, "that thought must begin by placing itself at the standpoint of Spinozism; to be a follower of Spinoza is the essential commencement of all Philosophy."[10] Not only Hegel, but Goethe, Schiller, Marx, and the young Schelling were much influenced by Spinoza. When Einstein was engaged in a philosophical dispute with Niels Bohr over the fundamental problems of quantum mechanics, he wrote that he would rather have 'old Spinoza' as a referee instead of Bertrand Russell or Rudolf Carnap.

Maybe that is why, with his customary arrogance, Bertrand Russell, in his *History of Western Philosophy*, writes that the whole of Spinoza's "metaphysic" is:

> [I]ncompatible with modern logic and with scientific method. *Facts* have to be discovered by observation, not by reasoning; when we successfully infer the future, we do so by means of principles which are not logically necessary, but are suggested by empirical data. And the concept of substance, upon which Spinoza relies, is one which neither science nor philosophy can nowadays accept.[11]

The whole point is that Spinoza, by not restricting himself to the narrow confines of empirical philosophy, was able to transcend the limits of the mechanistic science of the day. While Berkeley and Hume led philosophy into a blind alley (and they would have done the same to science, had it paid any attention to them, which fortunately it did not), Spinoza brilliantly showed the way forward. In spite of the ridiculous pretensions of Russell and his fellow logical positivists, who – without the slightest basis – put themselves forward as the supreme guardians of an alleged 'scientific method' arbitrarily defined by themselves, science proceeds in an entirely different way to that indicated in these lines.

In particular, the role of great hypotheses in pointing scientific research in the right direction has been fundamental. And, by definition, a hypothesis can only be based on a limited number of

---

10 G. W. F. Hegel, *Lectures on the History of Philosophy*, Vol. 3, p. 257.
11 B. Russell, *History of Western Philosophy*, p. 560.

'facts'. It must involve reasoning, and also courage and imagination. How much time and effort would have been saved if scientists had paid attention to Kant's nebular theory of the origin of the solar system, for example? On the other hand, how much time is now being wasted in the search for 'cold, dark matter', which is based upon no 'observed facts' whatsoever, and which is intended to support a cosmological hypothesis more fantastic than anything Spinoza ever thought of.

> It is to the highest credit of the philosophy of the time that it did not let itself be led astray by the restricted state of contemporary natural knowledge, and that – from Spinoza down to the great French materialists – it insisted on explaining the world from the world itself and left the justification in detail to the natural science of the future.[12]

Spinoza, by the strength of reason, and with the very limited scientific results available to him, arrived at one of the greatest hypotheses of all time. Breaking with Descartes, with his notion of a body without a soul and a soul without a body, he advanced the idea that body and mind are two attributes of one and the same thing. The universe is not composed of mind and matter, as alleged by Descartes' dualism. There is only a single Substance, which contains within itself all the attributes of thought and being. It is infinite and eternal, and possesses all the potential to give rise to the abundance of phenomena we see in the universe.

Spinoza gives this Substance the name of "God". But in reality, to make God equal to nature is to abolish God – a fact which was not lost on Spinoza's enemies when they accused him of atheism. In Spinoza's universe, infinite and eternal, and therefore uncreated and unbounded by heaven or hell, there is no room for a separate deity. Indeed, there is no room for anything whatsoever except Substance, which is just another way of saying nature.

Thus, in a strange way, the philosophy of Spinoza, despite its idealist appearance, is the real point of departure for materialism in the dialectical, that is, non-mechanical sense of the word. All that is

---

12 F. Engels, *Dialectics of Nature*, pp. 25-26.

necessary is to substitute the word 'matter' for 'God' and we get a perfectly consistent materialist position. As Marx wrote in a letter to Lassalle on 31 May 1858:

> Even in the case of philosophers who give systematic form to their work, Spinoza for instance, the true inner structure of the system is quite unlike the form in which it was consciously presented by him.[13]

The great admiration of Marx and Engels for Spinoza was revealed by Plekhanov, who recalls a conversation he had with Engels, by then an old man, in 1889:

> "So do you think", I asked, "old Spinoza was right when he said that *thought* and *extent* are nothing but two attributes of one and the same substance?" "Of course," Engels replied, "old Spinoza was quite right."[14]

The existence of the material universe is taken as an axiom. The model for Spinoza was geometry, which sets out with axioms: 'self-evident' assertions which require no proof. Yet the same people who are prepared to accept on trust the axioms of Euclid (which, incidentally, far from being self-evident truths, are open to serious objections) nevertheless display extreme reluctance to admit the reality of the material world, declaring this to be beyond our knowledge to assert. However, this same material world is the starting point of all our experience and knowledge. "God or a substance consisting of attributes, each of which expresses eternal and infinite essence, necessarily exists", proclaims Spinoza.[15] Moreover, matter can neither be created nor destroyed, only changed:

> Matter is the same everywhere, and its parts are not distinguished one from the other except in so far as we conceive matter to be affected in various ways, whence its parts are distinguished one from the other modally but not in reality. E.g., we can conceive water, in so far as it is water, to be

13 K. Marx, 'Letter to Ferdinand Lassalle, 31 May 1858', MECW, Vol. 40, p. 316.

14 G. V. Plekhanov, *Selected Philosophical Works*, Vol. 2, p. 339.

15 B. Spinoza, *Ethics*, p. 9.

divided and its parts separated one from the other: but not in so far as it is corporeal substance, for then it is neither separated nor divided. Again, water, in so far as it is water, can be made and destroyed, but in so far as it is substance it can neither be made nor destroyed.[16]

God thus has no existence separate and apart from the material world, which has not been created because it has always existed. He is 'free' – to obey the laws of nature, and so on. In other words, 'God' is only nature. This pantheism of Spinoza is really a thinly-disguised materialism. Despite its peculiar form (probably an unsuccessful attempt to ward off accusations of atheism), this is head and shoulders above the mechanistic outlook of contemporary scientists. Instead of the mechanical conception of matter being moved by an external force, here we have matter which moves according to its own inherent laws, it is 'its own cause'.

Thought can have no existence apart from Substance (matter). It is an attribute of matter organised in a certain way, "consequently thinking substance and extended substance are one and the same substance, which is comprehended through this and now through that attribute." In other words, thought and matter are "one and the same thing, but expressed in two ways".[17] This is a real breakthrough. In essence, we have here a correct assessment of the relation between thought and being; not, as in Descartes, a radical separation of the two, but their dialectical unity. Not thought opposed to matter, but matter that thinks. Here, Spinoza comes close to an overtly materialist position: "The mind", he says, "has no knowledge of itself save in so far as it perceives the ideas of the modifications of the body".[18] And again: "For the human body ... is affected by external bodies in many ways and disposed to affect external bodies in many ways. But the human mind ... must perceive all things which happen in the human body."[19]

---

16 Ibid., p. 16.
17 Ibid., p. 42.
18 Ibid., p. 59.
19 Ibid., p. 53.

This presentation was far superior to the crude conception of mechanical materialism which saw thought as a material substance secreted from the brain, like sweat from the sweat glands. Spinoza, following Descartes, says that thought differs from matter in that it has no extension. It is not a material thing, but the very function of the brain itself, its essential property. Thought is not merely an abstract contemplative activity, but the way in which thinking beings react to their environment at the conscious level. It is not possible to separate thought from all other human activities. Thought, as Spinoza understood, is one of the attributes of highly organised matter, nature that thinks, and not something opposed to nature:

> If this were so, it must seem most odd that consciousness and nature, thinking and being, the laws of thought and the laws of nature, should so closely correspond. But if we then ask what thought and consciousness are and whence they come, we find that they are products of the human brain and that man himself is a product of nature, who has developed in and along with his environment; whence it is self-evident that the products of the human brain, which in the last analysis are also products of nature, do not contradict the rest of nature's interconnections but correspond to them.[20]

Here thought and matter are different but not mechanically opposed, mutually exclusive opposites. Spinoza understood that matter ("Substance") contains within itself all that is necessary to give rise to thought. Given the right concatenation of factors, organic matter arises out of inorganic matter. And even the most primitive life forms can evolve to produce thinking beings. There is not, as Descartes thought, an absolute dividing line separating organic from inorganic matter, or man from the animals. In all these ideas, Spinoza showed himself to be far in advance of his times.

Spinoza believed that mastery over nature and the improvement of man were the main purpose of the pursuit of knowledge. In the

---

20 F. Engels, *Anti-Dühring*, p. 44.

field of ethics and morality too, he defends very advanced ideas. He correctly understood that morality was relative:

> As for the terms good and bad, they also mean nothing positive in things considered in themselves, nor are they anything else than modes of thought, or notions, which we form from the comparison of things with each other. For one and the same thing can at the same time be good, bad, and indifferent. E.g., music is good to the melancholy, bad to those who mourn, and neither good nor bad to the deaf. Although this be so, these words must be retained by us.[21]

He rejected the idea of free will, and instead advocated a thoroughly determinist position. There are no 'free' actions, in the sense that all actions are caused by something, whether we are aware of it or not. Spinoza was the first one to give a dialectical appraisal of the relation between freedom and necessity, when he pointed out that real freedom consists in the understanding of necessity. True freedom does not consist in denying the existence of the objective laws of nature, but in striving to understand them in order to gain mastery over them.

He opposed prejudice and superstition wherever he found them and, long before the French Enlightenment, decided to summon all prejudices to the "court of reason". For those who take refuge in the will of God, "the asylum of ignorance", he has nothing but contempt. In the following passage, he was undoubtedly speaking from painful personal experience:

> Thus again, when they see the human body they are amazed, and as they know not the cause of so much art, they conclude that it was made not by mechanical art, but divine or supernatural art, and constructed in such a manner that one part does not injure another. And hence it comes about that someone who wishes to seek out the true causes of miracles, and to understand the things of nature like a man of learning, and not stare at them in amazement like a fool, is widely deemed heretical and impious,

---

21 B. Spinoza, *Ethics*, p. 141.

and proclaimed such by those whom the mob adore as the interpreters of nature and the Gods.[22]

The basic idea of Spinoza's philosophy is monism – the idea that all things are one. All the myriad forms of existence, the shapes, colours, forms of movement, are only different expressions of the same Substance, which can assume an infinite variety of forms. These accidental, temporary phenomena he calls 'modi' (singular, modus). They are the forms which matter assumes, continually coming into being and disappearing, like the restless waves on a mighty ocean. But these transitory forms of being can have no separate existence independent from Substance, which is unbounded and eternal, and which, operating according to its own laws, must give rise to an unlimited number of particular, finite forms. These forms, in turn, are not free agents, but subject to natural laws which determine the existence of all things. Through the agency of reason, it is possible to understand these laws and thereby achieve freedom consciously to determine our actions and comprehend our true place in the universe.

This imposing philosophy is in complete accord with the discoveries of modern science. All the endless forms of organic and inorganic matter we see in the universe can be reduced to the same substance – molecules, atoms and subatomic particles. According to modern physics, a small number of quarks are put together in different ways to make hundreds of hadrons, which combine to form the nuclei of a hundred or so chemical elements. Together with leptons, they then make up atoms, which then combine to make molecules, out of which everything else is built. The same material substance therefore underlies all the forms of being in the universe. Of course, this picture is much more complicated than the one painted by Spinoza, who had only the scantiest of information to go on. A long period of scientific advance was necessary before his picture of the universe could be properly corroborated. But his hypothesis that everything comes from a common substance has been substantially vindicated.

---

22 Ibid., pp. 34-5.

The principle of monism can be interpreted either in a materialist or an idealist sense. Plato and Hegel were also monists, because they considered that the universe and everything in it was ultimately an expression of the Absolute Idea. Marx and Engels were materialist monists. Spinoza's case is peculiar. While formally he has to be considered an idealist, there is an element of ambiguity about his Substance which is certainly open to a materialist interpretation. This was quickly grasped by his contemporaries, Jews and Christians alike, who accused him of atheism. All kinds of heinous crimes and immoral ideas were attributed to him. For a long time after his death his name could hardly be mentioned in polite society. The German writer Lessing said that, in his day, a century later, people treated Spinoza 'like a dead dog'.

Despite all the calumnies, Spinoza's philosophy stands as a monument to the great and noble spirit that conceived it. His philosophy, which came very close to materialism, inevitably led him to draw the most advanced social conclusions, in contrast to the reactionary misanthropy of Hume and Berkeley. This comes across clearly in the pages of his masterpiece, *Ethics*:

> Man is a God to man. Yet it rarely happens that men live under the guidance of reason, but among them things are in such a state that they are usually envious of or a nuisance to each other. But nevertheless they are scarcely able to lead a solitary life, so that to many the definition of man as a social animal has been very attractive; and in truth things are so ordered that from the common society of men far more conveniences arise than the contrary. Let satirists therefore laugh to their hearts' content at human affairs, let theologians revile them, and let the melancholy praise as much as they can the rude and uncultivated life: let them despise men and admire the brutes – despite all this, men will find by experience that they can procure with mutual aid far more easily what they need, and avoid far more easily the perils which beset them on all sides, by united forces: to say nothing of how much better it is, and more worthy of our knowledge, to regard the deeds of men rather than those of the brutes.[23]

---

23 Ibid., pp. 161-2.

LEIBNIZ

> To see a World in a Grain of Sand,
> And a heaven in a Wild Flower,
> Hold Infinity in the palm of your hand,
> And Eternity in an hour.
> (William Blake, *Auguries of Innocence*.)

The monist views of Spinoza were challenged by his great contemporary, Gottfried Leibniz (1646-1716), yet another encyclopaedic mind. Leibniz was a mathematician, physicist, geologist, biologist, diplomat, librarian, and historian. He invented infinitesimal calculus, although Newton claimed to have done this earlier. In physics, he anticipated the law of preservation of energy. He is also considered to have been the founder of mathematical logic, although he did not publish his work on this subject.

An objective idealist, Leibniz nevertheless developed dialectics. In his *Philosophical Notebooks*, Lenin wrote that "Leibniz through theology arrived at the principle of the inseparable (and universal, absolute) connection of matter and motion."[24] Marx also expressed his admiration for Leibniz.[25] The basis of Spinoza's philosophy was the single universal substance. Leibniz also starts from the notion of substance but defines it differently. He sees it like living activity, internal motion, and energy. The fundamental difference with Spinoza is that, where he stressed the singleness of being, Leibniz lays all the emphasis on the multiplicity of the universe. For him, the entire universe is composed of an infinite number of substances which he calls 'monads'. The monads of Leibniz are similar to the idea of atoms. Whilst in Paris, Leibniz met and was influenced by the materialist Gassendi, who had revived interest in the atomistic philosophy of Democritus and Epicurus. For Leibniz, everything is made of monads, including ourselves. However, there

---

24 V. I. Lenin, 'Conspectus of Feuerbach's Exposition, *Analysis and Critique of the Philosophy of Leibniz*', LCW, Vol. 38, p. 379.

25 See 'Letter to Engels, 10 May 1870'.

are some peculiarities in this theory. To begin with, no monad is like another. Each is its own special world, impenetrable from without. Leibniz thought that no two things in the world were the same. Each monad (and there are an infinite number of them) is also a microcosm, which reflects the universe at large. It is a kind of embryo of the totality of things. Thus, the particular contains the universal.

The entire universe is only the sum total of all the monads. Everything is an aggregate of monads, even the human soul. Moreover, these monads are not dead matter, but centres of living activity, in constant movement and mutation. In many respects, this picture is a striking anticipation of the modern atomistic view of the universe. Leibniz most likely got his idea from observations through a microscope. Thus, he compares bodies to a fish pond in which the smallest drop of water is full of teeming life, although it cannot be said that the pond itself lives. Feuerbach compared Spinoza's philosophy to a telescope which makes objects visible to the human eye that are otherwise invisible because of their remoteness, whereas that of Leibniz is like a microscope which makes objects visible that are unnoticeable because of their minuteness and fineness. A monad is like an individual cell which contains all the information required to construct an entire body. In the same way, in *Capital*, Marx derives all the contradictions of capitalism from a single cell, the commodity.

Despite its idealistic form, there is here the germ of a profound idea and a dialectical concept of nature, based on movement, infinite connections, change and evolution from a lower to a higher stage. For example, he distinguishes between different levels of monads, from the lowest rank, analogous to the stage of inorganic nature, in which the life of the monads expresses itself only in the form of motion. There are higher stages, analogous to plants, animals, which culminate in the human soul. "Here is dialectics of a kind", commented Lenin, "and very profound, *despite* the idealism and clericalism."[26] What role does

---

26 V. I. Lenin, 'Conspectus of Feuerbach's *Exposition, Analysis and Critique of the Philosophy of Leibniz*', LCW, Vol. 38, p. 383.

God have in relation to the monads? Not very much, it seems. Leibniz makes God the "sufficient reason" of all the monads. Feuerbach considered him to be only half a Christian, atheist, or a cross between a Christian and a naturalist. As Schwegler remarks: "It was a hard matter for Leibniz to bring – without abandoning the presuppositions of both – his monadology and his Theism into unison."[27]

Leibniz's theory of knowledge is in opposition to the empiricism of Locke from the standpoint of objective idealism. Leibniz may be considered the father of German idealism. He is best known for his famous doctrine of "the best of all possible worlds", according to which it is impossible that there should be any more perfect a world than that which exists. This must have been a comforting thought for the wealthy aristocrats for whom Leibniz worked. But from a philosophical standpoint, their satisfaction would not really be justified. For Leibniz, there are an infinite number of possible worlds, but only one has been chosen by God. In other words, the world we live in at this particular moment is the "best" one because it is the only one. However, the same Leibniz writes in his Monadology number twenty-two: "Every present state of a simple substance is the natural consequence of its preceding state, in such a way that its present is big with its future."[28]

Leibniz's dialectical philosophy, which echoes Heraclitus and anticipates Hegel, was far from defending the idea of an unchanging status quo, "because all bodies are in a state of perpetual flux like rivers, and the parts are continually entering in or passing out."[29]

In the works of Descartes, Spinoza and Leibniz, we see brilliant conclusions reached on the basis of the developments in science. These achievements, however, were held back by the fact that science at this stage remained subordinate to traditional philosophy. Feuerbach grasped this contradiction in the works of these men when he said

---

27 A. Schwegler, *History of Philosophy*, p. 198.
28 G. W. F. Leibniz, *Discourse on Metaphysics: Correspondence with Arnauld, and Monadology*, p. 256.
29 Ibid., p. 267.

that: "Leibniz and Descartes are idealists only in a general sense, but when it comes to particular things they are materialists."[30] For science to advance – and with it philosophy – it had to release itself from what was known as Natural Philosophy and Metaphysics, so that thought could go from the realm of speculation to the realm of practice. Teodor Oizerman commented:

> The rationalistic systems of Descartes, Leibniz, and Spinoza, for all their theological assumptions, were related to the positive sciences. Seventeenth-century metaphysics "made discoveries in mathematics, physics and other exact sciences which seemed to come within its scope. This semblance was done away with as early as the beginning of the eighteenth century. The positive sciences broke away from metaphysics and marked out their independent fields. The whole wealth of metaphysics now consisted only of beings of thought and heavenly things, at the very time when real beings and earthly things began to be the centre of all interest."

> So, the connection between the metaphysical (mainly idealistic) systems and the positive sciences did not at all spring from the nature of idealism but from the fact that the positive sciences had yet to separate from philosophy. But when this process was in the main complete, it transpired that the metaphysical systems, with their claim to knowledge of some super-physical reality and the establishment of a closed system of perfect knowledge, ran into conflict with the actual development of scientific knowledge, which increasingly concentrated on vital, terrestrial problems. The metaphysical systems were discredited and were vanquished by French eighteenth-century materialism.[31]

---

30 L. Feuerbach, *Principles of the Philosophy of the Future*, *The Fiery Brook*, Verso, 2012, p. 185.

31 T. Oizerman, *The Making of the Marxist Philosophy*, pp. 293-4.

9. THE DEAD END
OF KANTIANISM

The German philosopher Immanuel Kant (1724-1804) marks the beginning of a turning point in philosophy. He was born in Königsberg, Prussia, where he spent most of his life. A liberal in politics, he was influenced by the ideas of Rousseau, and sympathised with the French Revolution, at least in the early stages. The other great influence on his thought was science, which at the time was making spectacular advances. Kant himself made an important contribution to science, particularly in his *General Natural History and Theory of the Heavens* (1755), where he put forward the nebular hypothesis for the formation of the solar system, a theory later developed by Laplace, and now generally accepted.

When Kant began his intellectual activity, German philosophy had reached a dead end. The brilliant flashes of inspiration that characterised the thought of Leibniz did not really add up to a coherent school of philosophy. After his death, Christian Wolff tried to turn it into a system, but succeeded only in vulgarising it. In Wolff's hands, Leibniz's profound intuitions about the world became transformed into the most arid formalism. Kant was repelled by this metaphysical speculation, which attempted to solve the mysteries of the universe, not by looking at nature, but by endless abstract reasoning. Meanwhile, in the real world, a new spirit was stirring. The natural sciences were developing quickly, especially in Britain and France. Even in sleepy Germany, where the Thirty Years' War had paralysed progress, there was a renewal of culture in the *Aufklärung*, the German equivalent of the French Enlightenment. Kant was the true child of his times.

His most important work, the *Critique of Pure Reason*, was first published in 1781 when he was fifty-seven years old, although it was subsequently revised in the second edition in 1787. In this work, Kant attempts to resolve the problem of knowledge, which had caused a crisis in philosophy, the clearest expression of which was the subjective idealism of Berkeley and the scepticism of Hume. Kant's declared aim was to finish off the old metaphysics, which:

> [A]ppears to furnish an arena specially adapted for the display of skill or the exercise of strength in mock-contests – a field in which no combatant ever yet succeeded in gaining an inch of ground, in which, at least, no victory was ever yet crowned with permanent possession.[1]

The great successes of natural science, especially in Britain, meant that knowledge could not be confined to mere abstract speculation, which sucked its theories out of its thumb. Determined to break with this 'metaphysics', Kant decided that it was necessary to go back to fundamentals. He decided to tackle the thorny question of how true knowledge was to be obtained. On the one hand, the striking advances of natural science pointed the way forward. All those questions about the nature of the universe and man's place in it could not be solved by abstract speculation, but only by observation and experiment.

The task of the sciences is not merely to collect a heap of facts. It is to obtain a rational insight into the workings of nature. For this, mere generalisations are insufficient. Thinking must not be passive but active, as Kant understood. It is not an accident that the title of his greatest work refers to Reason (*Vernunft*), which he clearly

1   I. Kant, *Critique of Pure Reason*, J. M. Dent & Sons Ltd, 1959, p. 11.

distinguishes from mere Understanding (*Verstand*). But are the forms of reason adequate to comprehend reality? Kant subjected these logical forms to a searching criticism, and showed that the traditional logic falls into a state of contradiction (antimony). Kant showed that it was possible to derive diametrically opposite conclusions from the same propositions. But in Kant, this contradiction remains unresolved.

KANT'S THEORY OF KNOWLEDGE

The relation of subject-object was a central question in philosophy for centuries. To simplify things, the mechanical materialists laid all the stress on the object (material reality, nature), leaving no role for the thinking subject, which was portrayed as a passive receptacle, whereas the idealists laid all the stress on the subject (mind, the Idea, etc.).

Kant asks what we can know, and how we can know it. This is one of the central questions of philosophy – the theory of knowledge or cognition ('epistemology'). We derive the greater part of our knowledge from observing the real world. From an early age, we see things, we listen, we touch, and so on. Gradually, we build up a picture of the world in which we live. This kind of knowledge is the knowledge of sense-perception. For empiricists like Locke, there is no other kind. Here Kant disagrees. In getting to know the world, the mind is not merely an empty vessel, which can be filled with any content (Locke described it as a *tabula rasa* – a blank slate). For Kant, the act of cognition is not passive, but active. We do not simply make a list of the things we see, but consciously select, order and interpret them. For this, the mind has its own method and rules. There are forms of thought which we apply, consciously or unconsciously, when we attempt to understand the information provided by our senses ('sense data').

Kant argues that there are two kinds of knowledge. While most knowledge is derived from experience, part of our knowledge is *a priori* (from the Latin meaning "from the beginning"), and not derived from experience. In Kant's opinion, we can only know what is given to us in sense experience. However, the things-in-themselves, which cause our sensations, cannot be known. Here, Kant is skating on thin ice. Although he denied it, these views seem to be similar to the subjective idealism of Hume and Berkeley. Kant changed some of his formulations in the second edition to try to avoid this conclusion. In the first edition, some of his formulations could be read so as to imply that the thinking subject might be the same thing as the object which it perceives. Later, he changed this, insisting that things outside ourselves certainly exist, but they manifest themselves to us only in appearance, not as they are in themselves.

According to Kant, there are some ideas which are not derived from sense-perception. This shows the difference between the philosophy of Kant and that of Locke, who held that all knowledge whatsoever came from the senses. By contrast, Kant claimed that some knowledge was inborn, for instance, the knowledge of space and time. If we make abstractions from all physical aspects of phenomena, he says, we are left with just two things – time and space. Now, time and space, together with motion, are the most general and fundamental properties of matter. The only way that it is possible to understand them is in relation to material things. But Kant was an idealist. He insisted that the notions of time and space were inborn. They did not come from experience, but were what he called *a priori*.

To support his idea, Kant uses a very peculiar mode of reasoning. He maintains that, whereas it is impossible to think of objects without time, it is quite possible to think of time without objects; the same in relation to space. In point of fact, space and time are inseparable from matter, and it is impossible to conceive of them as apart from matter.

Kant states that it is possible to imagine space with nothing in it, but impossible to imagine no space. But this is not so. Space without matter is just as much an empty abstraction as matter without space. In point of fact, time, space and motion are the mode of existence of matter, and can be conceived of in no other way. Kant's idea that time and space are subjective phenomena has been refuted by the discoveries of science.

In *Anti-Dühring*, Engels shows that the whole concept of *a priori* knowledge is false. All ideas are ultimately derived from reality, even the axioms of mathematics. It is true that, if we leave aside all the material qualities of a thing, all that is left is space and time.

However, these are now empty abstractions. They cannot stand on their own, any more than there can be fruit, without apples, pears, oranges etc.; or humanity, without human beings, and so on. The only difference is that the idea of fruit, or humanity, are abstractions of a particular kind of matter, whereas time and space are the most general features, or, more correctly, the mode of existence, of matter in general.

THE THING-IN-ITSELF

All human knowledge (cognition) is the product of two factors – the cognising subject and the cognised object. The raw material of knowledge is provided by the external object (the physical world), whereas the subject (the thinking mind) gives form and meaning to the information of the senses. Kant, unlike Berkeley, accepts the existence of an external world, without which there would be no possibility of knowledge, or experience. Nevertheless, Kant denies that it is possible to know things as they are 'in themselves'. We can only know appearances. His fundamental mistake was not to see the relation between appearance and essence. It is wrong to think that we can only know 'appearances'. When I know the property of the thing, I know the thing itself. There is nothing else to know; no 'beyond', no Thing-in-Itself.

Now it has been the conviction of every age that the only way of getting to know a thing was precisely by taking the material given to us by our senses, and analysing it by means of reflection. This, and nothing else, is the process of cognition. Here, for the first time, we are confronted with the assertion that there is some kind of difference between what we can see and experience and the 'real' nature of things. This is a most peculiar notion, and one which runs counter to all human experience. It therefore demands a very clear justification. But the fact is that Kant does not justify it at all. He merely asserts it in a dogmatic manner, which is the opposite of what he set out to do.

"It marks the diseased state of the age", remarks Hegel, "when we see it adopt the despairing creed that our knowledge is only subjective, and that beyond this subjective we cannot go."[2]

Hegel, like Kant, was an idealist, but he was an objective idealist, who never denied that it was possible to know the real world. Such objective idealism is far superior, with all its faults, to the complete confusion which comes from subjective idealism. It is therefore not surprising that in the 'diseased state' of our own age, it is Kant, not Hegel, who has found most favour with philosophers and scientists, who wish to convince us that we cannot really assert that the physical world exists, or that we cannot know what happened before the 'big bang' (and must not ask), or that the behaviour of subatomic particles depends exclusively on whether we are present to observe them.

Against this, we agree a hundred times with Hegel when he says that:

> [E]verything we know both of outward and inward nature, in one word, the objective world, is in its own self the same as it is in thought, and that to think is to bring out the truth of our object, be it what it may. The business of philosophy is only to bring into explicit consciousness what the world in all ages has believed about thought. Philosophy therefore advances nothing new; and our present discussion has led us to a conclusion which agrees with the natural belief of mankind.[3]

Evidently, at any given moment in time, we cannot know everything about a phenomenon. Truth is as infinite as the universe itself. But the entire history of human thought is characterised by a constant

---

2   G. W. F. Hegel, *Encyclopedia of the Philosophical Sciences, Part One: Logic* (Henceforth referred to as *Shorter Logic*), p. 35.

3   Ibid., p. 35.

movement from ignorance to knowledge. What we do not know today, we will discover tomorrow. Therefore, it is a serious mistake to confuse what is not known with what cannot be known. Kant's Thing-in-Itself is merely a way of indicating our present limitations. It is not a mystery, but a problem to be solved. What is today a Thing-in-Itself will tomorrow be a Thing-for-Us. This is the message of the whole history of thought in general, and science in particular.

In reality, the Thing-in-Itself is an empty abstraction. If we take away all the properties of an object which are knowable, we are left with precisely nothing. As J. N. Findlay, echoing Hegel, correctly observes: "The Thing-in-Itself which Kant holds to be unknowable is really the most completely knowable of abstractions; it is what we get when we deliberately leave out all empirical content and every vestige of categorical structure."[4] There is a fundamental difference between what is not known and what is unknowable. Kant here slides into agnosticism, the impotent doctrine that says that there are certain things which cannot be known, and therefore, that there are certain questions which cannot be asked. Findlay is harsh but not unjust when he concludes that "Kant, in short, is in a permanent philosophical muddle, and never knows where he has got to nor where he is going."[5] The notion of the unknowable Thing-in-Itself is undoubtedly the weakest part of Kant's philosophy, and for that very reason is practically the only bit which has been taken over by the modern philosophers and scientists.

The source of Kant's error was to regard appearance and essence as two mutually exclusive things. Thought, instead of being seen as a bridge uniting the thinking subject with the world, is conceived of as a barrier, something standing between the subject and the object. Kant conceives of thought as an instrument which we use to understand the world. This is an unsatisfactory formulation, as Hegel explains:

4 Ibid., p. xii.
5 Ibid., p. xiv.

A main line of argument in the Critical [i.e., Kantian – *AW*] Philosophy bids us pause before proceeding to inquire into God or into the true being of things, and tells us first of all to examine the faculty of cognition and see whether it is equal to such an effort. We ought, says Kant, to become acquainted with the instrument, before we undertake the work for which it is to be employed; for if the instrument be insufficient, all our trouble will be spent in vain. The plausibility of this suggestion has won for it general assent and admiration; the result of which has been to withdraw cognition from an interest in its objects and absorption in the study of them, and to direct it back upon itself; and so turn it to a question of form.[6]

Hegel points out that thought is not an 'instrument', like a tool which can be examined before commencing a job. We would be faced with the paradox that the 'tool' would have to examine itself, since thought can only be examined by thinking. To seek to know before we know is like the conduct of a man who refuses to go into the water until he has learnt how to swim. Men and women thought long before logic was ever conceived. In point of fact, the forms of thought, including logic, are the product of a very long period of human development, both mental and practical. The objects of the physical world are immediately given to us in sense-perception. But the matter does not stop there. The understanding gets to work on the information given to it by the senses. It is analysed, broken down into its parts. This is known as mediation in philosophy.

Marx's son-in-law, the French socialist Paul Lafargue, very wittily explains the practical consequences of the theory of the Thing-in-Itself:

The workingman who eats sausage and receives a hundred sous a day knows very well that he is robbed by the employer and is nourished by pork meat, that the employer is a robber and that the sausage is pleasant to the taste and nourishing to the body. Not at all, say the bourgeois sophists, whether they are called Pyrrho, Hume or Kant. His opinion

6 Ibid., p. 14.

is personal, an entirely subjective opinion; he might with equal reason maintain that the employer is his benefactor and that the sausage consists of chopped leather, for he cannot know *things-in-themselves.*

The question is not properly put, that is the whole trouble…

In order to know an object, man must first verify whether his senses deceive him or not…

The chemists have gone deeper – they have penetrated into bodies, they have analysed them, decomposed them into their elements, and then performed the reverse procedure, they have recomposed them from their elements. And from the moment that man is able to produce things for his own use from these elements, he may, as Engels says, assert that he knows the *things-in-themselves.* The God of the Christians, if he existed and if he had created the world, could do no more.[7]

Despite his undoubted genius, Kant did a disservice to philosophy and science by implicitly placing a limit on human knowledge. The theory of the unknowable, that part of Kant's philosophy which should have been allowed to quietly sink without trace, is precisely the one thing of Kant which has been taken over in our epoch by those, like Heisenberg, who wish to introduce mysticism into science. While Kant attempted a critique of the forms of logic (this was his great merit), he displayed a certain inconsistency, for example, in accepting the law of contradiction. This led him into new problems.

THE FORMS OF LOGIC

The most important aspect of the *Critique of Pure Reason* is Kant's criticism of logic:

That *Logic* has advanced in this sure course, even from the earliest times, is apparent from the fact that, since Aristotle, it has been unable to advance a step, and thus to all appearance has reached its completion.[8]

---

7 P. Lafargue, '*Le Matérialisme de Marx et l'Idéalisme de Kant*' ('Marx's Materialism and Kant's Idealism'), in *Le Socialiste*, 25 February 1900.

8 I. Kant, *Critique of Pure Reason*, p. 8.

An important part of Kant's inquiry concerns the nature of thought-forms in general, and particularly the forms of logic. Where do they come from? What do they represent? How far do they reflect the truth? It was to Kant's credit that he asked these questions, although he did not provide an adequate answer, being content to leave that to his successors. This question really goes to the heart of the fundamental question of all philosophy – the relation between thought and being, between mind and matter. Like Hegel, Kant had a very poor opinion of formal logic, a "specious art ... which gives to all our cognitions the form of the understanding."[9] Kant was the first one to distinguish between Understanding (*Verstand*) and Reason (*Vernunf*). Although it plays an important role, for Kant, *Understanding* is the lowest form of rational thinking. It takes things as they are, and bases itself on the registration and a superficial classification of the bare facts of existence. This is the basis of formal logic, and also 'common sense', which takes things to be just as they seem.

But the process of thinking does not stop at the level of understanding and immediate sense experience. In order to proceed towards a dialectical understanding we need the intervention of Reason, which goes beyond what is immediately given, breaks it down into its constituent parts, and puts it together again. This is the role of the Dialectic. Up until Kant, the art of dialectics had been virtually forgotten. It was regarded as mere trickery and sophism, the 'logic of illusion'. It was Kant's great achievement to restore dialectics to its rightful place in philosophy, as a higher form of logic.

Kant attempts to put human knowledge on a sound basis, by insisting that it must be based upon experience. However, this is insufficient. Initially, in the process of cognition, we are confronted with a confused mass of data, with no logical thread or necessary connection. This would not generally be thought of as real knowledge, still less scientific knowledge. We expect something

---

9 Ibid., p. 68.

more. In order to make sense of the information provided by the senses, it is necessary for reason to be active, not merely passive:

> They [the natural scientists] learned that reason only perceives that which it produces after its own design; that it must not be content to follow, as it were, in the leading-strings of nature, but must proceed in advance with principles of judgment according to unvarying laws, and compel nature to reply to its questions. For accidental observations, made according to no preconceived plan, cannot be united under a necessary law. But it is this that reason seeks for and requires. It is only the principles of reason which can give to concordant phenomena the validity of laws, and it is only when experiment is directed by these rational principles that it can have any real utility. Reason must approach nature with the view, indeed, of receiving information from it, not, however, in the character of a pupil, who listens to all that his master chooses to tell him, but in that of a judge, who compels the witnesses to reply to those questions which he himself thinks fit to propose.[10]

There is an important difference between the way that Kant and Aristotle understood the laws of logic. For Aristotle, these were laws of things, whereas, for the idealist Kant, they are laws of thought only. The nub of the matter is that, for Kant, the law of identity, for example, cannot be found in the objects themselves. It is merely applied to them by consciousness. Thus, for Kant, logic is only a convenient method for ordering and classifying things, whereas dialectics, as Marxists see it, derives its laws from the real world, and applies them back again. This mistaken conception of Kant has been carried over into modern logic and mathematics, where it is often asserted that laws, theorems, etc., are only formal ideas which are used for the sake of convenience, but which have no real relation to the objective world.

THE 'ANTINOMIES'

The most interesting part of the *Critique of Pure Reason* is known as the antinomies. In these, Kant shows the contradictions that

---

10 Ibid., pp. 10-11.

exist in thought. Thus, starting with the laws of formal logic, and applying them to the world of experience, Kant precedes to show the contradictions which arise. Kant takes this as proof of the unknowability of the Thing-in-Itself, instead of seeing that the contradictions are objective, and present in the phenomena themselves.

The fundamental problem here is: how do the forms of logic relate to the real world? The categories of formal logic tell us absolutely nothing about the real world. It was the task of science to discover the laws of the real world through observation and experiment. However, the picture of the world was never complete, since science would inevitably discover new fields all the time, and would have to constantly readjust its theories and propositions. This is the real process. However, Kant drew entirely different conclusions.

Not until Hegel was the reason for these contradictions explained. The problem arises from the nature of formal logic itself, which takes opposites to be mutually exclusive. For example, the logical category of identity presupposes its opposite – difference. When we say that something is, we think we have identified it. However, it only has identity in comparison to other things. John is John, because he is not Peter, Paul, etc. Thus, identity presupposes difference, and has no meaning in isolation. In general, things have no meaning unless taken together with their opposites. Life cannot be understood without death. North and south, right and left, male and female, good and bad, can only have meaning in relation to their opposites. The unity of opposites is a fundamental fact of existence.

Hegel later explained that pure, undifferentiated being is the same as nothing. If we merely confine ourselves to the assertion that a thing is, without explaining its concrete properties, internal contradictions, motion and change, and manifold relations, we do not really grasp the truth about it. Without further concretisation, simple being turns out to be an empty abstraction. This particular contradiction ("antimony") can only be resolved by understanding that being and not being are not mutually exclusive, but are combined in the process of becoming.

Similarly, the polar opposites cause and effect have to be united as interaction. If we attempt to isolate a particular cause and effect, we immediately land ourselves in a contradiction, since there are always an infinite number of causes which precede the given case; in fact, behind each isolated fact is the whole history of the universe. Similarly, if we attempt to understand a particular fact as a cause, we will enter into an endless chain of phenomena, following it in time, into infinity.

How to solve this contradiction? If we keep within the rules of formal logic, the only solution to Kant's antinomies is to deny the validity of exactly one half of its categories, recognising only the other half. The mediaeval Schoolmen, for example, declared chance (accident) to be a purely subjective concept, a product of ignorance of the causes. Everything in the universe was absolutely determined, in fact, preordained from the beginning to the end by the Supreme Being. Likewise, Identity was proclaimed to be absolute, and Contradiction rigorously prohibited by the traditional logic.

Kant points out in the section on the antinomies that contradiction is not just a trick of sophists, but is inevitable. The antinomies, where he gives two sets of proofs for two contrary propositions, are "not mere sophistries – are not fallacious, but grounded on the nature of reason..."[11]

Unfortunately for speculation – but perhaps fortunately for the practical interests of humanity – reason, in the midst of her highest anticipations, finds herself hemmed in by a press of opposite and contradictory conclusions, from which neither her honour nor her safety will permit her to draw back. Nor can she regard these conflicting trains of reasoning with indifference as mere passages at arms, still less can she command peace; for in the subject of the conflict she has a deep interest. There is no other course left open to her, than to reflect with herself upon the origin of this disunion in reason – whether it may not arise from a mere misunderstanding. After such an inquiry, arrogant claims would have to be given up on both sides; but the

11 Ibid., p. 304.

sovereignty of reason over understanding and sense would be based upon a sure foundation.[12]

The real resolution is the never-ending process of deepening knowledge:

> For it [reason] can give no answer to our question respecting the conditions of its synthesis – except such as must be supplemented by another question, and so on to infinity. According to it, we must rise from a given beginning to one still higher; every part conducts us to a still smaller one; every event is preceded by another event which is its cause; and the conditions of existence rest always upon other and still higher conditions, and find neither end nor basis in some self-subsistent thing as the primal being.[13]

Every answer only gives rise to a new question, and so on *ad infinitum*. There are no final answers. No end to the process. Therefore, dialectical thought is undogmatic and open-ended. The solution to the supposedly 'unsolvable' problems is given by the never-ending process of the history of science and human thought in general. The only way of resolving the contradictions in thought was by a complete overhaul of logic, breaking down the old rigid schemas, which did not and could not faithfully reflect the reality of a moving, changing, living, contradictory world. Hegel hailed Kant for reintroducing the notion of contradiction into logic.

> And to offer the idea that the contradiction introduced into the world of Reason by the categories of Understanding is inevitable and essential was one of the most important steps in the progress of Modern Philosophy.[14]

However, having posed the question, Kant was unable or unwilling to provide the answer: "But the more important the issue thus raised the more trivial was the solution."[15]

---

12 Ibid., p. 282.
13 Ibid., p. 284
14 G. W. F. Hegel, *Shorter Logic*, p. 77.
15 Ibid., p. 77.

Kant did not achieve this revolution. But his great merit was to point the way forward. Kant gave philosophy a new lease of life, by subjecting the old forms of thought to a thorough criticism, revealing their inherently unsatisfactory and contradictory nature. The *Critique of Pure Reason* showed that contradictions were inherent in thinking. In so doing, Kant reintroduced dialectics into philosophy. Hitherto, dialectics was regarded as a purely subjective method of reasoning. Kant showed that dialectics was neither arbitrary nor subjective, but an entirely valid method of reasoning.

Revolutionary though it was for its time, Kant's philosophy cannot be regarded as a satisfactory solution to the problems posed by it. More than anything, Kant's dialectic resembles the old Socratic dialectic of discussion. There is some merit in this. The struggle between opposed conceptions, in which due weight is given to the arguments of the other side, and arguments are put forward for and against in a rigorous way, can lead to a general increase in awareness of the questions involved. Yet there is something unsatisfactory about it; a kind of agnosticism; the superficial idea that "the truth is never all on one side," and so forth.

Kant's antinomies are only four in number. It was left to Hegel to point out that, in fact everything contains an "antimony" (contradiction):

> That true and positive meaning of the antinomies is this: that every actual thing involves a coexistence of opposed elements. Consequently to know, or, in other words, to comprehend an object is equivalent to being conscious of it as a concrete unity of opposed determinations.[16]

Kant's merit was to submit the traditional forms of logic to a thoroughgoing criticism. His defect lay in his subjectivist position on the theory of knowledge. This was the source of his main weaknesses – ambiguity, inconsistency and agnosticism. In failing to make a clean break with the traditional logic, while exposing its limitations, Kant landed himself in all kinds of insoluble contradictions, which

---

16 Ibid., p. 78.

he left unresolved. The problem of the relation between subject and object (thought and being) was only finally resolved by Marx and Engels, who pointed out that, ultimately, all the problems of philosophy are resolved in practice:

> All social life is essentially *practical*. All mysteries which lead theory to mysticism find their rational solution in human practice and in the comprehension of this practice.[17]

---

17 K. Marx, 'Theses on Feuerbach', MECW, Vol. 5, p. 5.

10. HEGEL'S REVOLUTION IN PHILOSOPHY

Incidentally, it is not difficult to see that our time is a time of birth and of transition to a new period. Spirit has broken with the previous world of its life and ideas, and is on the point of submerging it in the past; it is at work on its own transformation. Indeed, spirit is never at rest but always engaged in moving forward. But just as the first breath drawn by a child after its long, quiet nourishment breaks the gradualness of merely quantitative growth – a qualitative leap – and now the child is born, so the spirit that cultivates itself matures slowly and quietly into its new shape, dissolving bit by bit the structure of its previous world, whose instability is indicated only by isolated symptoms; the frivolity and boredom that infest the established order, the vague foreboding of something unknown, are heralds of approaching change. This gradual crumbling that did not alter the physiognomy of the whole is interrupted by the sunrise which, like lightning, all of a sudden reveals the contour of the new world.[1]

HEGEL'S 'VOYAGE OF DISCOVERY'

Georg Wilhelm Friedrich Hegel was born in Stuttgart in 1770. In his youth he was a follower, and then a collaborator of

---

1   G. W. F Hegel, *The Phenomenology of Spirit*, p. 8.

Schelling, whose radical views gained him a certain notoriety, until he made his peace with the Prussian authorities in later life. But Hegel soon moved on from his early efforts. Hegel's original contribution to philosophy begins in 1807 with the publication of *The Phenomenology of Spirit*. The period under consideration was one of storm and stress. France had erupted in revolution when he was a nineteen-year-old student. The French Revolution and the Napoleonic Wars set an indelible stamp on the entire epoch. In Hegel's own words, the "composition of the book was concluded at mid-night before the battle of Jena."

This work, which Hegel describes as his voyage of discovery was received with coldness and dissatisfaction by those who had previously been his teachers and friends.

The Phenomenology traces the development of thought through all its phases, proceeding from the lowest, most general and abstract, to the highest form, which he calls the Notion. Each form of knowledge is examined within its own conditions and limits, bringing out its dialectical relation to other forms of thought. Here, Hegel's method illustrates the importance of philosophy: it alone must consider and justify its own conceptions, unlike mathematics, which proceeds from given axioms which are accepted uncritically. Philosophy presupposes nothing, not even itself.

For the modern reader, the writings of Hegel present considerable difficulties – Abstract and abstruse, Engels called them. This is certainly true of *The Phenomenology*. At times, one has the impression that Hegel is being deliberately obscure, that he is challenging the reader to penetrate the complex and difficult edifice of dialectical thought. A large part of the difficulty, in fact, stems from the fact that Hegel was an idealist and that, therefore, the dialectic appears here in a mystified form. *The Phenomenology* is a good example of this.

Here, historical development appears in an idealistic fashion, as the development of self-conscious mind (or spirit). Nevertheless, it is possible to read Hegel, as Marx did, from a materialist point of view, bringing out the rational kernel of his thought. In *The*

Phenomenology, 'self-consciousness' reveals its activity in many ways, through sensation and perception, as well as through ideas. In all this, it is possible to perceive the dim outline of real processes that take place in nature, society, and the human mind. In contrast with previous idealist philosophies, Hegel displayed a lively interest in the facts of nature, human nature, and human history. Behind his abstract presentation, there lies a wealth of knowledge of all aspects of history, philosophy and contemporary science. Marx described him as the most encyclopaedic mind of the day.

Behind the 'abstract and abstruse' language, once the idealist mystification is stripped away, we see before us a fully fledged revolution in human thought. The Russian radical democrat Herzen referred to the Hegelian dialectic as "the algebra of revolution."[2] In an algebraic equation it is necessary to fill in the missing quantities. This was later achieved by Marx and Engels, who rescued the rational kernel of Hegel's philosophy after his death, and, by placing it on a materialist basis, gave it a scientific character. Commenting on Hegel's philosophy, Engels writes:

> This new German philosophy culminated in the Hegelian system. In this system – and herein is its great merit – for the first time the whole world, natural, historical, intellectual, is represented as a process, i.e., as in constant motion, change, transformation, development; and the attempt is made to trace out the internal connection that makes a continuous whole of all this movement and development. From this point of view the history of mankind no longer appeared as a wild whirl of senseless deeds of violence, all equally condemnable at the judgement-seat of mature philosophic reason and which are best forgotten as quickly as possible, but as the process of evolution of man himself. It was now the task of the intellect to follow the gradual march of this process through all its devious ways, and to trace out the inner law running through all its apparently accidental phenomena.[3]

---

2   A. Herzen, *My Past and Thoughts*, p. 237.

3   F. Engels, *Anti-Dühring*, p. 34.

HEGEL TODAY

Hegel was a genius who was far ahead of his time. Unfortunately, the level of the natural sciences at the beginning of the nineteenth century did not furnish enough information to allow him to apply his revolutionary new method to full effect, although he had some brilliant insights. Engels applied this method to science in *Dialectics of Nature*, a masterpiece of dialectical writing. But in our own time, science has furnished a wealth of material which shows the correctness of Hegel's fundamental ideas. It is a tragedy that the twentieth century lacked a Hegel to provide the necessary insights into these great discoveries.

Nowadays, many scientists adopt a contemptuous attitude towards philosophy, which they regard as superfluous to their requirements. They consider that the actual progress made by science places them far above philosophy. In reality, however, they are far below philosophy at its most primitive level. It is said that nature abhors a vacuum. In the absence of a consistent and worked-out philosophy, they fall prey to all kind of prejudices and false ideas which they unconsciously imbibe from the prevailing tendencies and mood in society in which they live. This flotsam and jetsam, together with a few confused recollections of bad philosophy they picked up at university, provide the sum total of the intellectual baggage of many supposedly educated people, including scientists. As Hegel humorously observed, these are "perfect equivalent of this journey and as good a substitute for it as chicory is reputed to be for coffee".[4]

For the last century-and-a-half, Hegel has been sadly neglected. The dominant schools of Western philosophy, Postmodernism, analytic philosophy and logical positivism (the latter of which was born partly as a reaction against Hegelianism), have treated Hegel rather as extreme Protestants treat the Pope of Rome. In turn, the views of this philosophical sect has influenced many scientists. One of the very few modern scientists in the West who has been prepared to give Hegel his due is the Belgian Ilya Prigogine, who

---

4 G. W. F. Hegel, *The Phenomenology of Spirit*, p. 31.

has developed the theory of chaos and complexity, a line of thinking which has much in common with dialectics. It is a very simple matter to dismiss Hegel (or Engels) because their writings on science were necessarily limited by the actual state of science of the day. What is remarkable, however, is how advanced Hegel's views on science actually were.

In their book *Order out of Chaos*, Prigogine and Stengers point out that Hegel rejected the mechanistic method of classical Newtonian physics, at a time when Newton's ideas were universally sacrosanct:

> The Hegelian philosophy of nature systematically incorporates all that is denied by Newtonian science. In particular, it rests on the qualitative difference between the simple behaviour described by mechanics and the behaviour of more complex entities such as living beings. It denies the possibility of reducing those levels, rejecting the idea that differences are merely apparent and that nature is basically homogeneous and simple. It affirms the existence of a hierarchy, each level of which presupposes the preceding ones.[5]

Prigogine and Stengers refer to the unjust neglect from which Hegel has suffered, precisely at a time when his criticisms of Newtonian mechanism had been shown to be correct:

> In a sense Hegel's system provides a consistent philosophic response to the crucial problems of time and complexity. However, for generations of scientists it represented the epitome of abhorrence and contempt. In a few years, the intrinsic difficulties of Hegel's philosophy of nature were aggravated by the obsolescence of the scientific background on which his system was based, for Hegel, of course, based his rejection of the Newtonian system on the scientific conceptions of his time. And it was precisely those conceptions that were to fall into oblivion with astonishing speed. It is difficult to imagine a less opportune time than the beginning of the nineteenth century for seeking experimental and theoretical support for an alternative to classical science. Although this time was characterised by a remarkable extension of the experimental

5 I. Prigogine and I. Stengers, *Order Out of Chaos*, p. 89.

scope of science and by a proliferation of theories that seemed to contradict Newtonian science, most of those theories had to be given up only a few years after their appearance.[6]

There are only a couple of things that need to be added to this. Firstly, what was valuable in Hegel's philosophy was not his system, but the dialectical method. Part of the reason why Hegel's writings are obscure is precisely that he tried to force the dialectic – which he developed brilliantly – into the straitjacket of an arbitrary idealist philosophical system. When it did not fit, he resorted to all manner of subterfuges and peculiar modes of reasoning which make the whole thing extremely convoluted and obscure.

However, we are firmly convinced that the main reason for the shameful conspiracy against Hegel has nothing to do with the obscurity of his style. That did not worry the university professors 100 years ago. Moreover, the obscurity of Hegel is nothing compared to the senseless linguistic meanderings of the logical positivists, who are held up as models of 'coherent thought', though nobody quite knows why. No, the real reason why Hegel became converted into a non-person is because it was realised that his dialectical philosophy was the point of departure for the revolutionary ideas of Marx and Engels. Poor old Hegel, conservative in real life, has been tried in his absence and found guilty by association.

The fear of Hegel's ideas is neither accidental nor mistaken. Even in the nineteenth century, the danger posed by the dialectic was clear to some. James Stirling, a prominent English 'Hegelian', wrote in 1867: "This dialectic, it appears to me, has led to much that is equivocal both in Hegel and in others, and may become a pest yet."[7] Even during his lifetime, the revolutionary implications of Hegel's philosophy began to disturb the Prussian authorities. The defeat of the French in 1815 ushered in a period of reaction all over Europe. The so-called Carlsbad decrees of 1819 subjected the universities in all areas under Prussian jurisdiction to inquisitorial control. The

---

6   Ibid., p. 90.

7   A. Schwegler, *History of Philosophy*, p. 445.

slightest non-conformity was looked upon as subversion. A stifling atmosphere of petty provincialism prevailed in the lands of the 'cabbage Junkers', as Marx later ironically called the Prussian feudal aristocrats.

In Berlin, where Hegel taught at the university, spiteful rumours were put in circulation by Hegel's enemies that his ideas were un-Christian, or even downright atheism. From then on, he was a marked man. Attacked by both Rationalists and Evangelicals, Hegel defended himself vigorously, pointing out that "all speculative philosophy on religion may be carried to atheism: all depends on who carries it; the peculiar piety of our times and the malevolence of demagogues will not let us want carriers."[8]

Such was the atmosphere of persecution that Hegel even considered moving to Belgium, as Marx later did. In 1827, he wrote a letter to his wife commenting that he had looked at the universities of Liège and Louvain with the feeling that they might one day provide him a resting place, "when the parsons in Berlin make the Kupfergraben completely intolerable for him". "The Roman Curia", he added, "would be a more honourable opponent than the miserable cabals of a miserable boiling of parsons in Berlin".[9] It is ironic that at the end of his life, the conservative and religious Hegel should be regarded as a dangerous radical. Yet there was more than a grain of truth behind the suspicions of the reactionaries. Hidden within the philosophy of Hegel was the germ of a revolutionary idea, which would transform the world. This, in itself, constitutes the most remarkable example of a dialectical contradiction!

In his *History of Philosophy* Hegel revealed the hidden dialectical relationship between different schools of thought, showing how different theories revealed different aspects of the truth, which do not so much contradict, as complement and complete one another. In the *Encyclopaedia of the Philosophical Sciences*, Hegel likewise

---

8 G. W. F. Hegel, *Shorter Logic*, p. xxxix.
9 Ibid.

attempts to show the whole of science as an integrally collective whole. It is not merely a collection of sciences or a dictionary of philosophical knowledge but science presented as a dialectically interrelated totality. This is a very modern conception.

Hegel did not set out to deny or demolish previous philosophy, but to summarise all previous schools of thought, and arrive at a dialectical synthesis. But in so doing, he pushed philosophy to its limits. Beyond this point, it was impossible to develop philosophy without transforming it into something different. It is possible to say that, since Hegel, nothing new has really been said on the main philosophical questions. Subsequent schools of philosophy, which purport to be new and original, merely rehash old ideas, invariably in a more superficial and unsatisfactory manner. The only real revolution in philosophy since Hegel was the one effected by Marx and Engels, which passes beyond the limits of philosophy as a merely intellectual exercise, and carries it into the realm of practice and the struggle to change society.

Hegel says in his *Phenomenology* that "the being of mind is its act, and its act is to be aware of itself." But in Hegel, thinking is not merely a contemplative activity. The highest form of thought, reason, does not merely accept the given facts, but works upon them and transforms them. The contradiction between thought and being, between 'subject' and 'object', is overcome in Hegel through the process of knowledge itself, which penetrates ever deeper into the objective world. From a materialist point of view, however, thinking is not an isolated activity, but is inseparable from human existence in general. Mankind develops thought through concrete, sensuous activity, not merely intellectual activity. By transforming the material world through labour, men and women also transform themselves, and, in so doing, develop and extend the horizon of their thinking. In embryo, the elements of this dialectical conception are already present in Hegel. What Marx did was to strip it of its idealist disguise, and express it in a clear and scientific manner.

THEORY OF KNOWLEDGE

As we have seen, one of the fundamental problems of philosophy is the relation between thought and being. What is the relation between consciousness (knowledge) and the objective world? Kant claimed that there was an unbridgeable gap between the thinking subject and the unknowable Thing-in-Itself. Hegel poses the question differently. The process of thinking is the unity of subject and object. Thought is not a barrier separating man from the objective world, but, on the contrary, is a process linking ('mediating') the two. Taking as its starting point the reality immediately given in sense-perception, human thought does not merely passively accept, as Locke imagined, but sets to work, transforming this information, breaking it down into its component parts, and putting it together again. Man uses rational thought to go beyond immediate reality. Dialectical thought, in analysing a given phenomenon, divides it into its component parts and demonstrates those contradictory features and tendencies which give it life and movement.

Scientific knowledge does not consist of a mere catalogue of particular items. If we say 'all animals', that is not yet zoology. Above and beyond the facts, it is necessary to discover laws and objective processes. It is necessary to uncover the objective relations between things, and explain the transitions between one state and the other. The history of science, like that of philosophy, is a permanent process of affirmation and negation, a ceaseless process and development, in which one idea negates another, and, in its turn, is negated in a never-ending process of deepening our knowledge of ourselves and the universe. A similar phenomenon may be seen in the mental development of the infant.

Hegel's great merit was to show the dialectical character of the development of human thought, from its embryonic phase, passing through a whole series of stages, and finally arriving at the highest stage of reason: the Notion. In Hegelian language, it is the process from being 'in itself' to being 'in and for itself', that is to say, from undeveloped, implicit being to developed and explicit being. The human embryo is, potentially, a human being, but it is not a human being in and for itself. In order to realise its full potential, a whole period of development is necessary, in which infancy, adolescence and middle age constitute necessary stages. The thought of a child evidently has an immature character. But even a correct idea expressed by a youth does not have the same weight as the same idea expressed by an old person, who has experienced life, and consequently has a deeper understanding of what these words actually mean.

In Hegel, the real development of human beings is presented in a mystical form, as the development of spirit. As an idealist, Hegel had no real conception of the development of society, although there are some brilliant anticipations of historical materialism in his writings. Thought appears here as an expression of the Absolute Idea, a mystical concept about which the only thing we learn, as Engels ironically put it, is that he tells us absolutely nothing about it. In reality, thought is the product of the human brain and nervous system, inseparable from the human body, which, in turn, depends upon food, which, in turn, presupposes human society and productive relations.

Thought is a product of matter that thinks, the highest achievement of nature. Inanimate matter possesses the potential to produce life. Even the lowest forms of life possess sensibility, irritability, which has the potential to produce, in higher animals, a nervous system and a brain. Hegel's 'self-consciousness' is merely a fantastic way of expressing the historical process by which real human beings gradually become conscious of themselves and the world in which they live. This does not come about easily or automatically, any more than the individual human being automatically acquires consciousness in the transition from infancy to adulthood. In both cases, the process takes place through a prolonged and often traumatic series of stages. The development of human thought, as reflected in the history of philosophy and science, and of culture in general, reveals itself as a contradictory process, in which one stage supersedes another, and, in its turn, is superseded. It is not a straight line, but one that is continuously interrupted, with periods of stagnation, faltering and even reversals, which, however, merely prepare the ground for new advances.

HOW THOUGHT DEVELOPS

The very beginnings of human thought, mind in its immediate and primitive stage, is sense perception: primitive humans, through his senses, begins by registering and memorising the data immediately provided by his environment, without understanding the true nature, causal relationships and laws which underlie them. From observation and experience, gradually the human mind proceeds to make a number of generalisations of a more or less abstract character. This process involves a long and laborious journey lasting several millions of years, extremely slow at first, but rapidly gathering momentum in the last ten thousand years. Yet, despite the colossal strides made by thought and science, ordinary thinking remains on quite a primitive level.

When we first consider any subject, we first form a notion of the whole, without grasping all the concrete content and detailed interconnections. It is merely a general outline and a bare abstraction. Thus, the Ionic philosophers and even Buddhism intuitively grasped the universe as a constantly changing dialectical whole. But this initial notion lacks all definition and concreteness. It is necessary to go further and provide the general picture with a definite expression, analysing and specifying the precise relations of its content. It has to be analysed and quantified. Without this, science in general is impossible. This is the difference between crude, immediate, undeveloped thought and science as such.

At the dawn of human consciousness, men and women did not clearly distinguish themselves from nature, just as a newborn baby does not distinguish itself from its mother. Gradually, over a long period, humans learned to distinguish, to cognize the world, by detecting focal points in the bewildering web of natural phenomena surrounding them, to observe, compare, generalise, and draw conclusions. In this way, over countless millennia, a series of important generalisations were built up from experience, which gradually came to crystallise into the familiar forms of thought which, because we are so familiar with them, we take for granted.

Common, everyday thought relies heavily on sense perception, immediate experience, appearances, and that peculiar hybrid of experience and superficial thinking called 'common sense'. These things are normally sufficient to carry us through life. But they are insufficient to arrive at a scientific understanding and, at a certain point, break down and become useless even for practical purposes. It is necessary to go beyond the immediate experience of sense perception, and to grasp the general processes, laws and hidden relations which lie beyond frequently deceptive appearance.

Ordinary human thought prefers to cling to what is concrete and familiar. It is easier to accept what is apparently fixed and well known rather than new ideas which challenge what is familiar and customary. Routine, tradition, custom and social convention represent a powerful force in society, akin to the force of inertia in mechanics. In normal periods, most people are reluctant to question the society in which they live: its morality, ideology and property forms. All kinds of prejudices, political ideas, 'scientific' orthodoxy are accepted uncritically, until some profound change in people's lives forces them to question what is.

Social and intellectual conformism is the commonest form of self-deception. Familiar ideas are taken to be correct just because they are familiar. Thus, the notion that private property, money and the bourgeois family are eternal and unchanging features of life has sunk deeply into the popular consciousness, although it bears no relation whatsoever to the truth. Dialectics is the direct opposite of this superficial and commonplace way of thinking. Precisely because it challenges familiar ideas, it frequently arouses fierce opposition. How is it possible to challenge the law of identity, which states what seems obvious, that 'A' equals 'A'? This so-called law is the logical reflection of a popular prejudice, that everything is what it is, and nothing else; that nothing changes. Dialectics, on the contrary, sets out from the opposite point of view, that everything changes, comes into being and passes away.

The empiricist thinker, who claims to take things 'as they are', imagines himself to be very practical and concrete. But, in reality, things are not always what they seem to be, and frequently turn out to be their opposite. This kind of immediate sensuous knowledge is the lowest kind of knowledge, like that of a baby. A really scientific understanding of reality requires us to break down the information provided by sense perception in order to get at the true nature of the things under consideration. A deeper analysis always reveals the contradictory tendencies which underlie even the most apparently fixed, solid, and immutable things, which eventually will lead to them being transformed into their opposites. It is precisely these contradictions which are the source of all life, movement and development throughout nature. In order to get a real understanding, it is necessary to take things, not just as they are, but also as they have been, and as they necessarily will become.

For simple everyday purposes, formal logic and 'common sense' are sufficient. But beyond certain limits it no longer applies. At this point dialectics becomes absolutely essential. Unlike formal logic, which cannot grasp contradictions and seeks to eliminate them, dialectics represents the logic of contradiction, which is a fundamental aspect of nature and thought. By a process of analysis, dialectics reveals these contradictions and shows how they are resolved. However, new contradictions always appear, thus giving rise to a never-ending spiral of development. This process can be seen in the entire development of science and philosophy, which takes place through contradictions. This is not an accident. It reflects the nature of human knowledge as an infinite process in which the solution of one problem immediately gives rise to new ones, which are in turn resolved, and so on *ad infinitum*.

If we set out from the most elementary form of knowledge at the level of sense-experience, the limitations of formal logic and 'common sense' very soon become clear. The mind simply registers the facts as we find them. At first sight, the truths of sense perception seem to be simple and self-evident. They can be confidently relied upon, but on closer examination, things are not so simple. What appears to be solid and reliable turns out not to be so. The ground begins to shift beneath our feet.

Sense-certainty sets out from the 'here' and the 'now'. Of this Hegel says:

> So we have to put the question to *sensory certainty* itself: *What is the This?* If we take the This in the twofold shape of its Being, as the *Now* and as the *Here*, the dialectic it has in it will receive a form as intelligible as the This itself is. To the question: *What is the Now?* we answer, for example: *The Now is the night.* In order to test the truth of this sensory certainty a simple experiment suffices. We write down this truth; a truth cannot lose anything by being written down, nor can it lose anything through our preserving it. If *now, this noon*, we look again at the written truth we shall have to say that it has become stale.[10]

This comment of Hegel recalls the famous paradoxes of Zeno in relation to motion. For example, if we wish to fix the position of an arrow flying, to say where it is now, the moment that we point to it, it has already passed, and therefore the 'now' is not something that is, but something that has been. Thus, what initially appears to be true, turns out to be false. The reason is to be found in the contradictory nature of movement itself. Movement is a process, not a collection of separate points. Similarly, time consists of an infinite number of 'nows', all taken together. Likewise, the 'here' turns out to be not a single 'here', but a before and a behind, and an above and a below, and a right and a left. What is here, as a tree, the next minute is here as a house, or something else.

DIALECTICAL AND FORMAL THINKING

The correct application of the dialectical method means that the investigator must completely immerse himself in the study of the object, examining it from all sides in order to determine the inner contradictions and necessary laws of motion which govern its existence. The classical example of this method is to be found in the three volumes of Marx's *Capital*. Marx did not invent the laws which

---

10 G. W. F. Hegel, *The Phenomenology of Spirit*, p. 44.

govern the capitalist mode of production in an arbitrary fashion, but derived them from a painstaking dialectical analysis of all aspects of capitalism, tracing its historical development and following the process of commodity production through all its phases.

In his *Philosophical Notebooks*, which contain a detailed study of Hegel's *Science of Logic*, Lenin points out that the first condition for dialectical thought is: "The determination of the concept out of itself (the thing *itself* must be considered in its relations and in its development)."[11] Or, put another way, the dialectical method sets out from "the *objectivity* of consideration (not examples, not divergences, but the Thing-in-itself)."[12]

The first and lowest form of thought is sense-perception, that is to say, the information immediately given to us by our senses – what we see, hear, touch, etc. This is followed by understanding (*Verstand*), which attempts to explain what is, but does so in a one-sided way, registering isolated facts. Broadly speaking, the understanding here is identical with formal logic, ordinary thinking, and 'common sense'. We see that a thing exists, that it is itself, and nothing but itself. There seems nothing more to be said. But, in reality, there is a great deal more to be said. The understanding presents things as isolated, fixed and unchanging. Reality, however, is not like that at all.

A more advanced form of thinking is what Hegel (and Kant) call Reason (*Vernunft*). Reason attempts to go beyond the immediate facts established by understanding, to break them down, dissolve them, and behind the apparently solid exterior appearances, to reveal the inner contradictory tendencies, which, sooner or later, will lead to profound transformations. "The battle of reason", says Hegel, "is the struggle to break up the rigidity to which the understanding has reduced everything."[13]

---

11 V. I. Lenin, 'Conspectus of Hegel's *Science of Logic*', LCW, Vol. 38, p. 221.

12 Ibid.

13 G. W. F. Hegel, *Shorter Logic*, p. 53.

The first principle of dialectical thought is absolute objectivity. The subject matter must be approached objectively, and the final result must not be anticipated in advance. We must absorb ourselves in the subject matter, until we grasp not just a series of isolated facts, but their inner connection and lawfulness. The laws of dialectics, unlike formal logic, are not arbitrary constructions which can be applied in an external manner to any particular content. They have been derived from a careful observation of the development of nature, society and human thought.

The usual forms of thought represented by formal logic can be applied to any subject matter in an external and arbitrary fashion. Indeed, the real content of the subject matter is entirely irrelevant to it. Formal logic, as expressed in the abstract law of identity ('A' equals 'A') appears to express an indisputable truth. In reality, it is an empty tautology, "monochrome formalism", or as Hegel says wittily, "the night in which … all cows are black – this is the naiveté of emptiness of cognition."[14]

The so-called law of identity is only an abstract form with no real content, incapable of movement or further development. It cannot be applied to the dynamic reality of a restless universe, in which everything constantly changes, comes into being, and passes away, and therefore cannot be considered self-equal. In the same way, the law of contradiction is false because every really existing thing contains both positive and negative. It is and it is not because it is in a constant state of movement and change. The only thing which does not change is change itself. All attempts to fix the truth as a one-sided and static thing are doomed to failure. The existence of contradiction is reflected intuitively in the popular consciousness in the form of proverbs and sayings which, however, because of their unsystematic and intuitive character, often contradict each other. For example, "One man's meat is another man's poison."

In science also we see contradictions at all levels, for example attraction and repulsion, north and south in magnetism, positive

---

14 G. W. F. Hegel, *The Phenomenology of Spirit*, p. 10.

and negative in electricity, action and reaction in mechanics, contraction and expansion, etc. As against formal logic, dialectics does not inflict itself on nature, but derives its categories from reality itself. Real dialectics has nothing in common with the caricature outlined by its critics, who try to present it as a subjective and arbitrary play on words. This is really the dialectic of Sophism, which, like formal logic, is also applied in an external manner to any given content with the intention of manipulating contradictions in a subjective manner. Nor does dialectics have anything in common with the gross oversimplification of the 'triad' (thesis, antithesis, synthesis), which was adopted by Kant and turned into a lifeless formula. Real dialectics attempts to discover, by means of a rigorously objective analysis, the inner logic and laws of motion of a given phenomenon.

HEGEL'S 'LOGIC'

The *Logic* of Hegel is one of the pinnacles of human thought. It is the systematic exposition and development of all the forms of thought, from the more primitive undeveloped thought, up to the highest form of dialectical reasoning, which Hegel calls the Notion.

He sets out with the most general proposition possible – that of 'pure being' – something that seems to require no further proof. From this extremely abstract idea, he proceeds, step by step, along a process which leads from the abstract to the concrete.

This process of reasoning proceeds by stages, in which each stage negates the previous one. The history of thought, particularly that of philosophy and science, shows that knowledge is acquired precisely in this way, in a never-ending process whereby we obtain an increasingly precise idea of the workings of the universe. In Hegel, each stage is no sooner affirmed than it is negated, and the result is a higher, richer, more concrete idea.

In general outline, Hegel's *Logic* can be divided into three main parts: The Doctrine of Being, The Doctrine of Essence (essential nature) and the Doctrine of the Notion. Hegel begins his philosophy with the most fundamental category of thought – the category of

Being. Evidently, anything which we consider must exist, before anything else. This seems to be the basis of all our knowledge. But things are not so simple as that. The bare statement of existence, without further details, does not get us very far. We want to know more. But the moment we pass from the abstract idea of being in general to a more concrete idea, being turns into its opposite. Hegel shows that being in general is the same as – nothing.

This idea seems strange, but actually can be seen to be true on many different levels. If we try to eliminate all contradiction from things, and cling to the idea that they just are, we arrive at the opposite conclusion, because there can be no being without not-being, just as there can be no life without death, and no light without darkness. People who have spent a long time in the Arctic know that the effect of unrelieved whiteness is the same as that of total blackness to the human vision.

It is, in fact, an empty abstraction, since it lacks all concreteness. In reality, the dialectical unity of being and nothing is becoming, that is the process of change. This is what Heraclitus meant when he said everything is and is not, because everything is in flux. Everyone knows from experience that things are frequently not what they seem to be. Things that appear to be stable, so that we can say 'they are', on closer examination turn out to be unstable, and change into something else, and they 'are not'. Moreover, this contradiction between being and not being is the basis of all life and movement.

In Hegel, the category of being represents the stage of primitive, undeveloped thought. It is thought only as a potential, like the thought of a small child, or early proto-humans. It is embryonic thought. An embryo begins as a single cell, with no clearly developed features. It is not clearly identifiable as a human being. In order to develop, it must first negate itself. Inside the cell, there are contradictory tendencies which give rise to a process of inner differentiation. When these conflicting tendencies reach a certain point, the cell divides in two. The original, undifferentiated cell has ceased to exist. It has been cancelled, negated. Yet at the same time, it has been preserved, and carried onto a higher level. The process is repeated many times, giving rise to increasing organisation and greater complexity, with more clearly distinguishable features, eventually giving rise to a fully-fledged human being.

The point is that, in real life, the negative side of things is equally as important as the positive. We are accustomed to look upon life and death as completely opposite poles. But in practice, they are two parts of the same process, and are inseparable. The process of life, growth and development can only take place through the constant renewal of all the cells of the organism, some dying, others coming into being. Even on the most primitive level, life involves constant change in which the organism constantly absorbs food from its surroundings and uses it to build itself, while getting rid of waste matter. Therefore, every living thing is and is not at the same time, because everything is in a constant state of flux. To be without contradiction is to lack all inner differentiation, to have no movement, to be in a state of static equilibrium – in a word, to be dead.

In the words of Prigogine and Stengers:

> The living cell presents an incessant metabolic activity. There thousands of chemical reactions take place simultaneously to transform the matter the cell feeds on, to synthesise the fundamental biomolecules, and to eliminate waste products. As regards both the different reaction rates and the reaction sites within the cell, this chemical activity is highly coordinated. The biological structure thus combines order and activity. In contrast, an equilibrium state remains inert even though it may be structured, as, for example, with a crystal.[15]

At first sight, these observations may seem like pointless subtleties. In point of fact, they are extremely profound reflections, which are not only applicable to thought, but also to nature. And, although it is not always obvious, the same is true of inanimate nature also. Indeed, Hegel considered that the two were inseparably linked. "Everything flows and nothing stays", said Heraclitus. "We step and

---

15 I. Prigogine and I. Stengers, *Order Out of Chaos*, p. 131.

we do not step into the same stream".[16] Hegel here is saying the same thing. At the heart of this philosophy is a dynamic view of the universe; a view which deals with things as living processes, not dead objects; in their essential interrelations, not separate bits and pieces, or arbitrary lists; as a whole, which is greater than the sum of the parts.

QUANTITY AND QUALITY

Everything can be seen from two points of view – quality and quantity. The fact that the world consists of a sum total of processes which are constantly changing does not mean that real things do not have a definite form of existence, an identity. However much an object changes, it remains, within certain limits, a qualitatively distinct form of existence, different from another. It is this qualitative definiteness which gives things stability, differentiates them, and makes the world so rich and boundlessly varied.

The properties of a thing are what makes it what it is. But this quality is not reducible to its separate properties. It is bound up with the object as a whole. Thus, a human being is not just an assemblage of bone tissue, blood, muscles, etc. Life itself is a complex phenomenon which cannot be reduced to the sum total of its individual molecules, but arises from the interactions between them. To use the modern terminology of complexity theory, life is an emergent phenomenon.

The relation of whole and parts was dealt with at length by Hegel, who wrote:

> The limbs and organs, for instance, of an organic body are not merely
> parts of it: it is only in their unity that they are what they are, and they
> are unquestionably affected by that unity, as they also in turn affect it.
> These limbs and organs become mere parts, only when they pass under
> the hands of the anatomist, whose occupation, be it remembered, is
> not with the living body but with the corpse. Not that such analysis is
> illegitimate: we only mean that the external and mechanical relation of

---

16 Quoted in Burnet, *Early Greek Philosophy*, p. 139.

whole and parts is not sufficient for us, if we want to study organic life in its truth.[17]

It is interesting to note that the latest ideas which have caught the imagination of an important section of the scientific community – the theories of chaos and complexity – were anticipated long ago by Hegel and, in many respects, received a much more comprehensive treatment in his hands. A case in point is his explanation of the transformation of quantity into quality, whereby an accumulation of small changes brings about a sudden change in quality.

In addition to the quality which defines the essential features of an object, all things possess quantitative features – a definite magnitude, number, volume, speed of its processes, degree of development of its properties, and so on. The quantitative side of things is that which permits them to be divided (actually or mentally) into their constituent parts and put together again. In contrast to quality, changes in quantity do not alter the nature of the whole, or cause its destruction. Only when a definite limit is reached, which is different in each case, do changes of quantitative character cause a sudden qualitative transformation.

In mathematics, the quantitative aspect of things is separated from their content and regarded as something independent. The extremely wide field of applicability of mathematics to spheres of natural science and technology with very different contents is explained by the fact that it deals purely with quantitative relations. Here, it is claimed, it is possible to reduce quality to quantity. This is the fundamental error of which Marx and Engels referred to as the metaphysical mode of thought, and which nowadays is termed reductionism. There is nothing in the real world that consists only of quantity, just as there is nothing which is pure quality. Everything in reality consists of the unity of quantity and quality, which Hegel called Measure.

Measure is the organic unity of quantity and quality. Every qualitatively distinct object, as we have seen, contains quantitative

17 G. W. F. Hegel, *Shorter Logic*, pp. 191-2.

elements which are mobile and variable. Living organisms grow at a certain rate. Gases and liquids are affected by variations in temperature. The behaviour of a water droplet or a heap of sand is determined by its size, and so on. These mutations, however, are necessarily bounded by definite limits, which are different in each case, but in practice can usually be discovered. Carried beyond this limit, quantitative changes bring about a qualitative transformation. In its turn, the qualitative change brings about a change in its quantitative attributes. There are not only changes of quantity to quality, but also the opposite process, where a change in quality causes a change in quantity. The critical points of transition from one state to another are expressed as nodal points in Hegel's nodal line of measurement.

ESSENCE

The Doctrine of Essence is the most important part of Hegel's philosophy, because it is here that he explains the dialectic in detail. Human thought does not stop at what is immediately given in sense perception, but seeks to go beyond it and grasp the thing-in-itself. Beyond appearance, we look for the essence of a thing. But this is not immediately accessible. We can see the sun and moon, but we cannot 'see' the laws of gravity. In order to go beyond appearance, the mind must be actively brought into play, to break down what we earlier learned through understanding. If the understanding is positive, asserting that a given thing 'is', dialectical reasoning is essentially negative, in that it dissolves what 'is', and reveals the inner contradictions, which will inevitably destroy it.

The contradiction which lies at the heart of all things is expressed as the idea of the unity of opposites. Dialectically, what seem to be mutually exclusive phenomena are actually inseparable, as Hegel explains:

> Positive and negative are supposed to express an absolute difference. The two however are at bottom the same: the name of either might be transferred to the other. Thus, for example, debts and assets are not two

particular, self-subsisting species of property. What is negative to the debtor is positive to the creditor. A way to the east is also a way to the west. Positive and negative are therefore intrinsically conditioned by one another, and are only in relation to each other. The north pole of the magnet cannot be without the south pole, and vice versa. If we cut a magnet in two, we have not a north pole in one piece, and a south pole in the other. Similarly, in electricity, the positive and the negative are not two diverse and independent fluids.[18]

In the process of analysis, Hegel enumerates a series of important stages: positive and negative; necessity and accident; quantity and quality; form and content; action and repulsion; and so on. One of the central features of Essence is that it is relative – everything is related to something else, in a universal web of interaction. The basic law of elementary knowledge (understanding) is the law of identity ('A' = 'A'). This is generally considered as the basis of all that we know. Up to a point, this is correct. Without the law of identity, coherent thought would be impossible. We ascertain the basic fact of existence, and focus our attention on a particular thing. However, identity presupposes difference. A cat is a cat, because it is not a dog, a mouse, an elephant, and so on. In order to establish identity, we must compare something to another.

In real life, nothing is purely itself, as implied by the law of identity, despite its apparently absolute character. Everything is determined by everything else. In that sense everything is relative. As Engels remarks:

The true nature of the determinations of 'essence' is expressed by Hegel himself (*Enzyklopädie*, I, paragraph 111, addendum): "In essence everything is *relative*" (e.g., positive and negative, which have meaning only in their relation, not each for itself).[19]

Not only that. Nothing is simple, as also implied in the law of identity. As we saw in relation to the simple cell or embryo, concrete

18 Ibid., p. 173.
19 F. Engels, *Dialectics of Nature*, p. 216.

being, as opposed to the purely abstract being of mere 'identity', must contain inner differentiation. Moreover, this differentiation contains the seeds of contradiction. In order to develop, in order to live, the cell must contain the tendency toward self-dissolution, towards division, towards negation. This inner tension is, in fact, the basis of all life. But it is also found in non-living objects, such as the phenomenon of surface tension in a drop of water, which holds the molecules in a certain order, and innumerable other examples.

The attempt to banish contradiction from thought has been an obsession of logicians for centuries. Hegel was the first one to show that, in fact, contradiction lies at the heart of everything that really exists. If we attempt to think of the world without contradiction, as traditional formal logic tries to do, all that we achieve is to introduce insoluble contradictions into thought. This was the real meaning of Kant's 'antinomies'. To separate identity and difference, to attempt to deny the existence of contradiction, leads thought into a barren and empty formalism.

APPEARANCE AND ESSENCE

Most people realise that 'appearances are deceptive'. However, this is only relatively true. In order to arrive at an understanding of the essence of a thing, we must begin by a thorough acquaintance with precisely these 'appearances', that is, with all the physical features, properties and tendencies we can observe. In the course of such an analysis, it will become clear that certain facts can be omitted as 'unessential' and, gradually, we will arrive at the most fundamental characteristics of the object under consideration.

It is very common to say about somebody: "Yes, but he's not really like that." The implication is that people are not what they seem to be. Appearance is one thing, but essence is supposed to be completely different. However, this is not quite true. If we only have a slight acquaintance with a person, then it is true that we cannot form an accurate impression of him or her on the basis of their conduct. It may be completely untypical. But if we have known people for a long time, we have sufficient reason to believe that we know them as they are. We precisely base ourselves on 'appearances' because there is nothing else to base ourselves on. The Bible says "by their fruits shall you know them",[20] and that is correct. As a man or woman lives and acts, so they are. There is nothing else to look for.

This was the fundamental error of Kant, when he tried to draw a line between appearances and some mysterious 'thing' that lay beyond experience which was supposed to be forever beyond human knowledge. In fact, once we know all the properties of a thing, we know the thing itself. We may be limited at any given moment in time by lack of information, but, in principle, there is nothing which is forever barred to human knowledge, except one thing – to know everything about an infinite universe. This is no real limitation, but simply an expression of the dialectical relation between the finite nature of individuals, and an infinite universe, which is constantly revealing new secrets. And although the particular knowledge of one person is finite, from one generation to another, the sum-total of knowledge and understanding of humanity increases. The process of learning is never-ending. Precisely in this lies its fascination and its beauty.

We set out from what is known, in order to discover what is not known. One thing leads to another. A doctor, basing himself on all his knowledge of medical science and past experience, carefully examines all the available symptoms and arrives at a diagnosis. A sailor will study the wind and tides in order to guess the possibilities of putting to sea. In this way, essence is manifested through appearance, although it requires a certain skill and understanding to pass from the one to the other.

One of the greatest errors it is possible to commit when dealing with the processes that occur in society is to approach them as static and fixed – that is to say, from the standpoint of formal logic. One frequently comes across this kind of thing – narrow-minded prejudice masquerading as 'practical wisdom'. It is said that 'people will never change', 'things will always be as they are', and 'there is

_____

20 Matthew 7:10.

nothing new under the sun'. This kind of superficial thought pretends to be profound, but really only reveals the kind of ignorance which is content with itself. No rational reason is given for such assertions. Occasionally an attempt is made to give it a biological basis, with vague references to something called 'human nature', from which we instantly deduce that the individual in question knows nothing whatsoever about humans or their nature.

This kind of mentality is strictly limited to its own narrow experience of the world of appearance in the most superficial sense. It is very much like a man who is constantly skating on the surface, without bothering to inquire about the thickness of the ice. Such a person may get away with it nine times out of ten. One day, however, he finds himself drowning in icy water. At that precise moment, he begins to realise that maybe the ice was not as solid as it looked.

'A' is 'A'. You are you. I am myself. People are people. A dollar is a dollar. Society is society. The trade unions are the trade unions. Such sentences seem reassuring, but in fact are empty of all content. Insofar as they express anything at all, it is the idea that everything is itself, and nothing changes. However, experience tells us something different. Things are constantly changing and, at a critical point, small quantitative changes can produce massive transformations.

FORM AND CONTENT

There are many contradictions in things. For instance, the contradiction between form and content. Every gardener knows that a seed carefully planted in a pot will produce a plant. Initially, the pot protects the young plant and helps it to thrive. But at a certain stage, the roots become too big for the space allowed. The gardener must remove it from the pot, or it will die. Similarly, the human embryo is protected by the mother's womb for nine months. At this point, a critical stage is reached in which, either the baby is separated from the mother's body, or both will perish. These are examples of the contradiction between form and content which are readily understood. Another example would be the way in which the forces which accumulate beneath the earth's crust eventually produce an earthquake.

Similar forces build up within society, which also has its 'fault-lines'. The action of these forces is no more visible than those that cause an earthquake. To the superficial observer, nothing is happening. Everything is 'normal'. The skilled observer, however, is able to detect the symptoms of subterranean activity in society, just as a competent geologist can read a seismograph. Trotsky once defined theory as the superiority of foresight over astonishment. It is the fate of superficial and empirical thought to be constantly astonished, like the man who fell through the ice. It is the price one pays for confusing appearance with essence and form with content.

The essence of a thing is the sum total of its most fundamental properties. The task of dialectical analysis is to determine these. In each case it will be found that there is a potential contradiction between the present state and tendencies which are tending to dissolve it. In classical mechanics, the idea of a perfect equilibrium plays a central role. Things tend to return to equilibrium. That is, at least, in theory. In real life, a perfect equilibrium is a rarity. Whenever equilibrium is reached, it tends to be temporary and unstable. Development and change presuppose this. In the intensive ward of a hospital, when a heart monitor reaches a state of 'equilibrium', i.e., a straight line, this signifies death of the organism.

When referring to the properties of a thing, it is customary to use the verb 'to have': fire has the property of burning; a human being has the properties of breathing, thinking, eating, etc. This gives the wrong idea. A child has an ice-cream. A woman has a dog. The relationship here is accidental and external, since the child and the woman could equally well not have these things, and still be a child and a woman. A thing does not 'have' properties – it is the sum-total of its properties. Take these away, and we are left with nothing, which is what Kant's Thing-in-Itself really was. This is an extremely important idea, which is only now beginning to be understood by scientists. The whole cannot be reduced to the sum of its parts, because in entering into a dynamic relationship, the parts themselves become transformed, and give rise to an entirely new situation, governed by qualitatively different laws.

This phenomenon can be seen in society. Trotsky pointed out that the working class, without organisation, is only "raw material for exploitation."[21] This fact is starkly revealed in periods like the present, when trade unions are eliminated or undermined in many workplaces. Historically, the movement of the workers to organise themselves brings about a complete transformation of the situation. Quantity becomes transformed into quality. Whereas individual workers are powerless, the class organised as a class has colossal power, at least potentially. Not a wheel turns, not a telephone rings, not a light bulb shines without the kind permission of the working class. In Hegelian language, the working class before it is organised, is only a class 'in itself' – that is, an unrealised potential. Once it becomes organised and conscious of its power, it becomes a class 'for itself'. Of course, Hegel was far from drawing such explicitly revolutionary conclusions from his dialectical method. Being an idealist, his main concern was to present the dialectic as the process of development of the Spirit. Real relations are stood on their head, and the real world is presented in a mystified form. But the real content constantly finds its way through the dense fog of idealism, like shafts of sunlight through the clouds.

In essence, everything is relative; that is to say, everything stands in relation to an Other, which conditions it, and in turn, is conditioned by it. Things are what they are thanks to their interrelations with other things. This also can be seen in society. Things which are commonly believed to be real entities are, in fact, the product of particular relationships, which have sunk so deeply into people's consciousness that they acquire the force of prejudice. Such a thing is the institution of monarchy:

> Naive minds think that the office of kingship lodges in the king himself, in his ermine cloak and his crown, in his flesh and bones. As a matter of

21 L. Trotsky, 'What Next? Vital Questions for the German Proletariat', *The Struggle Against Fascism in Germany*, p. 210.

fact, the office of kingship is an interrelation between people. The king is king only because the interests and prejudices of millions of people are refracted through his person. When the flood of development sweeps away these interrelations, then the king appears to be only a washed-out man with a flabby lower lip. He who was once called Alfonso XIII could discourse upon this from fresh impressions.

The leader by will of the people differs from the leader by will of God in that the former is compelled to clear the road for himself or, at any rate, to assist the conjuncture of events in discovering him. Nevertheless, the leader is always a relation between people, the individual supply to meet the collective demand. The controversy over Hitler's personality becomes the sharper the more the secret of his success is sought in himself. In the meantime, another political figure would be difficult to find that is in the same measure the focus of anonymous historic forces. Not every exasperated petty bourgeois could have become Hitler, but a particle of Hitler is lodged in every exasperated petty bourgeois.[22]

NECESSITY AND ACCIDENT

In further analysing the nature of being in all its different manifestations, Hegel deals with the relation between potential and actual, and also between necessity and accident ('contingency'). In relation to this question, it is important to clarify one of Hegel's most famous (or notorious) sayings: "What is rational is actual; and what is actual is rational."[23] At first sight, this statement seems mystifying, and also reactionary, since it seems to imply that all that exists is rational, and therefore justified. This, however, was not at all what Hegel meant, as Engels explains:

Now, according to Hegel, reality is, however, in no way an attribute predicable of any given state of affairs, social or political, in all circumstances and at all times. On the contrary. The Roman Republic

22 L. Trotsky, 'What Is National Socialism?', *The Struggle Against Fascism in Germany*, pp. 522-3.

23 G. W. F. Hegel, *Philosophy of Right*, p. 20.

was real, but so was the Roman Empire, which superseded it. In 1789 the French monarchy had become so unreal, that is to say, so robbed of all necessity, so irrational, that it had to be destroyed by the Great Revolution, of which Hegel always speaks with the greatest enthusiasm. In this case, therefore, the monarchy was the unreal and the revolution the real. And so, in the course of development, all that was previously real becomes unreal, loses its necessity, its right of existence, its rationality. And in the place of moribund reality comes a new, viable reality – peacefully if the old has enough common sense to go to its death without a struggle; forcibly if it resists this necessity. Thus the Hegelian proposition turns into its opposite through Hegelian dialectics itself: All that is real in the sphere of human history becomes irrational in the course of time, is therefore irrational by its very destination, is encumbered with irrationality from the outset; and everything which is rational in the minds of men is destined to become real, however much it may contradict existing apparent reality. In accordance with all the rules of the Hegelian method of thought, the proposition of the rationality of everything which is real is dissolved to become the other proposition: All that exists deserves to perish.[24]

A given form of society is 'rational' to the degree that it achieves its purpose, that is, that it develops the productive forces, raises the cultural level, and thus advances human progress. Once it fails to do this, it enters into contradiction with itself – that is, it becomes irrational and unreal, and no longer has any right to exist. Thus, even in the most apparently reactionary utterances of Hegel, there is hidden a revolutionary idea.

All that exists evidently does so out of necessity. But not everything can exist. Potential existence is not yet actual existence. In *The Science of Logic*, Hegel carefully traces the process whereby something passes from a state of being merely possible to the point where possibility becomes probability, and the latter becomes inevitable ('necessity'). In view of the colossal confusion that has arisen in modern science

---

24 F. Engels, *Ludwig Feuerbach and the End of Classical German Philosophy*, MECW, Vol. 26, pp. 358-9.

around the issue of 'probability', a study of Hegel's thorough and profound treatment of this subject is highly instructive.

Possibility and actuality denote the dialectical development of the real world and the various stages in the emergence and development of objects. A thing which exists in potential contains within itself the objective tendency of development, or at least the absence of conditions which would preclude its coming into being. However, there is a difference between abstract possibility and real potential, and the two things are frequently confused. Abstract or formal possibility merely expresses the absence of any conditions that might exclude a particular phenomenon, but it does not assume the presence of conditions which would make its appearance inevitable.

This leads to endless confusion, and is actually a kind of trick which serves to justify all kinds of absurd and arbitrary ideas. For example, it is said that if a monkey were allowed to hammer away at a typewriter for long enough, it would eventually produce one of Shakespeare's sonnets. This objective seems too modest. Why only one sonnet? Why not the collected works of Shakespeare? Indeed, why not the whole of world literature, with the general theory of relativity and Beethoven's symphonies thrown in for good measure? The bare assertion that it is 'statistically possible' does not take us a single step further. The complex processes of nature, society and human thought are not all susceptible to simple statistical treatment, nor will great works of literature emerge out of mere accident, no matter how long we wait for our monkey to deliver the goods.

In order for potential to become actual, a particular concatenation of circumstances is required. Moreover, this is not a simple, linear process, but a dialectical one, in which an accumulation of small quantitative changes eventually produces a qualitative leap. Real, as opposed to abstract, possibility implies the presence of all the necessary factors out of which the potential will lose its character of provisionality, and become actual. And, as Hegel explains, it will remain actual only for as long as these conditions exist, and no longer. This is true whether we are referring to the life of an individual, a given socioeconomic form, a scientific theory, or any natural phenomenon. The point at which a change becomes inevitable can be determined by the method invented by Hegel and known as the 'nodal line of measurement'. If we regard any process as a line, it will be seen that there are specific points ('nodal points') on the line of development, where the process experiences a sudden acceleration, or qualitative leap.

It is easy to identify cause and effect in isolated cases, as when one hits a ball with a bat. But in a wider sense, the notion of causality becomes far more complicated. Individual causes and effects become lost in a vast ocean of interaction, where cause becomes transformed into effect and vice versa. Just try tracing back even the simplest event to its 'ultimate causes' and you will see that eternity will not be long enough to do it. There will always be some new cause, and that in turn will have to be explained, and so on *ad infinitum*. This paradox has entered the popular consciousness in such sayings as this one:

> For the want of a nail, a shoe was lost;
> For the want of a shoe, a horse was lost;
> For the want of a horse, a rider was lost;
> For the want of a rider, a battle was lost;
> For the want of a battle, a kingdom was lost;
> ...And all for the want of a nail.

The impossibility of establishing a 'final cause' has led some people to abandon the idea of cause altogether. Everything is considered to be random and accidental. In the twentieth century this position was adopted, at least in theory, by a large number of scientists on the basis of an incorrect interpretation of the results of quantum physics, particularly the philosophical positions of Werner Heisenberg. We have dealt with this matter at length before.[25] Suffice it here to say that Hegel answered these arguments in advance, when he explained the dialectical relation between accident and necessity.

---

25 See A. Woods and T. Grant, *Reason in Revolt*.

Hegel explains that there is no such thing as true causality, in the sense of an isolated cause and effect. Every effect has a counter-effect, and every action has a counter-action. The idea of an isolated cause and effect is an abstraction taken from classical Newtonian physics, which Hegel was highly critical of, although it enjoyed tremendous prestige at that time. Here again, Hegel was in advance of his time. Instead of the action-reaction of mechanics, he advanced the notion of Reciprocity, of universal interaction. Everything influences everything else and is, in turn, influenced and determined by everything. Hegel thus re-introduced the concept of accident which had been rigorously banned from science by the mechanist philosophy of Newton and Laplace.

At first sight, we seem to be lost in a vast number of accidents. But this confusion is only apparent. Order emerges out of chaos. The accidental phenomena which constantly flash in and out of existence, like the waves on the surface of an ocean, express a deeper process, which is not accidental but necessary. At a decisive point, this necessity reveals itself through accident.

This idea of the dialectical unity of necessity and accident may seem strange, but it is strikingly confirmed by a whole series of observations from the most varied fields of science and society. The mechanism of natural selection in the theory of evolution is the best-known example. But there are many others. In the last half century, there have been many discoveries in the field of chaos and complexity theory which precisely detail how 'order arises out of chaos', which is exactly what Hegel worked out one and a half centuries earlier.

'Classical' chemical reactions are seen as very random processes. The molecules involved are evenly distributed in space, and their spread is distributed 'normally' i.e. in a Gauss curve. These kinds of reactions fit into the concept of Boltzmann, wherein all side-chains of the reaction will fade out and the reaction will end up in a stable reaction, an immobile equilibrium. However, in recent decades chemical reactions were discovered that deviate from this ideal and simplified concept. The most famous examples are the

Belousov-Zhabotinsky reaction, and the Brussels model devised by chaos theorist Ilya Prigogine.

Linear thermodynamics describes a stable, predictable behaviour of systems that tend towards the minimum level of activity possible. However, when the thermodynamic forces acting on a system reach the point where the linear region is exceeded, stability can no longer be assumed. Turbulence arises. For a long time, turbulence was regarded as a synonym for disorder or chaos. But now, it has been discovered that, what appears to be merely chaotic disorder on the macroscopic (large-scale) level, is, in fact, highly organised on the microscopic (small-scale) level.

Today, the study of chemical instabilities has become common. Of special interest is the research done on the phenomenon of the 'chemical clock' in Brussels under the guidance of Ilya Prigogine. The study of what happens beyond the critical point where chemical instability commences has enormous interest from the standpoint of dialectics. The Brussels model (nicknamed the 'Brusselator' by American scientists) describes the behaviour of gas molecules. Suppose there are two types of molecules, 'red' and 'blue', in a state of chaotic, totally random motion. One would expect that, at a given moment, there would be an irregular distribution of molecules, producing a 'violet' colour, with occasional flashes of red or blue. But in a chemical clock, this does not occur beyond the critical point. The system is all blue, then all red, and these changes occur at regular intervals.

> Such a degree of order stemming from the activity of billions of molecules seems incredible and indeed, if chemical clocks had not been observed, no one would believe that such a process is possible. To change colour all at once, molecules must have a way to "communicate". The system has to act as a whole. We will return repeatedly to this key word, communicate, which is of obvious importance in so many fields, from chemistry to neurophysiology. Dissipative structures introduce probably one of the simplest physical mechanisms for communication.[26]

_____

26 I. Prigogine and I. Stengers, *Order Out of Chaos*, p. 148.

The phenomenon of the 'chemical clock' shows how in nature order can arise spontaneously out of chaos at a certain point. This is an important observation, especially in relation to the way in which life arises from inorganic matter.

> "Order through fluctuations" models introduce an unstable world where small causes can have large effects, but this world is not arbitrary. On the contrary, the reasons for the amplification of a small event are a legitimate matter for rational inquiry.[27]

We must remember that Hegel was writing at the beginning of the last century, when science was completely dominated by classical mechanical physics, and half a century before Darwin developed the idea of natural selection through the medium of random mutations. He had no scientific evidence to back up his theory that necessity expresses itself through accident. But that is the central idea behind the most recent innovative thinking in science.

This profound law is equally fundamental to an understanding of history. As Marx wrote to Kugelmann in 1871:

> World history would indeed be very easy to make, if the struggle were taken up only on condition of infallibly favourable chances. It would on the other hand be of a very mystical nature, if "accidents" played no part. These accidents themselves fall naturally into the general course of development and are compensated for, again, by other accidents. But acceleration and delay are very dependent upon such "accidents" which include the "accident" of the character of those who at first stand at the head of the movement.[28]

Engels made the same point a few years later in relation to the role of 'great men' in history:

> Men make their history themselves, but not as yet with a collective will or according to a collective plan or even in a definitely defined, given society. Their efforts clash, and for that very reason all such societies

27 Ibid., p. 206.
28 K. Marx, 'Letter to Kugelmann, 17 April 1871', MESC, pp. 310-1.

are governed by *necessity*, which is supplemented by and appears under the forms of *accident*. The necessity which here asserts itself amidst all accident is again ultimately economic necessity. This is where the so-called great men come in for treatment. That such and such a man and precisely that man arises at that particular time in that given country is of course pure accident. But cut him out and there will be a demand for a substitute, and this substitute will be found, good or bad, but in the long run he will be found.[29]

THE NOTION

In Hegel's dialectic the supreme achievement of thought is the Notion. The development of the Notion is described by Hegel as a process which proceeds from abstract to concrete. It signifies a deepening of knowledge, and a development from a lower to a higher degree of understanding, of the development from potential to actual. At the beginning, the Notion is referred to as 'in itself', or implicit. It is later developed, and becomes the Notion 'for itself', or explicit. In its highest form it is the union of both these aspects, 'in and for itself'. In the Notion the process of development reaches its highest point. What was only implicit at the beginning now becomes explicit. It is a return to the starting point, but on a qualitatively higher level.

In his main work, *The Science of Logic*, Hegel does not end with the Notion, but goes on to the Absolute Idea, of which all that can be said is that he tells us absolutely nothing about it. This is typical of the contradictions Hegel's idealism landed him in. The dialectic cannot lead to an Absolute Idea, or any other final solution. To imply that there is an end to the process of human knowledge conflicts with the letter and spirit of dialectics. So the Hegelian philosophy ended up in an insoluble contradiction. This could only be solved by a radical break with all of previous philosophy.

The epoch-making quality of Hegel's philosophy consisted in the fact that, by summing up the whole history of philosophy in such a comprehensive way, he made it impossible to proceed any further

---

29 F. Engels, 'Letter to Starkenburg, 25 January 1894', MESC, p. 518.

along the traditional philosophical lines. Secondly, the dialectical method, which he perfected, provided the basis for a whole new world outlook, one that did not confine itself to the analysis and criticism of ideas, but involved an analysis of the history of society and a revolutionary criticism of the existing social order. Hegel's great contribution was well expressed by Engels in *Anti-Dühring*:

That [the] Hegel[ian system] did not solve the problem [it propounded] is here immaterial. Its epoch-making merit was that it propounded the problem. This problem is one that no single individual will ever be able to solve. Although Hegel was – with Saint-Simon – the most encyclopaedic mind of his time, he was limited, first, by the necessarily limited extent of his own knowledge and, second, by the limited extent and depth of the knowledge and conceptions of his age. To these limits a third must be added. Hegel was an idealist. To him the thoughts within his brain were not the more or less abstract pictures of actual things and processes, but, conversely, things and their evolution were only the realised pictures of the 'Idea', existing somewhere from eternity before the world existed. This way of thinking turned everything upside down, and completely reversed the actual connection of things in the world. Correctly and ingeniously as many individual groups of facts were grasped by Hegel, yet, for the reasons just given, there is much that is botched, artificial, laboured, in a word, wrong in point of detail. The Hegelian system, in itself, was a colossal miscarriage – but it was also the last of its kind. It was suffering, in fact, from an internal and incurable contradiction. Upon the one hand, its essential proposition was the conception that human history is a process of evolution, which, by its very nature, cannot find its intellectual final term in the discovery of any so-called absolute truth. But, on the other hand, it laid claim to being the very essence of this absolute truth. A system of natural and historical knowledge, embracing everything, and final for all time, is a contradiction to the fundamental law of dialectic reasoning. This law, indeed, by no means excludes, but, on the contrary, includes the idea that systematic knowledge of the external universe can make giant strides from age to age.[30]

---

30 F. Engels, *Anti-Dühring*, pp. 34-5.

Hegel's dialectic was brilliantly conceived, but ultimately deficient, because it was limited to the domain of thought. Nevertheless, it contained the potential for a major departure in thought, one that was to radically alter not just the history of philosophy, but that of the world. To paraphrase Hegel, what was present in itself (i.e. potentially) in his work became a realised idea – an idea in and for itself in the revolutionary doctrine of Marxism, where philosophy finally gives up its character as a one-sided abstract, mental activity, and enters the realm of practice.

Aristotle already explained the relationship between potential and actual. At all levels of nature, society, thought, and even the development of individual human beings from childhood to maturity, we see the same process. Everything that exists contains within itself the potential for further development, that is, to perfect itself, to become something different to what it is. The whole of human history can be seen as the struggle of humanity to realise its potential. Ultimately, the aim of socialism is to create the necessary conditions whereby this goal can be finally realised, that men and women can become actually what they always were potentially. Here, however, we have already left the dimly-lit study of the philosopher, and stepped out into the broad daylight of human life, activity and struggle.

11. FROM HEGEL TO MARX

HEGELIANISM AT A DEAD END

With Hegel, we reach the pinnacle of the history of philosophy as a system of ideas. Here, the development of each branch of the system is so complete and comprehensive, that one feels that all that has to be said has already been said. All that is left is to spin an infinite number of variations on the same themes, as in the intricate sound-world of J. S. Bach.

But, at the moment of its greatest triumph, the Hegelian system began to enter into irreversible decline and dissolution. The crisis of Hegelianism can be simply explained. Hegel carried his all-embracing system so far that it really exhausted the possibilities of philosophy as such. The problems he raised could not be resolved within the limits of a purely ideal system. The inherent weakness of Hegel's method was that, as an idealist, he did not set out from real, concrete, sensuous human thought, but from an idealist abstraction, which he called self-consciousness. In his *Phenomenology of Spirit*, Hegel sets out from an elementary, embryonic stage of consciousness, proceeding through a whole series of stages, which in their totality embrace the entire history of human thought, from religion, through the history of philosophy, to science.

Hegel's dialectical method was a huge advance over the earlier philosophy, and it contained many profound insights and flashes of genius. In places (notably, in *The Philosophy of History*) he comes close to materialism. But, since his starting point was idealism, the real world is here expressed only in an indirect and distorted manner. For this reason, in the end, despite all its undoubted profundity and its many brilliant insights, Hegelian philosophy found itself at an impasse.

The starting point and culmination of the *Science of Logic* was the Absolute Idea. The problem here was that Hegel stood the relation between subject and object on its head. His method is objective in the sense that it clearly establishes the relation between real things and processes, and their reflection in consciousness. However, in Hegel, thought alienates itself from itself, enters the material world and develops and unfolds within it, only to return to itself at the end of a lengthy evolution, as the Absolute Idea – a universal that has been enriched with all the wealth of the particular.

The Absolute Idea is thought that has become conscious of itself. But, in reality, it is precisely the other way around. Here, reality is only alienated thought, whereas the exact opposite is the real state of affairs. To tell the truth, the entire edifice was merely a ghostly echo of reality. *Thought is matter that has become conscious of itself.* We do not think only with our mind but with all our senses – with our whole body in fact. What links humans with the external world (nature) is not the abstract thinking of individuals but collective human sensuous activity – social labour, which transforms nature, and at the same time transforms humankind itself.

HEGELIANISM AFTER HEGEL

Some philosophers tried to continue where Hegel had left off in his own terms, i.e. within the framework of traditional philosophy. The Hegelian Right were represented by men like Karl Friedrich Göschel, Johann Philipp Gabler, Johann Karl Friedrich Rosenkranz and Johann Eduard Erdmann. They based themselves on the weakest, most conservative side of Hegel.

For them, the Hegelian dialectic had been carried to its completion, and all that was required was the mechanical repetition of old phrases, which could be applied in an external manner to any content. This, more than anything, resulted in the discrediting of dialectics, which many began to see as a mere exercise in verbal tricks and sophistry. These self-proclaimed disciples of Hegel possessed all of the master's defects and none of his virtues. Their attempts signally failed to produce anything of interest, and are far inferior to the writings of the great man. They are now no longer a footnote to history. Their writings contain nothing of note and their names have long been consigned to a well-earned oblivion.

HEGELIANISM AS A TOOL OF REACTION

For the Right Hegelians, the autocratic Prussian state represented the highest point of all social development. In this, they seemed to be following in the footsteps of their master. But in reality, this represents only one side of Hegel's thought – the weakest and least interesting side. Hegel, whose philosophical views were undoubtedly both mystical and idealist, was (at least in his later years) conservative in his political views and tended to support the Prussian Absolutist state. Yes, all this is true and well known. But it does not exhaust the matter under discussion and does not do justice to the essential, dialectical nature of Hegel's thinking.

In fact, the German authorities were quick to grasp the subversive and revolutionary implications of Hegel's dialectic. Realising the danger posed by it, the philosophical establishment in Germany made every effort to distance itself from Hegel, preferring to support the 'Back to Kant' movement. But in other countries, Hegelianism was eagerly welcomed for its conservative side. That was particularly the case in Britain, where the mystical, idealist elements of Hegel were seen as a useful antidote to materialism.

HEGELIANISM IN THE ANGLO-SAXON WORLD

By this time, religion was fighting a desperate rearguard action against the advance of science, in particular the evolutionary ideas of Charles

Darwin, which posed a direct threat to the idea of Creation, and even to the existence of God the Supreme Creator. It was precisely the fear of materialism – with its subversive and revolutionary connotations – that explains the otherwise inexplicable popularity of Hegelianism in British universities in the last decades of the nineteenth century.

The British academic establishment searched for a philosophical weapon to strike down the monster of materialism, and found it in Hegelian idealism. As John Passmore points out: "In Germany, Hegelianism had completely failed to arrest the progress of materialism; *the fact remains that it was introduced into Great Britain to fulfil that very purpose.*"[1] Similarly, in the USA, the St. Louis Hegelians thought they had found in his philosophy "a sword wherewith to smite the three-headed monster of anarchy in politics, traditionalism in religion and naturalism in science".[2]

We have the astonishing spectacle of German philosophy (or, more accurately, a caricature of German philosophy) being imported into British universities, while the 'theory of knowledge' – that handmaiden of English empiricism – was exported to Germany, where it was met with equal enthusiasm. For a time, the traditional roles were reversed, with not very positive results in either case. Typical of the British school of vulgarised Hegelianism was the work of J. H. Stirling, *The Secret of Hegel* (1865), of which some remarked that: "If Hegel had a secret, Stirling kept it well!" While the great man was still alive, he received scant attention from the British philosophical establishment, whose obsession with empiricism gave rise to a deep-seated mistrust of abstract thought and broad theoretical generalisations which has been the enduring weakness of all Anglo-Saxon philosophy up to the present day.

THE DISSOLUTION OF THE HEGELIAN SCHOOL

In Germany, where the inner decay of the Hegelian School had led to its dissolution into a number of squabbling sects, the situation

---

1   J. Passmore, *A Hundred Years of Philosophy*, p. 51, my emphasis.
2   Ibid., p. 51.

was different. After the death of Hegel in 1831, his School inevitably disintegrated and fell to pieces, a victim of its own internal contradictions. The decay of Hegelianism was bound to provoke a reaction, and it did. The Hegelian School split into two wings – the right and left. One expression of this was Marxism, which led away from philosophy altogether (at least, philosophy as hitherto understood).

It was Marx and Engels who rescued the healthy kernel of Hegel's thought from oblivion and restored it as dialectical and historical materialism. The early writings of the founders of scientific socialism clearly display their Hegelian origins. The real settling of accounts with Hegel can be traced to *The Holy Family*, *The German Ideology* and, particularly, the famous 'Theses on Feuerbach'. But Marxism did not spring, ready formed and armed, like Athena from the head of Zeus. Marx and Engels first had to pass through the preparatory school of the Hegelian Left.

THE HEGELIAN LEFT

As we have noted, the Hegelian Right produced not one figure worthy of mention. Far more interesting was the left wing that crystallised around a group of radical German freethinkers, formed in opposition to the conservative reactionaries. Known variously as the Young Hegelians (*Junghegelianer*), the Left Hegelians (*Linkshegelianer*), or the Hegelian Left (*die Hegelsche Linke*), these brave young men attempted to draw radical conclusions from Hegel's philosophy.

This was no accident. The Young Hegelians were the product of the religious, philosophical, and political ferment in Germany at that time. This was the period between the Revolution of 1830 in France, which overthrew the reactionary Bourbon monarch Charles X, and the wave of revolutions that swept Europe – including Germany – in 1848 and 1849. The Hegelian Left represented the radical wing of Hegel's followers. Active in the 1830s and 1840s, they interpreted Hegel's ideas in the spirit of German liberalism. Their leading members were David Strauss, Arnold Ruge, Max Stirner, and Bruno and Edgar

Bauer. But they also included Ludwig Feuerbach and Moses Hess. The young Marx and Engels were also initially involved in this movement.

Despite its revolutionary claims, this school was entirely preoccupied with abstract philosophical questions and the criticism of religion, reflected in the publication in 1835 of *The Life of Jesus* (*Das Leben Jesu*) by David Strauss. This was a critical analysis of the Bible, in which Jesus is portrayed as an ordinary historical personality. Strauss explained this by the traditional persistence of mythological ideas. Later, Bruno Bauer argued that religion was a false consciousness, and that the person of Jesus was a fiction. The radical critique of the New Testament carried out by Strauss and Bruno Bauer represented an important step forward in biblical studies. It laid the basis for the writings of Marx and Engels on religion, and later Kautsky's masterly work of historical materialism, *The Foundations of Christianity*.

These were very bold and advanced theories for those times. It took courage to challenge the ideas of the church in the context of general reaction and suffocating censorship. But although they made some advances, their general approach remained idealist, and therefore was condemned to sterility. One of the main concerns was the question of how false consciousness arises in society and becomes a power over the minds of men. The abstract nature of the Young Hegelians' discussions was partly a result of the strict laws of censorship. But art, literature and religion were the only fields where some degree of critical thought were permitted.

In about 1840, political arguments emerged in the ranks of the Young Hegelians, when the enthronement of Friedrich Wilhelm IV led to a certain relaxation of press censorship. Nevertheless, their pronouncements on religion, philosophy and politics were veiled in an obscure and abstract terminology, characterised by the repeated use of the word 'critique'. This was later satirised by the writings of Marx and Engels such as *The German Ideology* and *The Holy Family*. Despite its radical-sounding phraseology, the debate between the two major Young Hegelians – Strauss and Bauer – remained within the bounds of Hegel's idealist system. Strauss maintained that the evangelical legends resulted from a spontaneous, subconscious, mythological creativity on the part of the early Christian communities, an expression of the people's spirit.

On the other hand, Bauer sees the origin of the Bible stories in the activity of certain outstanding religious preachers, who consciously created the myths that constitute a necessary element in the historical development of human self-consciousness. Bauer finally emerged victorious from his polemics with Strauss. His subjective idealist philosophy of self-consciousness became the main theoretical plank of Left Hegelianism. But essentially, nothing had changed. Both Strauss and Bauer criticised Hegel from different points of view, but without ever breaking free from the basic ground of idealism.

THE LIMITATIONS OF THE LEFT HEGELIANS

The revolutionary implications of Hegel's philosophy were already implicit in the writings of the Left Hegelians, although in a confused and still idealist manner. In order to carry it any further, a complete overturn was required: the total abandonment of idealism and the transition to materialism. But the Left Hegelians were incapable of making that transition. In fact, they were moving in quite the opposite direction. Hegel at least was an objective idealist, whose thought was not merely profound but actually came close to reality on many occasions. The way forward from Hegel – the only possible path of advance – was materialism.

In attempting to erect an alternative to Hegel, the Left Hegelians fell into the trap of extreme subjectivism. Subjective idealism is not superior to objective idealism, but far inferior to it. It is the emptiest, most superficial and least rewarding of all schools of philosophical thought. And it has dominated what passes for philosophy for the whole of the twentieth century. The main characteristic of the writings of the Left Hegelians was extreme individualism, according to which the motive force of history was the 'critically thinking individual'. By contrast, they regarded the masses as the 'enemy of the spirit' and progress, and had no notion of real social or economic development. This reduced all their revolutionary rhetoric to empty phrases.

Their 'critique' led them, on the one hand, to a rejection of any form of Christianity and on the other hand, to a most peculiar variant of philosophy ('radical egoism') advocated by Max Stirner in his book *Der Einzige und sein Eigentum* (*The Ego and its Own*). This was one of the founding documents of anarchism and a clear proof of its relationship to bourgeois individualism. In essence, this was really only an idealised aspiration towards liberal (bourgeois) democracy.

But this confused jumble of radical-sounding ideas had far-reaching effects when it entered the brain of a young Russian radical called Mikhail Bakunin, who proclaimed that "the joy of destruction in itself is a creative joy". This confused school of thought was a complete dead-end, which, by 1844, had ceased to exist as a coherent force, although some of the writings of Bauer still provided something of interest. The bankruptcy of the Hegelian left was finally exposed in the writing of Ludwig Feuerbach.

LUDWIG FEUERBACH

Between Hegel and Marx stands the tragic figure of Ludwig Feuerbach (1804-1872). He was the first one to challenge Hegel from a materialist standpoint. In his *Critique of the Hegelian Philosophy*, he characterised Hegelianism as "*the last refuge, the last rational mainstay for theology.*"[3] Born at Landshut in Bavaria, the young Feuerbach started to study theology in Heidelberg, but within a year abandoned it and, at the age of twenty, went to Berlin to study philosophy under Hegel. He immediately fell under the spell of the great man, and he became an ardent Hegelian. He later became a professor of philosophy at Erlangen.

Although he was identified with the Hegelian Left, Feuerbach was alienated by its empty rhetoric and abstract idealism, and finally became dissatisfied with the whole business. He set out to make a thorough criticism of Hegel's philosophy from the standpoint of materialism, describing Hegelian idealism as: "the last grand attempt

---

3   L. Feuerbach, *Preliminary Theses on the Reform of Philosophy*, *The Fiery Book*, p. 168.

to restore a lost and defunct Christianity through philosophy".[4] Feuerbach correctly understood that the roots of Hegel's idealism (in fact, of *all* idealism) lay in religion: "Modern philosophy", he wrote, "proceeded from theology; it is itself nothing else but theology dissolved and transformed into philosophy".[5]

And he decided to take an axe to the very roots of idealism by attacking religion itself. This he did in his book, *The Essence of Christianity*. The appearance of this epoch-making work in 1841 had revolutionary consequences. Feuerbach's materialist reading of religion in *The Essence of Christianity* was an important step forward, pointing the way towards a final break with idealism. The impact it had at the time is difficult to overstate. To his contemporaries, he seemed like Prometheus, the Titan who dared to steal fire from the gods and give it to humans. This represented a great philosophical revolution.

Especially great was his impact on the young Marx and Engels. Engels later wrote: "Enthusiasm was universal: we were all Feuerbachians for a moment."[6] He alone was willing to carry out an open break with Hegel's idealism. In place of the old mysticism, he boldly proclaimed an entirely new vision – the materialist doctrine of the unity of humankind and nature:

> Matter is an essential object for reason. If there was no matter, reason would have no *stimulus* and no *material* for thought and, hence, no content. One *cannot give up* matter without *giving up reason;* one *cannot acknowledge matter without acknowledging reason.*[7]

His move to materialism was a bold one. It required great courage, especially in the given context of general European reaction and the

---

4   L. Feuerbach, *Principles of the Philosophy of the Future*, *The Fiery Brook*, p. 206.

5   Ibid., pp. 202-3.

6   F. Engels, *Ludwig Feuerbach and the End of Classical German Philosophy,* MECW, Vol. 26, p. 364.

7   L. Feuerbach, *Principles of the Philosophy of the Future*, *The Fiery Brook*, p. 198.

repressive Prussian state. It provided inspiration to the young Marx and Engels. But ultimately, it failed. Feuerbach regarded human consciousness mainly as a reflection of nature, while also stressing that man came to comprehend his own nature and his relations with other men. Ultimately, however, his conclusions are extremely weak. His only alternative to the domination of religion is education, morality, love, and even a new religion.

Although Feuerbach's materialism still suffered from defects that prevented him from developing the extremely promising premises that he had discovered, he pointed the way to the revolutionary philosophy of dialectical materialism, which was finally developed by Marx and Engels. At first, Marx and Engels were under the influence of Feuerbach. But very soon they became aware of his failings. They were disappointed by Feuerbach's reluctance to draw all the conclusions from his own ideas. His writings, especially *The Essence of Christianity*, contain valuable insights on the subjects of alienation and the connection between idealism and religion. He was extremely critical of the idealist nature of Hegelian dialectics.

Feuerbach made philosophy come down from the clouds of speculation to the human level – to normal, material human beings who are derived from nature and are an integral part of it. That was an important step forward. But his materialism was not capable of answering the questions that it posed. At the centre of Feuerbach's philosophy is man. But Feuerbach takes man, not as a social being, but as an abstract individual. As such, this philosophy bore very little relation to the real world of men and women. Real history and real social development are conspicuous by their absence in the writings of Feuerbach.

Despite its limitations, *The Essence of Christianity* still retains considerable interest for its brilliant insights into the social and historical roots of religion. Feuerbach regards religion as the alienation of man, in which human traits are made objective and treated as a supernatural being. It is as if man suffers from a kind of split personality, and contemplates his own essence in God. For Feuerbach, the central problem of alienation is religious – in worshipping God, men and women worship their own alienated being:

> Man – and this is the secret of religion – objectifies his being, and then again makes himself the object of this objectified being, transformed into a subject, a person. He is an object to another being.[8]

This idea was undoubtedly correct, but left completely out of account the real mainspring and origin of all alienation – the alienation of labour from itself in the form of surplus value in the process of capitalist production. Through their collective labour, the workers create an alien power – capital – which confronts them and enslaves them. In Feuerbach's writings, Man appears in a one-sided, abstract and unreal manner. The real, historical men and women only appear with the advent of Marxist philosophy.

The problem with Feuerbach and some other Left Hegelians (Moses Hess) is that he merely said no to Hegel, negating his philosophy by simply denying it. His main mistake was, to use the German expression, to throw the baby out with the bath water. In rejecting Hegel's philosophy, he also rejected its rational core – dialectics. This explains the one-sided character of Feuerbach's materialism, which caused its downfall.

Feuerbach paid a heavy price for his radical views. He was persecuted savagely by the authorities. Dismissed from the university in 1830, he spent his last years a tragic and virtually forgotten figure in an obscure village. Somebody once remarked that the saddest phrase in any language is 'might have been'. This is truer of Feuerbach than any other philosopher. Having spent the greater part of his life in the wilderness, in the end, his destiny, like a philosophical John the Baptist, was to prepare the way for others. His defence of materialism paved the way for the philosophical revolution carried out by Marx and Engels. His most important role was to act as a catalyst for the new movement.

The revolution of 1848 consigned the ideas of Feuerbach and the Hegelian Left to oblivion. Ideas which had seemed radical before

---

8   L. Feuerbach, *The Essence of Christianity*.

now appeared irrelevant. Only the revolutionary programme of Marx and Engels stood the test of fire. Feuerbach did not understand the revolution, and remained aloof from the new movement founded by Marx and Engels, although, to his credit, at the end of his life he joined the German Social Democratic Party.

AN EXTRAORDINARY COLLABORATION

> When I visited Marx in Paris in the summer of 1844, our complete agreement in all theoretical fields became evident and our joint work dates from that time.[9]

These few words by Engels mark the beginning of one of the most famous and extraordinarily fruitful collaborations of all time, the one between Karl Marx and Friedrich Engels. For many years, the enemies of Marxism (and even some who pretend to be Marxists) have attempted to drive a wedge between these two giants. They have tried by all manner of means to 'prove' that what Engels wrote, for example, in the field of philosophy, was not what Marx believed, and so on, and so forth.

This stupid falsification is instantly disproved by even the most cursory reading of the voluminous correspondence between the two men, which fills nine bulky volumes of the *Marx-Engels Collected Works* (English edition), dating from 1844 right up to Marx's death in 1883. These letters show just how closely the two men worked together, and how they jointly worked out and developed the theories of scientific socialism. Since both Marx and Engels were extremely scrupulous in all matters pertaining to theory, neither would ever allow any differences to pass without comment. But no serious differences are to be found. The only disagreement arose on questions of a secondary or tactical nature, such as which side would eventually emerge victorious in the American Civil War.

Such matters did not reveal any serious differences between Marx and Engels, either on theoretical principles or methodology. So closely

---

9   F. Engels, 'On the History of the Communist League', MECW, Vol. 26, p. 318.

identified were their ideas that Marx often asked Engels to write articles in his (Marx's) name. This close collaboration – cemented by a lifelong personal friendship – commenced when the two young men threw themselves eagerly into the battle of ideas, crossing swords with the Young Hegelians, but also pointing out the limitations and deficiencies of Feuerbach's ideas.

The united front of Marx and Engels immediately bore fruit with the publication of one of the seminal works of Marxist philosophy, *The Holy Family, or the Critique of Critical Criticism*, written between September and November 1844 and first published in February 1845. It dealt a mortal blow to the Left Hegelians.

Marx and Engels subjected the philosophical ideas of the Left Hegelians to a withering criticism, spiced with the most biting irony. They demolished the subjective idealist conception of self-consciousness, explaining that sensuously perceived reality exists irrespective of the consciousness of the observer. They pointed out that the world continues to exist even when the subject is not present to perceive it. That is something that most people accept without question. But philosophers are a strange breed, and the subjective idealists are stranger than most. Of Bruno Bauer, they wrote that he is "transforming the world *outside himself* into an *appearance*, a mere fancy of *his* brain, and afterwards declaring this *fantasy* to be what it really is, i.e., a mere fantasy".[10]

They pointed out that subjective idealism inevitably ended up in extreme individualism, the elevation of the individual hero as the mainspring of history, and a contemptuous rejection of the role of the masses as a historical agent. On this they wrote: "Critical criticism, by lumping humanity together in a spiritless mass, gives the most striking proof how infinitely small real human beings seem to speculation."[11] On 1 August 1844, Marx wrote to Feuerbach about the *Literatur-Zeitung*, the monthly magazine of Bruno Bauer:

In his critical Berlin *Literatur-Zeitung*, *Bruno Bauer*, my friend of many years standing – but now rather estranged – has provided fresh proof of

10 K. Marx and F. Engels, *The Holy Family*, MECW, Vol. 4, p. 140.
11 Ibid., p. 40.

how difficult it is for Germans to extricate themselves from the contrary one-sidedness. I don't know if you have read the journal. It contains much covert polemic against you.

The character of the *Literatur-Zeitung* can be reduced to the following: "Criticism" is transformed into a transcendental being. These Berliners do not regard themselves as *men* who *criticise*, but as *critics* who, *incidentally*, have the misfortune of being men. They therefore acknowledge only one *real* need, the need of *theoretical* criticism. People like Proudhon are therefore accused of having made some "*practical*" "*need*" their point of departure. This criticism therefore lapses into a sad and supercilious intellectualism. *Consciousness* or *self-consciousness* is regarded as the *only* human quality.[12]

Marx quotes Bauer's view that philosophy, or rather, 'criticism', to use the Young Hegelian jargon, should not display feeling or passion. Bauer says literally:

The critic should participate neither in the sufferings nor in the joys of society; he should know neither friendship and love, nor hate and envy; he should be enthroned in a solitude, where only the laughter of the Olympian Gods over the topsy-turviness of the world resounds occasionally from his lips.[13]

Marx goes on to say:

Love, for example, is rejected because the loved one is only an "*object*". Down with the object. This criticism thus regards itself as the only *active* element in history. It is confronted with the whole of humanity as a *mass*, an inert mass, which has value only as the antithesis of intellect. It is therefore regarded as the greatest crime if the critic displays *feeling* or *passion*, he must be an *ironical ice-cold sophos*.[14]

This criticism of 'Critical Criticism' is systematically developed in *The Holy Family*, where Marx and Engels prove that Bauer's subjectivist

---

12 K. Marx, 'Letter to Ludwig Feuerbach, 11 August 1844', MECW, Vol. 3, p. 356.
13 Quoted ibid., p. 356.
14 Ibid., p. 356.

philosophy merely carries to a logical end the basic idea of Hegel's *Phenomenology of Spirit:* the substance must rise to self-consciousness.

Instead of these lifeless abstractions, the founders of scientific socialism proceeded from real, material men and women in society, real history, not the spirit world of idealist 'Self-Consciousness'.

MARX'S REVOLUTION IN PHILOSOPHY

Marx's materialism had nothing in common with the old mechanical ('metaphysical') materialism. In fact, it owed an immense debt to Hegel. But whereas the latter had turned the real relation between subject and object on its head, Marx inverted the relation, placing it once more with its feet firmly on material grounds.

On 20 August 1859, in an article on Hegel in *Das Volk*, No. 16, Engels wrote a brief but highly illuminating account of the philosophical revolution carried out by Karl Marx:

> Since Hegel's death hardly any attempt has been made to develop any branch of science in its specific inner coherence. The official Hegelian school had assimilated only the most simple devices of the master's dialectics and applied them to everything and anything, often with ridiculous incompetence. Hegel's whole legacy was, so far as they were concerned, limited to a mere template, by means of which any subject could be shaped aright, and to a list of words and phrases whose only purpose was to turn up at the right moment, when ideas and positive knowledge were lacking. Thus it happened, as a professor at Bonn has said, that these Hegelians understood nothing but could write about everything. And that is what it came to. For all their conceit these gentlemen were, however, sufficiently conscious of their weakness to avoid major problems as far as possible. The old pedantic learning held its ground because of its superior positive knowledge, and then with Feuerbach's renunciation of the speculative method, Hegelianism gradually fell asleep, and it seemed that science was once more dominated by the old metaphysics with its fixed categories...

> Here there was, therefore, a question to be solved which was not connected with political economy as such. How was science to be dealt with?

There was, on the one hand, the Hegelian dialectic in the quite abstract, "speculative" form in which Hegel had left it, and on the other hand the ordinary, essentially Wolffian, metaphysical method, which had again come into vogue and which was used by bourgeois economists to write their bulky rambling volumes. The second method had been theoretically so demolished by Kant and particularly by Hegel that its continued use in practice could only be rendered possible by inertia and the absence of an alternative *simple* method. The Hegelian method, on the other hand, was in its *existing* form quite inapplicable. It was essentially idealist, while the task here was to elaborate a world outlook more materialist than any previous one. Hegel's method took as its point of departure pure thought, whereas here the starting point was to be inexorable facts. A method which, according to its own avowal, "came from nothing through nothing to nothing" was in this shape by no means suitable. It was, nevertheless, the only element among the entire available logical material which could at least serve as a point of departure. It had not been subjected to criticism, had not been overthrown; none of the opponents of the great dialectician had not been able to make a breach in its proud edifice. It has been forgotten because the Hegelian school did not know how to apply it. Hence, it was first of all essential to subject the Hegelian method to thoroughgoing criticism.

What distinguished Hegel's mode of thinking from that of all other philosophers was the exceptional historical sense underlying it. However abstract and idealist the form employed, the development of his ideas runs always parallel to the development of world history, and the latter is indeed supposed to be only the proof of the former. Although this reversed the actual relation and stood it on its head, yet the real content was invariably incorporated in his philosophy, especially since Hegel – unlike his pupils – did not rely on ignorance, but was one of the most erudite thinkers of all time. He was the first to try to demonstrate that there is development, an intrinsic coherence in history, and however strange some things in his philosophy of history may seem to us now, the grandeur of the basic conception is still admirable today, compared with either his predecessors or those who following him ventured to advance general observations on history. This monumental conception of history pervades the *Phenomenology*, the *Aesthetics* and the *History of Philosophy*, and the material is everywhere set forth historically, in a definite historical context even if in an abstract distorted manner.

This epoch-making conception of history was the direct theoretical precondition of the new materialist outlook, and already this constituted a connecting link with the logical method as well. Since, even from the standpoint of "pure thinking", this forgotten dialectics had led to such results, and had moreover with the greatest ease coped with the whole of the former logic and metaphysics, there had, at all events, to be more to it than sophistry and hair-splitting. But criticism of this method, which the entire official philosophy had evaded and still evades, was no small matter.

Marx was and is the only one who could undertake the work of extracting from the Hegelian logic the kernel containing Hegel's real discoveries in this field, and of establishing the dialectical method, divested of its idealist wrappings, in the simple form in which it becomes the only correct mode of the development of thought. The working out of the method which underlies Marx's critique of political economy is, we think, a result hardly less significant than the basic materialist outlook.[15]

THE THESES ON FEUERBACH

Perhaps the most important of the early writings of Marx were the *Theses on Feuerbach*. They were an important step on the way to breaking with the one-sided materialism of Feuerbach and striking out in a new direction. These few concentrated sentences contain a philosophical revolution. Let us begin with the first thesis:

> The chief defect of all previous materialism (that of Feuerbach included) is that things, reality, sensuousness are conceived only in the form of the *object, or of contemplation*, but not as *sensuous human activity*, *practice*, not subjectively. Hence, in contradistinction to materialism, the *active* side

---

15 F. Engels, 'Karl Marx, *A Contribution to the Critique of Political Economy*', MECW, Vol. 16, pp. 472-5.

was set forth abstractly by idealism – which, of course, does not know real, sensuous activity, as such.[16]

This phrase of Marx has often caused a certain puzzlement. Its meaning is not immediately clear, nor can it be made clear unless we place it in the context of the history of philosophy. Yet the idea contained within it is the starting point for the development of dialectical materialism, and of Marxism in general.

The old materialism was one-sided in that it considered human thought in a static, passive and contemplative way. Man was merely an observer of nature, taking note of 'the facts':

> The mind to it is in itself void, a mere mirror of the external world, a dark room into which the images of the things without fall, without any contribution or action on its part; its entire contents are due to the impressions made on it by material things.[17]

The early, mechanical materialism was unable to solve this problem and arrive at a scientific understanding of the real relationship between subject and object. This is what Marx deals with in his 'Theses on Feuerbach'. The early materialism was limited by the level achieved by the science of the day, which was very rigid and mechanical in nature (Engels referred to it as the 'metaphysical outlook', although we use the word metaphysics differently today).

Mechanics sees the relation between subject and object in a simplistic, static and one-sided way: pushing, pulling, lifting, inertia, levers, pulleys etc. All motion is imparted from without. Newton's mechanical universe required the Almighty to give it a push to set it in motion, but after that it worked perfectly, like clockwork. The relationship was passive and one-sided.

In this clockwork universe, there is little or no room for subjective activity and creative initiative. Every action is predetermined by Nature's Eternal Laws. By contrast, the idealists exaggerated the role of

---

16 K. Marx, 'Theses on Feuerbach', MECW, Vol. 5, p. 3.

17 A. Schwegler, *Handbook of the History of Philosophy*, pp. 180-1.

the subject, seeing it as all-important. They even derived the existence of the object from the subject.

The conception of the activity of the subject was contained and developed by the objective idealist, Hegel. That is what Marx meant when he said that the subjective element was developed by the idealists, not the materialists. It was the bringing together of the two elements, the concept of activity of the subject of the idealists and the notion of the objectivity of the material world, which was the key to solving the problem.

THE SECOND THESIS

> The question whether objective truth can be attributed to human thinking is not a question of theory but is a *practical* question. Man must prove the truth, i.e., the reality and power, the this-worldliness of his thinking in practice. The dispute over the reality or non-reality of thinking which is isolated from practice is a purely *scholastic* question.[18]

The problem of knowledge (epistemology) has occupied a central place in philosophy for centuries. But this so-called problem only arises when human knowledge is regarded a) as something separate from a physical body, and b) as something separate from the material world.

Marx and Engels exposed the false premises that lie at the roots of the epistemology of idealism. It is really a kind of swindle that begins by separating the general definition of individual things from their concrete reality and then proceeds to present the general definition as the source and the prime cause of the objects of sensory perception.

For instance, the general concept 'fruit' is separated from real fruits, and declared to be the true substance of pears, apples and oranges. From the standpoint of speculative idealism, the distinction between apples, pears and oranges is immaterial. But in actual life, that is not at all the case. Nobody has ever eaten an abstract 'fruit', but only apples, oranges and so on. Engels pointed out that a mineralogist who confined himself to stating that all minerals are modifications

---

18 K. Marx, 'Theses on Feuerbach', MECW, Vol. 5, p. 3.

of "the Mineral in general", instead of studying their real qualitative
distinctions, "would be a mineralogist only in *his imagination*."[19]

But does that mean that abstractions are of no value, that they are
merely the arbitrary products of our imagination? Not at all! Abstract
thought is a most powerful tool for penetrating the secrets of nature
and enabling human beings to gain mastery over it. In defining the
nature of things, we can arrive at their hidden essence, the general
traits that give them their specific identity. Without such abstract
generalisations, rational thought would be impossible. In fact, as
Hegel pointed out, it would be impossible even to utter the simplest
sentence (Mary is a woman, this is a house, Fido is a dog) without
turning a particular into a universal.

Yet the abstractions of thought did not drop from the clouds.
They are all ultimately derived from observation of material things
and experience of the real world, and would have absolutely no value
unless they closely corresponded to the real, material world. This
process has taken place over a very long time – so long, in fact, that
the real origins of human thought and language have long sunk into
oblivion.

Long before men and women developed the idea of a circle, they
had observed a countless number of round objects: the sun, the moon,
a tree trunk cut in half and so on. From these observations, eventually
we arrive at the idea of 'roundness', and hence a circle. Nobody has ever
seen an abstract circle in real life, because such a thing has never existed
and never will exist. The idealists conceive of abstractions as if they
had real existence. The material world for them is merely a crude and
imperfect imitation of the Idea. In reality, it is the other way around.
As Aristotle, 'the great definer', pointed out long ago: "But of course,
there cannot be a house in general, apart from particular houses."

THE RATIONAL KERNEL OF HEGEL

It was left to Marx and Engels to carry Hegel's criticism of Kant to
its logical conclusion – a complete break with idealism. But whereas

---

19 K. Marx and F. Engels, *The Holy Family*, MECW, Vol. 4, p. 58.

Feuerbach rejected Hegel's ideas in their totality, Marx and Engels understood that the Hegelian philosophy contained a very important truth: the dialectic. In Hegel, the dialectic remained obscured, its profound truths hidden in a mass of abstract and abstruse reasoning. Stripped of its mystical and idealist wrapping and placed on a sound scientific (materialist) basis, Hegel's dialectic provided the starting point for a real philosophical revolution.

It required the genius of a Marx to discover the rational kernel that lay hidden in the pages of Hegel's *Logic* and apply it to the real, material world. He also explained that the deficiency of Feuerbach's "anthropological materialism" is that here the individual is conceived of as an abstract entity. But real human activity (labour) is not the activity of isolated individuals. It is necessarily collective in its very essence.

The problem of the relation between subject and object (thought and being) was finally resolved by Marx, who pointed out that, ultimately, all the problems of philosophy are resolved in practice: "The dispute over the reality or non-reality of thinking which is isolated from practice is a purely *scholastic* question."[20] Materialism rejects the notion that mind, consciousness, soul etc., is something separate from matter. Thought is merely the mode of existence of the brain, which, like life itself, is only matter organised in a certain way. Mind is what we call the sum total of the activity of the brain and the nervous system. But, dialectically, the whole is greater than the sum of the parts.

The idealists persist in presenting consciousness as a 'mystery', something that we cannot comprehend. Hiding behind this stubborn attempt to place an absolute limit on what mere mortals are allowed to know lurks the murky spirit world of religious superstition and all the rest of the wretched mumbo-jumbo that science ought to have consigned to a museum long ago. Despite everything, science continues its onward march, tearing down one by one, all the old mysteries and forcing religion to retreat, step by step, loudly protesting its right to exist.

---

20 K. Marx, 'Theses on Feuerbach', MECW, Vol. 5, p. 3.

The materialist view corresponds closely to the conclusions of science, which is gradually uncovering the workings of the brain and revealing its secrets. And there is no final limit to this process of human development. What we do not know today, we are sure we shall know tomorrow, or the day after tomorrow. The final truth of materialism is provided, not by abstract debates in university seminar rooms, but by social development and the history of science. Humankind does not merely contemplate nature but actively transforms it, and this ceaseless productive activity is what demonstrates the correctness or otherwise of ideas, as Engels explains:

> The most telling refutation of this as of all other philosophical quirks is practice, namely, experimentation and industry. If we are able to prove the correctness of our conception of a natural phenomenon by bringing it about ourselves, producing it out of its conditions and making it serve our own purposes into the bargain, then the ungraspable Kantian "thing-in-itself" is finished. The chemical substances produced in the bodies of plants and animals remained just such "things-in-themselves" until organic chemistry began to produce them one after another, whereupon the "thing-in-itself" became a thing for us...[21]

SUBJECTIVE IDEALISM

A further complication arises when we reach the stage of subjective idealism, which emerged as a definite trend with Berkeley and Hume and passed into the philosophy of Kant, where it continued to cause endless confusion. Kant was a philosopher of stature. His great merit was to subject the traditional forms of logic to a thoroughgoing criticism. But his Achilles' heel was to be found in his subjectivist position on the theory of knowledge, which he unfortunately took over from the vulgar empiricist David Hume.

Here was the source of his main weaknesses – ambiguity, inconsistency and agnosticism. As has been explained, in failing to make a clean break with the traditional logic, while exposing

---

21 F. Engels, 'Ludwig Feuerbach and the End of Classical German Philosophy', MECW, Vol. 26, pp. 367-8.

its limitations, Kant landed himself in all kinds of insoluble contradictions (antinomies), which he left unresolved. In Kant's theory of knowledge we have a one-sided view of consciousness, which is presented as a *barrier* that is supposed to shut us off from the 'external' world. In fact, we are part of this world, not separate from it, and consciousness does not separate us but *connects us to it*. The relationship of humans to the physical world from the very beginning was *not contemplative but active*. As the great German Poet Goethe said: "*Am anfang war die Tat!*" – In the beginning was the *Deed!*

We do not only think with our brain, but with our whole body. Thinking must be seen, not as an isolated activity ("the ghost in the machine", as Gilbert Ryle caricatured René Descartes' dualist theory of mind and body)[22] *but as part of the whole human experience, of human sensuous activity and interaction with the world and with other people.* The act of thinking must be seen as part of this complex process of permanent interaction, not as an isolated activity that is mechanically juxtaposed to it. The great genius Hegel came close to discovering the truth, but despite his colossal intellectual power, he failed to make the decisive leap from theory to practice, blinded as he was by his idealist preconceptions.

Kant's subjective idealism had been thoroughly demolished by Hegel from the standpoint of objective idealism. But it raised its head once more after the death of the great man and, in one disguise or another, has been the dominant trend in bourgeois philosophy ever since. It received a definitive answer in the second of Marx's 'Theses on Feuerbach'. The arguments of subjective idealism and the subject-object problem can only be thoroughly demolished when we adopt the standpoint of practice and approach the theory of knowledge from a concrete historical point of view, and not from the standpoint of empty and static abstraction.

In embryo, the elements of this dialectical conception are already present in Hegel. What Marx did was strip it of its idealist disguise,

---

22 See G. Ryle, *The Concept of Mind*.

and express it in a clear and scientific manner. Hegel says in *The History of Philosophy* that "the being of mind is its act, and its act is to be aware of itself." But in Hegel, thinking is not merely a contemplative activity. The highest form of thought, which he calls Reason, does not merely accept the given facts, but works upon them and transforms them.

The contradiction between thought and being, between 'subject' and 'object', is overcome in Hegel through the process of knowledge itself, which penetrates ever deeper into the objective world. In Hegel, however, instead of genuine human men and women we have the abstraction of Self-Consciousness. The real struggle of historical forces is expressed in the shadowy form of the struggle of ideas. No further progress was possible without a complete break with Hegelian idealism. This transition was accomplished by Marx and Engels after their break with the abstract materialism of Feuerbach.

THE 'ALGEBRA OF REVOLUTION'

The nineteenth century Russian revolutionary democrat Alexander Herzen once described the dialectic as the "algebra of revolution".[23] When Marx and Engels freed the rational kernel of Hegel's philosophy from its idealist prison, they transformed dialectics into a powerful weapon for revolutionary action:

> Thus dialectics reduced itself to the science of the general laws of motion, both of the external world and of human thinking – two sets of laws which are identical in substance, but differ in their expression in so far as the human mind can apply them consciously, while in nature and also up to now for the most part in human history, these laws assert themselves unconsciously, in the form of external necessity, in the midst of an endless series of seeming accidents. Thereby the dialectic of concepts itself became merely the conscious reflex of the dialectical motion of the real world and thus the Hegelian dialectic was placed upon its head; or rather, turned off its head, on which it was standing, and placed upon its feet. And this

---

23 A. Herzen, *My Past and Thoughts*, p. 237.

materialist dialectic, which for years was our best means of labour and our sharpest weapon...[24]

THE THIRD THESIS ON FEUERBACH

In his third thesis on Feuerbach, Marx wrote:

> The materialist doctrine concerning the changing of circumstances and upbringing forgets that circumstances are changed by men and that the educator must himself be educated. This doctrine must, therefore, divide society into two parts, one which is superior to society.
>
> The coincidence of the changing of circumstances and of human activity or self-change can be conceived and rationally understood only as *revolutionary practice.*[25]

Here at last thought is united with activity – not the one-sided purely intellectual activity of the scholar but real, sensuous human activity. But this inevitably leads us to revolutionary conclusions. From the standpoint of materialism, the development of men and women is determined by the material conditions of their existence. This is really a self-evident proposition, even when we take into consideration the genetic element that undoubtedly has a role to play in this development.

The biological accidents of birth provide the basic raw material for the physical and mental development of individual men and women. But it is objective circumstances that will ultimately decide the way in which this development proceeds. Albert Einstein was a genius, and it is not excluded that his genius would have sooner or later expressed itself in one way or another, independently of the conditions of his life. But if he had been born the son of a landless labourer in an Indian village, would his genius have realised its full potential?

He may have acquired an impressive level of skills in the planting of rice or perhaps even risen to the rank of a village artisan. Maybe,

---

24 F. Engels, 'Ludwig Feuerbach and the End of Classical German Philosophy', MECW, Vol. 26, p. 383.

25 K. Marx, 'Theses on Feuerbach', MECW, Vol. 5, p. 4.

or maybe not. But would he have developed the theory of relativity that transformed science in the twentieth century? The question answers itself. The mere assertion that material conditions determine the lives of men and women does not exhaust the matter. If the material conditions of the masses constitute an insuperable obstacle that prevents millions of people from realising their true potential as human beings, if it suffocates that creative spark that exists in every individual, to one extent or another, then it follows that these objective conditions must be changed.

The argument that is frequently advanced by reformists to counter the idea of revolution is that it is necessary to 'educate the masses'. Sometimes one even hears a variant of the same false idea expressed by so-called Marxists. They try to explain the absence of a successful socialist revolution by referring to the alleged 'immaturity' of the masses, who are not yet worthy to carry out a revolution, presumably because they have not yet read the three volumes of Marx's *Capital!* In order to succeed, the workers must gather round the rostrum of the sectarians who will 'educate' them and eventually present them with a Certificate of Maturity. Armed with this portentous document, the masses could then proceed to take power the very next morning at precisely nine o'clock.

Answering this ridiculous nonsense, Marx pointed out wittily, it is not the masses who need such a certificate, but precisely the 'educators' who need educating. These sophistical arguments are merely a cunning and cynical defence of the status quo. For it is precisely the objective conditions of life under capitalism that constitute an impenetrable barrier between the mass of the population and access to culture.

Society is divided into 'thinkers' and 'doers', which the Bible describes as "the hewers of wood and the drawers of water."[26] Contempt for manual labour is at once a reflection of bourgeois prejudice and an attempt to justify the structures, morals and values of bourgeois society, a society in which the Ego (the 'individual') is said to rule

---

26 Joshua 9:21.

supreme. The mainspring of human history is presented as the actions and volition of individual protagonists, whether heroes or villains.

In reality, however, the individuality of the great majority is crushed and enslaved to the individuality of a tiny handful that own and control the means of production and thus the key to life itself. And to tell the whole truth, even this minority is subject to forces that they do not control. Although the masses who create the wealth of society make up the overwhelming majority of humankind, they have no history and no name; their voices are silenced and their existence largely ignored. For over 10,000 years, society has been dominated by a tiny privileged minority that has held in its hands a monopoly on culture.

Marx explained that social being determines consciousness. In order to change people, it is necessary to change their conditions of existence. But how is society to be changed? That is the question! A fundamental change in society cannot be achieved by passive contemplation or endless speculative discussions in the philosophy departments of universities, but only by the collective revolutionary action of the oppressed masses themselves. And the masses do not learn from books, but from the concrete experience of the class struggle.

THE EIGHTH THESIS ON FEUERBACH: TOWARDS THE COMMUNIST MANIFESTO

All social life is essentially *practical*. All mysteries which lead theory to mysticism find their rational solution in human practice and in the comprehension of this practice.[27]

These words represent a decisive break with the past. They are a recognition of the need to develop an entirely new way of thinking: a new type of philosophy that was, in effect, *a non-philosophical theory*.

From a materialist point of view, thinking is not an isolated activity, but is inseparable from human existence in general. Marx says that

27 K. Marx, 'Theses on Feuerbach', MECW, Vol. 5, p. 5.

labour, material production, is man's species-life. That is to say, *labour is the mode of existence of human beings*. This specific distinction of man from animal is not a natural one, but emerges and develops in the process of production throughout human history, from the fashioning of the first crude stone axes to the building of computers, robots and space travel.

Humankind develops thought through concrete, sensuous activity – not merely intellectual activity, but collective human labour. By transforming the material world through labour, men and women also transform themselves and, in so doing, develop and extend the horizon of their thinking. The power of labour lies in the combination of the efforts, strivings and creativity of a vast number of individual men and women. It is this magical combination that gives rise to all the wonders of civilisation.

In the power of human labour, we see the concrete realisation of what Hegel called the unity of the Particular and the Universal. Yet this necessary unity has been stubbornly denied. The thoughts and actions of humankind are presented, not as a collective activity, but as the work of isolated individuals. Behind this one-sided view lies a deep-seated prejudice that elevates mental labour to the most important, if not the sole element in human progress, while the role of manual labour is relegated to insignificance.

The enslavement of one class by another does not originate with capitalism. It has existed in different forms for thousands of years, a fact that Marx and Engels examined in great detail in their writings on historical materialism. The outlines of this theory are already seen in *The German Ideology* (notably in the first chapter entitled 'Feuerbach'). It finally emerges in a finished form in one of the greatest and most influential documents in world history: *The Communist Manifesto*, which for the first time places human history on a scientific basis, starting with a bold statement: "The history of all hitherto existing society is the history of class struggles".[28]

---

28 K. Marx and F. Engels, *The Communist Manifesto, Classics of Marxism Volume One*, p. 3.

And it ends with a stirring proclamation:

> Let the ruling classes tremble at a communistic revolution. The proletarians have nothing to lose but their chains. They have a world to win.
>
> *Workers of All Countries, Unite!* [29]

A PERIOD OF DECLINE

For the past one-and-a-half centuries, the realm of philosophy has resembled an arid desert with only the occasional trace of life. The age of giants has passed away without trace. The treasure trove of the past, with its ancient glories and flashes of illumination, has vanished. Its fire is utterly extinguished. This desert that still calls itself philosophy is inhabited by a tribe of eunuchs and squabbling pygmies. In this intellectual wasteland one would search in vain for any source of illumination.

The complete emptiness of modern bourgeois philosophy is something that has been increasingly noted, even by the philosophers themselves. Peter Unger spent decades working as a celebrated analytic philosopher at the University of New York, having been tutored by the guru of that philosophy, A. J Ayer. What conclusion did he finally draw?

In 2014 he published a book with the interesting title, *Empty Ideas: A Critique of Analytic Philosophy*. In an article defending the book, he states the following:

> [D]uring the last five decades, there has been offered hardly any new thoughts whose truth, or whose untruth, makes or means any difference as to how anything ever is as concern [sic] concrete reality, except for ever so many perfectly parochial thoughts, ideas about nothing much more than which words are used by which people, and how various of these people use these words of theirs – and nothing any deeper than that.[30]

---

29 Ibid., p. 35.
30 P. Unger, 'A Taste of Empty Ideas', *3 Quarks Daily*, 30 June 2014.

I would only add that the same thing can be said of every other product of modern bourgeois philosophy, and for a period considerably longer than five decades.

The constant semantic fiddling and fussing about the meaning of words resembles a dog that never tires of chasing its own tail. It calls to mind the convoluted debates of the medieval Schoolmen who argued endlessly over the sex of angels, and how many can dance on the head of a pin. It is hard to say what is worse: the intolerable pretensions of so-called postmodernism, or the obvious emptiness of its content. The fact that this tedious playing with words could be given the name of philosophy at all is proof of how far modern bourgeois thought has declined.

Hegel wrote in the *Phenomenology*: "By the little with which the human spirit is satisfied, we can judge the extent of its loss." That would be a fitting epitaph for all the bourgeois philosophy after Hegel and Feuerbach. Bourgeois philosophy has long ago entered into the stage of senility where it is only capable of incoherent babbling and constant wearisome repetition of old stories that no longer evoke any reaction other than a sense of irritation and boredom. It is, to quote Shakespeare: *Sans teeth, sans eyes, sans taste, sans everything.*

THE END OF PHILOSOPHY

The beginning of the new spirit is the product of a wide-ranging revolution in various forms of culture, the reward of a complicated, tortuous journey and of an equally immense and strenuous effort. The beginning is the whole that has returned into itself from succession as well as extension, the resultant *simple concept* of the whole. But the actuality of this simple whole consists in this: these configurations that have become moments again develop anew and take on a configuration, but now in their new element, in the sense that has emerged.[31]

We now arrive at a final parting of the ways. We have followed all the vicissitudes of philosophy over two-and-a-half millennia. We have participated in its triumphs and its failures. We have had occasion to

---

31 G. W. F. Hegel, *The Phenomenology of Spirit*, p. 9.

marvel at the colossal achievements of the human intellect and admire the astonishing sweep and boldness of its vision. We have been in the presence of some of the greatest thinkers who have ever lived. But now the history of philosophy has run its course, and having done so, returns once again to its starting point.

Philosophy, as we have seen, commences with the Greeks. The early Ionian philosophers were materialists who believed that material objects possessed life, or rather that matter is invested with a kind of innate life force, or energy. That is the exact meaning of hylozoism. It is what Thales meant when he said that all things are full of gods (*daimon*). All the early Greek philosophers taught that there is a form of life in all material objects. They regarded the magnet as alive because of its attractive powers. This apparently showed that matter possessed the inherent power of movement. This astonishing insight anticipated the discoveries of modern science by two-and-a-half millennia.

It would seem that we have completed a great circle and have now returned to our point of departure. But the evolution of thought and science is not an endless circle, but rather a spiral, in which one theory negates another, while retaining all that was viable and progressive in the earlier stages. Philosophy in the old sense of the word has said everything worthwhile that it had to say. It has served its purpose, and in so doing, it has exhausted all the progressive potential that it once possessed. Philosophy today is only a pitiful shadow of its former self.

This is no accident. The great mysteries over which it used to ponder have been largely solved by the discoveries of science, which prefers the trusty weapons of experiment and observation to the useless pastimes of empty speculation and mystification. The materialism of the Greek pre-Socratic philosophers was a brilliant anticipation, but it was really in the nature of an inspired guess. They lacked the necessary scientific proof for their assertions, because the productive forces had not yet reached the level required to furnish such proofs. We do not have to return to the fantastic theories of Thales, Anaximander and Heraclitus, because we have at our disposal all the wealth of information provided by the march of science over many decades and centuries.

A NEW DEPARTURE

Precisely at this point we have arrived at an entirely new point of departure, a fundamental parting of the ways with all previous philosophy. It finds its expression in what is perhaps the greatest and most important of Marx's Theses on Feuerbach: the celebrated eleventh thesis. These words, which have echoed like a clarion call down the ages, are like a breath of fresh air. At long last, philosophy finally emerges out of the dark and airless cellar to which it was confined for centuries by scholastic speculation and is dragged, blinking, into the light of day.

Here philosophical thought – the highest, most sublime achievement of the human spirit – for the first time ceases to be merely a contemplative activity and becomes a formidable weapon in the struggle to change society. We have now left the dimly lit study of the philosopher, and stepped out into the broad daylight of human life, activity and struggle. Finally, philosophy ceases to be a monopoly of a privileged handful of thinkers. It becomes in practice what it always was in potential.

Marx pointed out that ideas in themselves have no history and no real existence. They fight no battles and win no victories. The real battles of history are fought by men and women. And in most circumstances, they are moved in the first instance, not by ideas alone, but by material circumstances. The instinctive, elemental revolutionary movement of the masses is the mainspring of the socialist revolution. But all history shows the limitation of spontaneous action.

In order to succeed, the working class must be armed with the necessary ideas, methods and programme. And Marx explained that ideas become a material force when they grip the minds of the masses. Here is where scientific thought ceases to be an idle occupation and joins hands with humanity – not the lifeless abstractions of "Self-Consciousness" or "World Spirits" or Feuerbach's abstract anthropological construction, but real, breathing, living, struggling, fighting men and women. And we, the militant defenders of the new world outlook, while embracing all that was progressive, truthful and enduring in the philosophies of the past, proudly proclaim on our banner the words of Marx:

> The philosophers have only *interpreted* the world in various ways; the point is to *change* it.[32]

32 K. Marx, 'Theses on Feuerbach', MECW, Vol. 5, p. 5.

BIBLIOGRAPHY

Ali, Ameer Syed, *Short History of the Saracens*, Macmillan, 1955.

Allegro, John M., *The Dead Sea Scrolls and the Christian Myth*, Abacus, 1979.

Aristotle, *Metaphysics*, J.M. Dent and Sons, 1961.

Atkinson, William C., *A History of Spain and Portugal*, Penguin Books, 1961.

St Augustine, *Eighty-Three Different Questions*, Catholic University of America Press, 1982.

Averroes, 'The Decisive Treatise', On the Harmony of Religion and Philosophy, Luzac, 1961.

Bacon, Francis, *The Advancement of Learning*, J.M. Dent & Sons Ltd, 1962.

Antti, Balk, P,. *Saints and Sinners: An Account of Western Civilization*, Thelema Publications, 2008.

Berkeley, George, *Principles of Human Knowledge*, Fontana Library, 1962.

Bernal, J, D., *Science in History*, Watts and Co, 1954, p. 122.

Blake, William, *Auguries of Innocence*.

Bouquet, A, C., *Comparative Religion*, Penguin Books, 1971.

Burn, A, R., *The Pelican History of Greece*, Penguin Books, 1966.

Burnet, John, *Early Greek Philosophy*, Adam and Charles Black, 1963.

Childe, Gordon, V., *What Happened in History*, Penguin Books, 1965.
— *Man Makes Himself*, Fontana Library, 1966.

Cohn, Norman, *The Pursuit of the Millennium*, Oxford University Press, 1970.

Descartes, Rene, *A Discourse on Method*, J.M. Dent & Sons Ltd, 1969.

Donaldson, Margaret, *Children's Minds*, Fontana Press, 1978.

The New Encyclopaedia Britannica: Macropaedia, Encyclopaedia Britannica, 1993.

Engels, Friedrich, *Anti-Dühring*, Wellred Books, 2017.
— *Dialectics of Nature*, Wellred Books, 2012.

Farrington, Benjamin, *Greek Science*, Penguin Books, 1963.

Feuerbach, Ludwig, *The Essence of Christianity*, Prometheus Books, 1989.
— *The Fiery Brook*, Verso, 2012.

Feynman, Richard, P., *The Feynman Lectures on Physics*, Addison-Wesley Publishing Company, 1965.

Fiorio, Soraya, F., 'The Killing of Hypatia', 16 January 2019, *Lapham's Quarterly*, Available at: https://www.laphamsquarterly.org/roundtable/killing-hypatia (accessed on 20 August 2021)

Forbes, R, J., and Dijksterhuis, E, J., *A History of Science and Technology*, Penguin Books, 1963.

Frazer, Sir James, G., *The Golden Bough*, Macmillan, 1983

Gibbon, Edward, *The Decline and Fall of the Roman Empire*, The Modern Library, 1932.

Heath, Thomas, L,. *A History of Greek Mathematics*, Oxford University Press, 1921.

Hegel, G. W. F., *The Phenomenology of Spirit*, Oxford University Press, 2018.
— *The Science of Logic*, Cambridge University Press, 2010.
— *Lectures on the History of Philosophy*, University of Nebraska Press, 1995.
— *The Philosophy of History*, Dover Publications, 1956.
— *Philosophy of Right*, Cambridge University Press, 2003.
— *Encyclopedia of the Philosophical Sciences, Part One: Logic,* Oxford University Press, 1978.

Herzen, Alexander, *My Past and Thoughts*, University of California Press, 1982.

Hippocratic Writings, Penguin Books, 1983.

Hobbes, Thomas, *Leviathan*, J.M. Dent and Sons Ltd, 1962.

Hooper, Alred, *Makers of Mathematics*, Faber, 1961.

Huizinga, Johan, *The Waning of the Middle Ages*, Penguin Books, 1972.

Hume, David, *A Treatise of Human Nature*, J.M. Dent and Sons, 1968.

Irving, Washington, *The Conquest of Granada*, A.L. Burt, 1900.

Kant, Immanuel, *Critique of Pure Reason*, J.M. Dent & Sons Ltd, 1959.

Kautsky, Karl, *Foundations of Christianity*, S.A. Russell, 1953.

Keats, John, *On First Looking into Chapman's Homer*.

Leibniz, Freiherr von, G, W., *Discourse on Metaphysics: Correspondence with Arnauld, and Monadology*, Open Court, 1916, p.256.

Lenin, Vladimir, I., *Collected Works*, Lawrence and Wishart, 1960.

Lucretius, Titus, C., *The Nature of the Universe*, Penguin Books, 1952.

Marx, Karl, *Grundrisse*, Penguin Books, 1973.

Marx, Karl, and Friedrich Engels, *Marx and Engels Collected Works*, Lawrence and Wishart, 1975.
— *Marx and Engels Selected Correspondence*, 1846-1895, Lawrence and Wishart, 1936.
— *Classics of Marxism Volume One*, Wellred Books, 2017.

Michel de Montaigne, *An Apology for Raymond Sebond*, Penguin Books, 1987.

Nixey, Catherine, T*he Darkening Age: The Christian Destruction of the Classical World*, Pan Books, 2018.

Oizerman, Teodor, I., *The Making of the Marxist Philosophy*, Progress Publishers, 1981, pp. 293-4.

Pasnau, Robert, *Theories of Cognition in the Later Middle Ages*, Cambridge University Press, 1997.

Passmore, John, *A Hundred Years of Philosophy*, Penguin Books, 1972.

Peterson, John [Ed.], *The Revolutionary Philosophy of Marxism*, Wellred Books, 2018.

Plato, *Republic*, Penguin Books, 1987.
— *Timaeus*, Lowe & Brydone, 1892.

Plekhanov, Georgi, V., *Selected Philosophical Works*, Progress Publishers, 1976.

Pope, Alexander, *Epitaph: Intended for Sir Isaac Newton*.

Prigogine, Ilya, and Stengers, Isabelle, *Order Out of Chaos: Man's New Dialogue with Nature*, Flamingo, 1985.

Russell, Bertrand, *History of Western Philosophy*, Routledge, 1991.

Ryle, Gilbert, *The Concept of Mind*, Hutchinson's University Library, 1951.

Schwegler, Albert, *Handbook of the History of Philosophy*, Oliver and Boyd, 1890.

Scruton, Roger, *Spinoza*, Oxford University Press, 2002.

Sismondi, Jean, *A History of the Italian Republics*, Peter Smith, 1970.

Spinoza, Baruch, *Ethics*, J.M. Dent, 1993.

Tawney, Richard, H., *Religion and the Rise of Capitalism*, Pelican, 1948.

Tertullian, *Apologeticus*, William Heinemann Ltd, 1931.

The Corpus of Roman Law, Vol. 1, *The Theodosian Code* (*Codex Theodosianus*), Princeton University Press, 1952.

Thomson, George, *The First Philosophers*, Lawrence and Wishart, 1955.

Trotsky, Leon, *The Chinese Revolution*, Haymarket, 2010.
— *My Life*, Wellred Books, 2018.
— *The Struggle Against Fascism in Germany*, Pathfinder Press, 1971.

Unger, Peter, 'A Taste of Empty Ideas', *3 Quarks Daily*, 30 June 2014, available at: https://3quarksdaily.com/3quarksdaily/2014/06/a-little-taste-of-some-empty-ideas.html (accessed on 20 August 2021)

White, Andrew, D., *A History of the Warfare of Science With Theology in Christendom*, D. Appleton and Co., 1910.

Woods, Alan, and Grant, Ted, *Reason in Revolt*, Wellred Books, 2012.

LIST OF TITLES BY WELLRED BOOKS

Wellred Books is a UK-based international publishing house and bookshop, specialising in works of Marxist theory. A sister publisher and bookseller is based in the USA.

Among the titles published by Wellred Books are:

Anti-Dühring, Friedrich Engels

Bolshevism: The Road to Revolution, Alan Woods

Chartist Revolution, Rob Sewell

China: From Permanent Revolution to Counter-Revolution, John Roberts

The Civil War in France, Karl Marx

The Class Struggles in France, 1848-1850, Karl Marx

The Classics of Marxism: Volume One and Two, Various authors

Dialectics of Nature, Friedrich Engels

The Eighteenth Brumaire of Louis Bonaparte, Karl Marx

The First Five Years of the Communist International, Leon Trotsky

The First World War: A Marxist Analysis of the Great Slaughter, Alan Woods

Germany: From Revolution to Counter-Revolution, Rob Sewell

Germany 1918-1933: Socialism or Barbarism, Rob Sewell

History of British Trotskyism, Ted Grant

The History of Philosophy, Alan Woods

The History of the Russian Revolution: Volumes One to Three, Leon Trotsky

The History of the Russian Revolution to Brest-Litovsk, Leon Trotsky

The Ideas of Karl Marx, Alan Woods

Imperialism: The Highest Stage of Capitalism, V. I. Lenin

In Defence of Marxism, Leon Trotsky

In the Cause of Labour, Rob Sewell

Lenin and Trotsky: What They Really Stood For, Alan Woods and Ted Grant

Lenin, Trotsky and the Theory of the Permanent Revolution, John Roberts

Marxism and Anarchism, Various authors

Marxism and the USA, Alan Woods

Materialism and Empirio-criticism, V. I. Lenin

My Life, Leon Trotsky

Not Guilty, Dewey Commission Report

The Origin of the Family, Private Property and the State, Friedrich Engels

The Permanent Revolution and Results & Prospects, Leon Trotsky

Permanent Revolution in Latin America, John Roberts and Jorge Martin

Reason in Revolt, Alan Woods and Ted Grant

Reformism or Revolution, Alan Woods

Revolution and Counter-Revolution in Spain, Felix Morrow

The Revolution Betrayed, Leon Trotsky

The Revolutionary Philosophy of Marxism, John Peterson [Ed.]

Russia: From Revolution to Counter-Revolution, Ted Grant

Spain's Revolution Against Franco, Alan Woods

Stalin, Leon Trotsky

The State and Revolution, V. I. Lenin

Ted Grant: The Permanent Revolutionary, Alan Woods

Ted Grant Writings: Volumes One and Two, Ted Grant

Thawra hatta'l nasr! - Revolution until Victory!, Alan Woods and others

What Is Marxism?, Rob Sewell and Alan Woods

What Is to Be Done?, V. I. Lenin

To order any of these titles or for more information about Wellred Books, visit wellredbooks.net, email books@wellredbooks.net or write to Wellred Books, PO Box 50525, London E14 6WG, United Kingdom.